Becoming a Father

Becoming a Father

Charlie Lewis

Open University Press

Milton Keynes · Philadelphia

Open University Press
Open University Educational Enterprises Limited
12 Cofferidge Close
Stony Stratford
Milton Keynes MK11 1BY, England

and

242 Cherry Street
Philadelphia, PA 19106, USA

First Published 1986

British Library Cataloguing in Publication Data
Lewis, Charlie
  Becoming a father.
  1. Fathers
  I. Title
  306.8′742   HQ756

  ISBN 0-335-15128-0
  ISBN 0-335-15127-2 Pbk

Library of Congress Cataloging in Publication Data
Main entry under Title:
Lewis, Charlie
  Becoming a father.

  Includes bibliographical references and index.
  1. Fathers – United States – Psychology.
  2. Father and child – United States.   I. Title.
  HQ756.L476 1986   306.8′742   86-2635
  ISBN 0-335-15128-0
  ISBN 0-335-15127-2 (pbk.)

Text design by Nicola Sheldon
Phototypeset by Dobbie Typesetting Service, Plymouth, Devon
Printed in Great Britain by Alden Press, Oxford

For Rosemary and Tom

who transformed fantasy into reality

Contents

Acknowledgements

I would like to thank the following people for their much appreciated help:

First and foremost, the one hundred fathers, and their wives, who agreed so willingly to take part in this study.

My ex-colleagues at Nottingham University: John and Elizabeth Newson persuaded me to undertake this research and were encouraging throughout my seven years in Nottingham. Tony Hipgrave must also take some of the blame, as he had extolled the virtues of fatherhood research over many a game of bowls in the summer of 1978. Dady Key kindly interviewed the mothers whose accounts are discussed here. Susan Gregory, always supportive, made many constructive changes to the final draft of this book. I must also thank those people who gave me help with statistics and computing (Chris Blunsdon, John Newson, Paddy Reilly, Brian Sharratt, Simon Lalonde, Jeanette Lilley and Michelle Thirlaway), who helped to transcribe my interviews (Jo Newson, Jane Rayner, Barbs Gregson, Rosemary Smith, Dady Key, Joy Rayner, Beryl West and Rob Lewis), who displayed their typing and secretarial skills for me (Penny Radcliffe, Alison Q. Cumberpatch, Brian Sharratt, Rosemary Smith, Beryl West, Joy Rayner, Caroline Thorpe, Maggie Broom and Betty Reid) and who gave me their technical help (Tony Falla, Steve Sharp, Howard Martin, Carl Espin and Mike Burton). The Science Library staff at Nottingham (notably Caroline Thorpe, Margaret Williams and Shirley Lander) provided a superb service.

For financial support: the Social Science Research Council, the Susan Isaacs Memorial Fellowship Trustees at London University's Institute of Education, the Department of Psychology Board for Postgraduate Study (for awarding me a Gertrude Cropper Scholarship) and Child Development Research Unit at the University of Nottingham and the Research Board and Department of Psychology at the University of Reading.

The Child Health Department in Nottingham, particularly Dr More and Mrs Johnson, for allowing me to select my sample from their records and helping me with the selection procedure.

Finally, my thanks go to John Hockey for his wisdom on men and masculinity, Suzette Heald, Tom (TNT) Lewis and Mary Douglas for their comments on earlier papers on men, pregnancy and childbirth, Lars Jalmert for providing information about paternal roles in Sweden, Lorna McKee for her insight into the transition to fatherhood, Rudolph Schaffer for commenting on the report upon which this book was based, John Skelton for his patience and Mick Gregson for running with me every day when I lived in Nottingham and discussing fatherhood as we plodded along.

Part One
Fatherhood Research

1   Fathers in Psychological Research: Contrasting Images and Confused Theories

Emergent Fathers:
Are Men Becoming More Involved in Parenthood?

In recent years fathers have entered the limelight in many ways. They feature centrally in many popular accounts of family life; in films like *Kramer vs Kramer*, in television situation comedies like *Father's Day*, in frequent women's magazine articles, in books written especially for men (e.g. Jackson 1984, Johnson 1984) and in the United States in programmes designed to encourage their participation in family life (Klinman and Kohl 1983). Widespread comment was made about John Lennon's parenting role shortly before his death, and now Prince Charles's involvement receives frequent coverage. At the same time, the past ten years have witnessed an explosion of research, particularly that in which men are observed interacting with their young children, with the aim of assessing whether men influence their children's development (Lamb 1981a, Pedersen, 1980a).

With few exceptions accounts of the contemporary father's role make three interrelated claims: firstly, that there has been a dearth of literature on men's family roles until very recently; secondly, that the father's role has been very limited in previous generations; thirdly, and most importantly, that contemporary men are considered to be increasingly involved in family life – no longer on the periphery, they are at last becoming 'fathers'. This is what I term the 'emergent' view of fatherhood. Typical descriptions of this image of contemporary male domesticity read:

> We find ourselves in the late 1970s, in the midst of a series of reconsiderations. Previously accepted models of womanhood, of work, of family life, of the relationship between work and family life, are being scrutinised, examined, remade. Many women, assigned in the past to roles of caring for children, keeping the home, supporting their menfolk, are exploring the world of paid employment, taking on and

1

sharing the bread-winning responsibilities previously held mainly by men. Many men, feeling burdened by too-restrictive definitions of masculinity and manliness, are seeking to blend work life and family life, making efforts to become and stay involved in the daily responsibilities of child care, learning more about the frustrations and the joys of deep and regular participation in the lives of their children.

(Fein 1978a: 327)

Father is changing as never before. He is still inside the economic prison, often encased in attitudes of the past, and still largely ignored. Old inequalities tenaciously persist. But there is something restless about the modern father. In the past we might have said he was flexing his muscles. But perhaps what he is doing is looking into his heart.

(Jackson 1984: 27)

Future generations of children will derive greater comfort from their contact with fathers who are competent both inside and outside the family. Such a change in male behaviour will generate a more caring society and eventually promote greater understanding between nations.

(Winn 1979: 35)

Similar views are often expressed by parents themselves. However, this 'emergent' view of fatherhood is too simplistic and utopian. The contrast between yesterday's uninvolved man and today's 'super-dad' is hardly supported by firm data.

This book attempts to unravel some of the contrasting views of fathering. I shall consider husbands' and wives' accounts of the fathers' adjustment to parenthood over the first year of their child's life. Before examining these accounts, this first chapter asks just why our understanding of fatherhood remains unclear. It divides into four sections. In the first, I will analyse each of the claims made by proponents of the emergent view. I shall suggest that this image of fatherhood is hard to substantiate. The second section considers an opposing viewpoint, that parental roles continue to be clearly differentiated. Again such a perspective, while supported by more evidence, does not completely illuminate the father's role. Indeed, in the third section I shall argue that theoretical perspectives on the father's role have emerged within a wider debate on the social position of women. The fourth section introduces my own research and outlines the way it might clarify our understanding of fatherhood, not only by realizing its complexities and the contradictions within it, but also by examining it in relation to the social institution of motherhood.

Problems in Understanding Fathers: a Closer Look at the Emergent View

Belief 1: Fathers have only recently been discovered by family researchers
In keeping with the emergent view, it is clear that the emphasis on *mothers* in the literature ostensibly about (Rapoport *et al.* 1977) and for (De Frain

1975 and 1977) parents far outweighs the attention given to fathers. This is hardly surprising since women have continued to take the major responsibility for child-rearing throughout the industrial world. However, a closer look at the literature reveals far more discussion on the paternal role than contemporary authors suggest. Reviews of fatherhood research over the past fifty years continue to make a statement of 'fact' that men have been almost completely omitted from parenting studies (Gardner 1943, Jackson 1984, Lamb 1975, Nash 1965, Tasch 1952). Nash (1965), for example, made the claim that there has been little written about fathers, but managed to write a thirty-six-page review of the literature. In fact he commented upon this contradiction in his conclusion.

Indeed, it seems absurd to assume that men have been completely ignored. Since the Second World War fathers have been considered in studies of pregnancy (Landis 1950), women and work (Komarovsky 1953), the family (Bott 1957) and child-rearing (Newson and Newson 1963), to mention but a few areas of academic interest. While they were included mainly in research on families and child development, they have received attention in their own right. For a start, there has been a trickle of publications on child care written especially for men. In the 1950s, for example, English and Foster (1953), like others before them (see, for example, Walker and Walker 1928), wrote a parentcraft manual for fathers. In keeping with the emergent view of fatherhood, they stressed the importance of the man's involvement:

> No baby is born 'bad'. He does not inherit a tendency toward evil. He *becomes* unkind or cantankerous or suspicious, or deceitful because of what happens to him, literally, from the moment of his birth. And right there is where the great good hope of a brighter future for mankind lies. It lies with parents. It lies with fathers more than they have ever fully understood before. It lies with *you*.
>
> (English and Foster 1953: 19)

Research on the nature of fathers' roles was also more abundant than is recognized. Gardner (1943) and Tasch (1952), for example, interviewed men about their involvement in family life. As in all research areas, interest in fathers undoubtedly ebbed and flowed. After the Second World War studies of forces veterans as fathers were fashionable (e.g. Elder 1949, Stoltz *et al.* 1954, Underwood 1949). In the late 1950s fathers again received attention. A symposium of the International Council of Psychologists, in 1961, discussed 'Fathers' Influence in the Family' (Layman 1961). At this conference Layman reported the number of citations of fatherhood research in the second half of the 1950s. In that period, forty-two articles were referenced under the topic of fatherhood in the citation index 'Psychological Abstracts'. While this is only a fifth of the articles on motherhood (there were 202), it still suggests that previous writers did not simply forget men.

The reason why fathers failed to gain a central position in our understanding of the family cannot be put down to an oversight on the part of researchers.

Belief 2: In previous generations fathers were not involved in child-rearing

As Fein stated above, recent accounts of 'traditional' families depict a less involved male. Is there evidence to support this view? A close look at the data suggests, firstly, that measuring changes in family patterns is difficult; and secondly, that historical accounts of the father usually are too vague to inform us about the paternal involvement of men in times gone by.

Massive social changes from one generation to the next make it difficult to measure shifts in fathers' roles. Since the Second World War we have witnessed many upheavals in the practice, and in our expectations, of child care. For example, employment patterns for both men and women have been subject to continual change. The most dramatic alteration has been the number of women, particularly mothers, entering the labour force (Ratner 1980). However, with the increases in shift-work (Young and Willmott 1973), paid leave (English Tourist Board 1979) and, most recently, unemployment, it is clear that employment patterns for men are also subject to change. In addition there has been much written about the difference between family structures of today and those of the early post-war years (Rapoport *et al.* 1977). Most notable has been the rapid increase in single-parent families (Finer 1974). Such changes are easily visible, although difficult to measure specifically, particularly when we attempt to assess their impact upon stereotypes of men's participation in fathering, and their actual involvement. At the same time there have been less dramatic or visible movements in the daily routines of family life. For example, the post-war years have witnessed changes in technology and labour-saving devices like automatic washing-machines. These necessarily alter the nature of housework (Young and Willmott 1973) and also influence parents' roles and their expectations about the domestic division of labour.

In the midst of these changes (and the above list is far from exhaustive), it is difficult to *measure* any alteration in men's roles, if indeed change has been consistent. As we see in the evidence presented in reviews of the patterns of fathering in recent years (e.g. Beail and McGuire 1982a), very few longitudinal comparisons of fathers' roles have been made. Most historical accounts resort to stereotypical descriptions of patriarchy and the 'traditional' family as if no evidence needs to be provided to prove their pervasiveness in former times. Yet these historical portrayals of fatherhood are hardly convincing since they display a facility for carefree over-generalization (Bloom-Feshbach 1981, Nash 1976). Bloom-Feschbach, for example, devotes two or three pages of commentary to historical periods that lasted for centuries. As a recent commentator suggests, 'Most evidence for the role of the father in history is little more than anecdotal. Such evidence is usually a surface response and conforms to what is believed to be a social norm'. (Lummis 1982: 53).

It is important to mention the work of Lummis here. His focus of interest is much less broad-sweeping than that of others: 'To comment on the role of the father in history briefly and yet relevantly will require a focus that is specific in time and place' (Lummis 1982: 43). He collected an oral history of a twenty-four-year period (1890–1914) from people who were born into an East Anglian fishing community at the end of the last century. His work serves as an excellent counter-example to those studies that rely upon the received wisdom of historical stereotypes. Lummis starts by documenting the agreed opinion that at the turn of the twentieth century working-class fathers, including those in the fishing trade, tended to be brutal, drunken and aloof from their families – very similar to Walter Morel in D. H. Lawrence's *Sons and Lovers* (1913). In contrast, the recollections of Lummis's respondents suggest that East Anglian fathers during this period were unlike the stereotype, and many were very participant members of the household.

We cannot infer from this evidence that all fathers at the turn of the century were highly involved with their families, and Lummis is at pains to point out the specificity of his data. However, it serves to warn us that we should also avoid making general statements about 'the father' in history – or in the present – without clear documentary evidence of men's actual involvement, or lack of it. Lummis's work is not unique, and many historical accounts show the plurality of family structures in history (Everslea and Bonnerjea 1982). As McKee and O'Brien (1982b) state, it is likely that, as now, historical patterns of father involvement have varied according to regional, occupational, class and ecological factors. Certainly the evidence since the 1930s suggests that variations within generations may be more important than those between them (Pedersen and Robson 1969), and the data from forty years ago hardly suggests that fathers were as uninvolved as contemporary opinion suggests (Gardner 1943, Tasch 1952).

Belief 3: Recently men have started to become highly involved in and committed to child care

In light of the evidence presented in this study, Chapter 10 will examine this proposition directly. Here I will consider the historical context of this belief. Is the present generation unique in suggesting that men are becoming more participant in family life?

The answer seems to be no. A brief consideration of what has been written about fathers and marital relationships suggests just why our understanding of fatherhood has remained blurred and confused. A cursory glance at the literature on marriage indicates that the emergent image of fatherhood – the view that men are starting to become involved in family life – is as old and perhaps as prominent as the notion of patriarchy. Histories of family research, like that of Lasch (1977), show that each generation tends to reproduce the same ideals as the last, even if in a slightly modified form. We see in Mowrer's (1930) analysis of the family, for example, a review of a considerable number of studies on the notion of 'companionate marriage', which developed in the 1920s. Mowrer maintained that a reciprocal form of marriage was developing in order to reduce the tensions and imbalance of 'orthodox' conjugal forms, where the husband's word was law. This argument has distinct parallels with that of Fein, quoted above.

In the 1940s similar views were propounded. The word 'companionate' was replaced by the term 'developmental' in order to describe the emergent sense of the new style of marriage. Writings on marriage (Lindeman 1942) and more specifically on fathers (Elder 1949) carried an air of optimism about contemporary trends in the father's role in the family:

> The traditional conception of the family holds that the father is head of the house, that the mother is entrusted with the care of the house and of the children and that in return for the unselfish devotion of the parents to their duties, the children owe their parents honour and obedience. Today these values are being discarded by those who are creating developmental families based upon inter-personal relations of mutual affection, companionship, and understanding, with a recognition of individual capabilities, desires and needs for the development of each member of the family, be he father, mother or child.
>
> (Elder 1949: 98)

Similar beliefs were restated by Mogey (1957) in his analysis of fatherhood in the century 1855–1955. Mogey's central belief was that the key figure in the family is the father: 'the role of the father is the most important factor in family stability' (Mogey 1957: 234). Mogey uses the term 'participant' to describe the 'modern father' of the 1950s; and although he is more specific in his reasons for the 'reintegration' of men into the family, the gist of his argument bears a strong resemblance to the previous writers cited above:

> As the working week becomes shorter, the occupancy of single family houses, house ownership, and house repairing more general, the word 'companionship' becomes too passive a word to describe the relations between a man and his family. This newer father behaviour is best described as participation, the re-integration of fathers into the conspicuous consumption as well as the child rearing styles of family life.
>
> (Mogey 1957: 238)

Since Mogey, the same theme has been echoed numerous times (see, for example, Blood and Wolfe 1960, Goode 1963). Perhaps the most detailed statement of the 'emergent' perspective is Young and Willmott's (1973) *Symmetrical Family*. While the same historical arguments are again presented, these authors are more guarded about the balance of marital power. Young and Willmott propose that the emergent family is not necessarily an androgynous one, where both adults have the same role. Couples come to perform complementary rather than equal functions. So a husband might 'help' his wife with housework and she might assist in his task of providing for the family. Despite this broadening of the emergent perspective the belief that fathers are becoming increasingly involved links the symmetrical family ideal with its predecessors.

A Contrasting View: the 'Differentiation' Perspective

The belief that men are becoming more involved in family life has been contrasted with a converse view of parenthood – that the sex roles of parents remain sharply differentiated. Such a belief has been espoused by strange bedfellows. In the first place, conservative theorists have argued that men and women occupy distinct roles within society generally and in its microcosm, the family. Parsons and Bales (1955) are most clear in their description of the 'instrumental' role of men, which signifies the detachment and control needed to survive in the harsh economic world. This is contrasted with the 'expressive' female role, which is passive, nurturant and family-centred. Similar sentiments are expressed in psychological accounts of the family. The obvious examples are Bowlby (1954) and Winnicott (1965), who asserted that the mother played the key part in the child's emotional development, while the father serves to support his wife and child somewhat in the background. Such a view, expressed most clearly after the Second World War, was by no means restricted to academic publications (e.g. Lundberg and Farnham 1947). Like the 'emergent' view of fatherhood, such a differentiation perspective can be traced back as far as McDougall (1908) and many other earlier writers (Rose 1985).

At the same time the idea that parents' roles are sharply differentiated has been propounded by more radical authors. These hold that men actively withdraw from family life and abrogate their responsibilities. Often this belief has been expressed in opposition to the emergent view. For example, in her discussion of women in the 1950s, Komarovsky questioned the belief that fathers were becoming more involved:

> Can we seriously expect that a democratic family (which more than any other group requires mutuality) can endure if we make one member the specialist in family virtues? . . .

> Isolated from his children, a father all too often feels he is 'just the guy who foots the bills'. Fathers need a richer experience of fatherhood.
>
> (Komarovsky 1953: 250, 252)

Rather than suggesting a 'merging' of adult sex roles, feminist authors have continued to document the discrepancy between the ideal of equality and the reality of sexual inequality in the work-place (e.g. Bird 1968, Holter 1972, Russo 1976). This view can again be traced back many decades (e.g. to Hollingworth 1916). However, as a result of the wave of feminist writing in the 1970s researchers have focused increasingly on 'domestic politics' (McKee 1982, Oakley 1979). Men's contributions to housework (Oakley 1974) and child care (see Chapter 6) have been regarded with an increasingly critical eye.

The dramatic re-emergence of interest in women has been so influential that it has given rise to two areas of discussion about men. Firstly, there is a body of literature on what is termed 'men's liberation'. Perhaps as a result of their origins in the women's movement, these accounts depict the male personality as domineering and deviant. Frequent mention is made, for example, of men's 'social incompetence' or their 'inability' to develop emotionally intimate relationships, particularly with other men (Balswick and Peck 1971, Davids and Brannon 1976, Farrell 1974, Fasteau 1974, Lewis 1978, Rubin *et al.* 1980). Farrell (1974) likens the male personality to a 'machine', as witnessed in the impersonal philosophies of Locke, Mill and Adam Smith. The most comprehensive publication of this literature (Solomon and Levy 1982) reads more like a psychiatric report than an account of personality. As Lederer (1982) writes in his critique of the book, the authors describe men as being brutal in their muscular strength, aggressive, assertive, success-oriented, the cause of international violence, lacking in artistic sensitivity, impatient, competitive, emotionally isolated and incapable of intimacy with women and children.

The second area of theoretical reflection on men comes from recent developments in object relations theory, within psychoanalysis. The writings of Dinnerstein (1978) and Chodorow (1978) suggest that the very differentiation of parental roles has distinct and lasting effects on boys and girls, such that adult sex roles reproduce themselves from one generation to the next. Boys, for example, are forced to reject their close relationship with their mothers during the pre-Oedipal period. As men, they later develop ambivalent relationships with women, since they both desire the sort of intimacy they received from their mothers and fear rejection from such an attachment figure.

Is the 'differentiation' view valid?
While there is much evidence to support the differentiation perspective, particularly that proposed by recent radical authors, there is plenty to suggest that making such a clear distinction between mothers and fathers exaggerates and even distorts our perception of their roles. This has been demonstrated most clearly in recent critiques of conservative proponents of the differentiation view (Morgan 1975, Rapoport *et al.* 1977). Like earlier

authors (Hacker 1957, Mead 1954, Slater 1961), these critiques of Bowlby and Parsons reveal the mismatch between theory and data in their distinction between involved motherhood and supportive fatherhood.

Close examination of these conservative accounts exposes their over-simplicity. Consider the following extract from Parsons and Bales's (1955) most influential analysis of family life. Here a co-author admits that the evidence shows that marital roles are not as different as their instrumental–expressive dichotomy suggests. So he has to resort to cultural values and stereotypes in order to make his case:

> From certain points of view the American middle-class family approaches to equal allocation (or no 'allocation') of instrumental and expressive activities. The universalistic value schema (in which women are 'just as good as men') coupled with the general attitude toward the explicit expression of authority ('I'm agin it') apparently constitutes the limiting case of no differentiation at all. Underlying this broad value-schema, however, a rather clear differentiation occurs. In the distribution of instrumental tasks the American family maintains a more flexible pattern than most societies. Father helps mother with the dishes. He sets the table. He makes formula for the baby. Mother can supplement the income by working outside. Nevertheless, the American male, by definition, must 'provide' for his family. He is responsible for his wife and children. There is simply something wrong with the American adult male who does not have a job.
>
> (Zelditch, in Parsons and Bales 1955: 339)

The more recent radical perspective also exaggerates the divisions between parents' roles, although not so obviously. Chodorow's model of sex-role development has been amplified in interesting ways with reference to fathers (Richards 1982) and men in general (Seidler 1985). Yet its determinism, pessimism and polarization of sex roles leave it open to criticism (e.g. Lasch 1985). Indeed, evidence from couples who have successfully broken with convention and exchanged roles suggests that patterns of dependence within families are not so universally determined (Ehrensaft 1985).

The Emergent and Differentiation Views in Perspective

The emergent and differentiation perspectives obscure our understanding of fatherhood, since neither provides us with a detailed account of the man's role in the family. This has effects on both men themselves and those who study them. A common theme in the literature on fathers throughout this century suggests that they find their role confusing. For example, when summarizing the literature on fathers in the 1930s pearl Gardner (1943: 16) stated that many men regarded their role with 'perplexed bewilderment', especially about what their function was in the child's development, but also in the way they experienced fatherhood. This feeling is apparent in work since Gardner's (e.g. Backett 1982, Josselyn 1956). Authors have repeatedly stated that fathers rarely seem to be have a clear 'job description' of their role, and many find paternal involvement confusing at times.

The confusion felt by fathers carries over into research. They have been considered extensively, but only in relation to other issues. The most important of these is the preoccupation with the position of women, which has dominated social thinking at intervals throughout this century. The paternal role seems to be rediscovered with every wave of feminism (e.g. Pleck and Brannon 1978). As Richards (1982) and others before him suggest, only rarely have authors paused to examine fathers in their own right:

> interest and research in changes in men's social roles have been eclipsed by the voluminous concentration on the more spectacular developments and contradictions in feminine roles, and changes in masculine roles have been treated largely as a reaction and adjustment to the new status of women. Possibly one reason why masculine social roles have not been subject to scrutiny is that such a concept has not clearly emerged. Men have stood for mankind and their problems have been identified with the general human condition. It is a plausible hypothesis, however, that men as well as women suffer from the lack of generally accepted, clearly defined patterns of behaviour expected of them.
> (Hacker 1957: 227)

The father in the literature on the 'transition to parenthood'
The theoretical neglect of fathers is demonstrated by a brief consideration of the literature on the 'transition to parenthood' (Rossi 1968). This is an area of research that should throw much light upon our understanding of fatherhood, since men have consistently received attention in studies over the past thirty years. However, as in other areas their experiences have been largely overlooked.

This tradition has been dominated by the debate between those who regard early parenthood as a 'crisis' (Dyer 1963, Le Masters 1957) and those who find no such crisis (Hobbs 1965 and 1968, Hobbs and Cole 1976, Knox and Gilman 1974). In the 1970s researchers developed an interest in the influences of a new baby upon the family as a whole (Lamb 1978). Detailed longitudinal and cross-sectional studies examined the transition in more detail (Cowan *et al.* 1978, Cowan and Cowan 1981, Entwisle and Doering 1981, Gladieux 1978, Grossman *et al.* 1980, Hoffman and Manis 1978, Shereshefsky and Yarrow 1973). Yet close examination of the bulk of these reveals a persistence with the search for a crisis. One study, for example, took the following starting-point:

> The process of becoming parents seems best understood as a time of normal developmental crisis with accompanying upheaval in physiology, roles, values and relationships (Bibring, 1959; Le Masters, 1957). Questions are raised, change is demanded; feelings of disequilibrium

and anxiety are present until new resolutions are achieved. A pregnancy is a critical turning point in the life of a woman and her family.

(Grossman *et al.* 1980: 4)

A more serious problem for our purposes concerns the treatment of fathers. While a few studies have attempted to examine the differences in the ways fathers and mothers experience this period (e.g. Miller and Sollie 1980), only two studies have focused exclusively on men (see Roopnarine and Miller 1985). The literature thus tends to treat men in one of two ways. Some adhere to the differentiation perspective and assume that men are not centrally involved in the process of parenting. No evidence is given to support this view, which is implicit in many studies:

> One important function of the man, who has been less engulfed from the beginning, is to use his separateness to help his wife gain some distance from her trial involvement with the newborn and to reduce her inevitable anxieties about the vulnerabilities of the new infant and, for first-time mothers, of herself as a mother.
>
> (Grossman *et al.* 1980: 171)

As this book will show, many men do feel 'less engulfed' than their wives, but it is not necessarily the case that all men do.

Alternatively, men may be considered to be involved but overawed by the changes that occur during the perinatal period. For example, Leibenberg (1973: 105), in her contribution to the Shereshefsky and Yarrow study, gives no support for her assertion that 'Pregnancy is a period of heightened dependency for the man when he needs mothering himself.' Later she argues that fathers increase their working hours after the arrival of the child in order to cut themselves off from their wives and as 'a protection against the outbreak of serious neurotic phenomena' (Leibenberg 1973: 107). Again she offers a psychological explanation without considering a variety of other possibilities. For example, a man may need to work more after delivery to compensate for the loss of his wife's earnings or because caring for the child exerts greater economic pressure upon him.

While these studies stress the importance of fathers as sources of emotional support to their wives, in the last analysis men's perceptions of the transition have been treated as unimportant unless they react in a 'pathological' way to the arrival of a child (Lewis 1982b).

This Study

This study, which took place in 1979–80, set out to examine fathering from the man's point of view. Numerous authors have argued that we should attempt to consider the social psychology of the father's role (Eiskovits 1983,

Pedersen 1980b, Richards 1982). Indeed, this project was initiated at a time when researchers from a wide variety of disciplines were pointing simultaneously at the great gap in our knowledge of the father's experience of parenthood (McKee and O'Brien 1982b). The most direct influence comes from a tradition of work that was developed recently in Britain. In the late 1970s an inter-disciplinary group of researchers formed the Fatherhood Research Group, united in the view that men were somehow being neglected in family research. As a result a first wave of father-centred research was published (Beail and McGuire 1982a, McKee and O'Brien 1982a). Similar moves have been apparent in the United States (Hanson and Bozett 1985; Lewis and Salt, 1986). These publications argue that 'better theoretical formulations are required and . . . these must be derived from a consideration of the social institution of fatherhood' (Richards 1982: 59).

This first wave of writing on fathers sketched out some of the issues concerning men as parents. The aim of the research reported in the present book was to discover something about the 'social institution' of fatherhood, by asking men to describe in full the nature of their roles and the depth and breadth of their experiences. It focuses upon the first year of fatherhood. This period in family development is interesting for many reasons. To begin with, the child is at his or her most helpless, so care is necessary for his or her survival. In addition, parents' roles become more clearly defined during this stage (see Chapter 6); and, as the literature on the transition to parenthood shows (La Rossa 1977), parents' feelings may be accentuated.

The specific methods employed in this study derive from two main sources. Firstly, John and Elizabeth Newson's (1963 and 1968) study of mothers' attitudes towards child-rearing examined the range of contemporary child care patterns, by interviewing large numbers of mothers about a wide variety of topics. Like them, I attempted to obtain an extensive picture of fatherhood, by interviewing men from across the social spectrum about their involvement in child care. Secondly, Ann Oakley's (1979) detailed analysis of women's experiences of early motherhood underlines the complexities of their adjustment to parenthood and reveals the over-simplicity of most writing on the 'transition to parenthood'. Like Oakley, I wanted to report the accounts of fathers in detail to consider just why they appear to experience their role with 'perplexed bewilderment'.

As the following chapters will suggest, men describe many inherent contradictions in the ways their duties are defined and perceived. Their feelings are not unrelated to the contrast between the emergent and differentiation images of fatherhood. They may, for example, feel both a need to involve themselves in child care, but also pressure to spend much of their waking day at work, providing for their families. Such dilemmas are examined throughout this book. The following discussion avoids many of the issues raised in the growing literature on men, with its focus on the relationship between instrumental masculinity and the early socialization of males. Instead it attempt to build up a picture of how fathers' involvement develops along with the changing needs of the child (Lewis *et al.* 1982) and in negotiation with their wives (Backett 1982).

While fathers are the primary concern of the study, it would be impossible to examine their parenting in isolation. I pointed out above that theorists have attempted to see either the similarities or the differences between the roles of couples as parents. Few have examined mothering and fathering in relation to the fact that fatherhood is a socially constructed phenomenon (Malinowski 1927a and 1927b, Mead 1950/62). As the accounts of parents will suggest, early parenthood is a time when a man's fathering role very much depends on the nature of his explicit relationship to and implicit relationship with the mother of the child.

Plan of the book
This chapter has discussed the reasons why this study undertook an examination of fathering from the man's point of view. Chapter 2 will outline the methods used to discover more about the nature of the father's role. Since this study is exploratory in nature it aims to examine fathers' experiences in both breadth and depth. Chapter 2 will therefore be partly concerned to describe how a methodology incorporating both quantitative and qualitative techniques has been used.

The remaining chapters divide into two distinct sections. Part Two (Chapters 3 to 7) examines the development of the father–infant relationship from before the child's arrival until his or her first birthday. Chapter 3 describes men's impressions of their wives' pregnancies. This period in a couple's transition to parenthood serves as a very good starting-point for the study, since the man's role is necessarily limited by his physiological make-up. Men describe pregnancy as a time when they attempt to share their wives' experiences (in keeping with the emergent image of fatherhood), and yet their roles are necessarily differentiated. The apparent contradictions in the man's pregnancy role continue, through the delivery (Chapter 4) and into the child's early life (Chapters 5 and 6), although social definitions of the man's fathering role become increasingly more important than physiological limitations. Chapters 5 and 6 examine the development of men's participation in the daily care of their infants. While previous studies suggest a confusion in the way men perceive their roles, these chapters indicate that certain child care activities are accepted as being 'appropriate' for fathers, while others are considered less so. In light of his practical role, Chapter 7 describes the development of the father's relationship with his child. The nature of their contact and the way a father perceives his child often seem to relate to one another.

Part Three of the book (Chapters 8 to 10) takes a broader look at the social context of fatherhood, considering it from a number of angles. Chapter 8 examines the father's marital relationship, since parenthood and marriage appear to influence one another in contrasting ways. Chapter 9 looks more specifically at the father's own involvement in parenthood. Throughout this study I suggest that he usually adopts an involved role but one which is less involved than that of his wife. In contrast to the men's liberation literature, Chapter 9 suggests that men have a great deal of personal investment in their roles as fathers. Chapter 10 re-examines a number of issues raised in the book. It considers the closeness of father–child relationships over a much longer time period. This exercise suggests that the stage on which this study focuses is one when men may well be closer to their children than at later times in the life-cycle. It also questions the emergent belief that fathers are becoming more involved in family life.

2 One Hundred Fathers

Introduction

> Researchers, in common with the couples they observe, are restricted
> in what they can see. There is in the nature of scientific enquiry an
> element of partiality. To study in detail is to narrow the field of vision;
> to select one area of investigation is to ignore another. . . . [The
> research process is] an artefact in the sense that it has been segregated
> from the wider context of which it is part.
>
> (Clulow 1982: 20)

Recent years have witnessed a dramatic shift in the way researchers have
examined the methods they use. No longer is it acceptable to assume that
behaviour observed in a laboratory or responses gleaned from an interview
are simple 'facts', which the psychologist merely records in order to make
sense of the social world. As Clulow states above, the research act is 'an
artefact' in that the end product records only a narrow area of experience.

This chapter will describe how I 'narrowed' my field of vision, to focus
upon a sample of one hundred fathers. The discussion divides into two
parts. The first describes some details of the sample; and the second gives
an account of the nature of the interaction between the fathers and myself
and the synthesis of their accounts that will be presented in the following
chapters. Because research findings derive from the methods on which they
are based, it is necessary to spell out in some detail how I collected my
'data'. It is all too tempting to sweep all the limitations of a study under
the carpet, so I hope that here the limitations as well as the strengths of
this research project will become apparent.

Obtaining a Sample

Lessons from other studies

Fathers are a notoriously difficult group to study. Like researchers, they
tend to work during the day – at least in times of high employment. A
number of authors have written (e.g. Richards *et al.* 1977) that the reluctance
of researchers to work at unsocial times of the week (at evenings and
weekends) has prevented men from featuring centrally in many studies.
As a result most of the 'data' on fathers gleaned from interview studies

actually comes from research involving their wives (e.g. Cleary and Shepperdson 1979 and 1981, Newson and Newson 1963, Pedersen and Robson 1969, Richards *et al.* 1977). Young mothers are not only a captive audience; they are also generally more accepted as authorities on, and caretakers of, young children. The Newsons, for example, had a little problem in collecting their 709 mothers, and only 1.6 per cent of those approached refused to participate in their study.

While mothers' accounts of their husbands' role in the family are of interest, there is a tendency simply to accept them as valid and objective. In their study of husbands and wives, for example, Blood and Wolfe (1960) admitted that men and women differ in their opinions, but they adopted the policy of interviewing only women on the grounds that these differences were not highly significant. However, they did not justify this assertion. Such assumptions came under severe criticism, particularly since Safilios-Rothchild's (1969) critique of the validity of wife-centred family studies.

The track record of research involving fathers is not impressive. The main review of sampling biases in studies of parents suggests that, while mothers refuse to participate in studies as much as their husbands, fathers are more likely to break their appointment with a researcher (Wollett *et al.* 1982). As secondary care-givers, men are less accessible, and there is not the cultural acceptability of using them as a source of data for academic research. many investigations have as a result to abandon 'objective' means of obtaining samples – in terms of both finding men and enlisting their participation. They have used personal contacts (De Frain 1975), volunteers through newspaper advertisements (Entwisle and Doering 1981) and attenders at Lamaze childbirth classes (Fein 1976). All these sampling procedures have the dubious advantage of attracting a particular breed of 'keen' father. Some attempts have been made to select men in a more random manner.

Table 2.1   Participation rate in studies of the transition to parenthood involving fathers

	Numbers of fathers approached	Participated	Success rate %
Grossman *et al.* (1980)	127	75	(59)
Knox and Gilman (1974)	382	102	(27)
La Rossa (1977)	28	16	(57)
La Rossa and La Rossa (1981)	30	18	(60)
McKee (1979)	27	13	(48)
Moss (1981)	124	89	(72)
Pressman (1980)	283	66	(23)

Table 2.1 gives a breakdown of the recent interview studies of the transition period that both pay specific attention to fathers and also report their success rate. This list of studies is not comprehensive and does not represent all the research on fathers during this period, mainly because many studies (e.g. Manion 1977, Rendina and Dickerscheid 1976) fail to report their rate of losses. The table shows that the response rate in all these studies is below three-quarters of those approached; in three of the seven examples presented fewer than 50 per cent of the men contacted actually participated in the study.

The study's main sample
The present study shares the same methodology as that employed by the Newsons in their research more than twenty years ago (Newson and Newson 1963). Like their longitudinal study it was based in the same city, using the same access to a sample. It was carried out in Nottingham, England's twentieth largest urban district (*Whittaker's Almanack*, 1983), and within one of the ten biggest conurbations in the country. This geographical area has the dual advantage of being sizeable – where all social class groups and many occupations are represented – yet, at the same time, self-contained.

The sample was drawn from the records kept by the Child Health Department in Nottingham. These contain a list of registered births in the city and the current addresses of children. I selected at random as many fathers per week as I was able to interview – usually one for each weekday for the duration of the study. The sample was not truly 'random', as I shall outline below.

Table 2.2 gives a breakdown of the losses from the sample. In all 124 men were approached to participate, and 100 finally interviewed. Not all the twenty-four 'drop-outs' actually refused to become involved. While child-health records are updated as frequently as possible, twelve families were not known at the address given. Indeed, three homes had been demolished! Six men were not resident with their families at the time of interview. Two were separated, two were in prison, and two were reported to be away working. In slight contrast to other studies, only six fathers refused to participate. One middle-class man wrote to refuse to co-operate and gave no reason. Three of the five working-class refusers gave no reason.

Table 2.2   Losses from the sample

Approached	*124*
Interviewed	100
Refused	6
Not known at address/no reply	12
In prison (2), separated (2), away 'working' (2)	6

One man saw 'no point' in the research, and the last suspected that I was connected in some way with the local Social Services Department.

While, as in other studies, the participation rate of the men approached is not 100 per cent, the low number of refusers suggests that this sample is as representative as possible of married men resident with their families. In all 84 per cent of all the selected men and 94 per cent of those with whom I made contact agreed to participate. However, as I shall now outline, the sample is not representative of the population as a whole.

The Newsons (1963) interviewed more than seven hundred mothers. They could thus use a completely random selection procedure and still end up with a sample with large numbers of families from each social class and with different numbers of children. Having the available time and resources to interview only one hundred fathers, I set certain constraints in order to obtain a sample from across the spread of the class spectrum. I imposed three limitations upon my 'random' selection procedure, all of which were possible, given the information available in the child-health records.

Firstly I selected only first and second births. A random sample of one hundred would have yielded some first and second children plus a handful of later births. With the exception of the La Rossas' second study (1981), the 'transition to parenthood' literature has almost universally concentrated upon the arrival of a first child. I wanted to compare the accounts of first-timers and second-timers to test an assumption in much of the literature that the first child effects psychological change in the parent, while subsequent children do not.

However 'neat' researchers try to make their samples they always encounter problems. During the course of the study four men were found to have more than two children – not all of them were on the local child-health records since they were the product of previous marriages. For the sake of convenience these fathers were included in the sample of second-timers.

The second way in which this sample was not selected at random lay in its social class make-up. As only one hundred men were to be interviewed I decided to restrict the class composition, as measured by the UK Registrar General's Classification of Occupations (1970), in two ways. Firstly, I eliminated members of the occupational group of semi-skilled workers in his 'Social Class IV', who are less homogeneous than the others. Secondly, having followed convention and combined the two small social groups of professional and managerial, I limited the number of men selected from each of the four groups in the sample to 25, consisting of 15 first-timers and 10 second-timers – see Table 2.3.

Although Table 2.3 shows an even distribution of the fathers into social class groups, the allocation of men to these groups was not always simple. The Registrar General's list of occupations is extensive, but a few men labelled their jobs in ways not classified by him. I therefore had to infer

Table 2.3 Description of the sample by occupational/social class background (UK Registrar Generals classification, 1970)

| | Middle class | | Working class | |
| | | | III (m.) | |
	I/II (Professional/ managerial)	III (w.c.) (White-collar, e.g. clerical)	(Skilled manual, e.g. trades)	V (Unskilled labourers)
Numbers of first-born children	15	15	15	15
Numbers of second-born children	10	10	10	10
Total: (n = 100)	25	25	25	25

in these cases from what the man had said about the nature of his work. More importantly, it was difficult to fit some men into a social class group. Many had changed jobs since their occupation had been listed on the child-health records, and in three particular cases this caused problems, since the change in occupation represented a change in occupational class membership. For example, one father had been a dispatch clerk for six years, before changing eight weeks before his interview to become a coal-miner. As he seemed to be set on a career as a miner he was categorized accordingly. The two disabled and seven unemployed men were allocated to the category they had occupied before they stopped working.

Despite these problems in allocating fathers to their respective occupational groups, the sample appears to represent a broad spectrum of the population. Furthermore each group does seem to be distinguishable on measures other than that of occupation, as we see in Table 2.4. It shows that in terms of their ages and educational qualifications there was a tendency for couples belonging to the same occupational groupings to fit similar patterns. Mothers' and fathers' ages (measured by whether they are older or younger than twenty-five) and educational qualifications (measured by their attainment of CSEs or not) were related to social class membership.

On other measures differences were also apparent. For example, half the manual workers were born into families with four or more children, while only eight of the fifty white-collar workers came from such large families. These correlations suggest that the Registrar General's classifications serve to distinguish groups of people with widely different experiences.

Table 2.4   Age and education ranges
of mothers and fathers
(according to father's occupational class)

| | | | Social class | | |
		III	III (w.c.)	III (m.)	V
A g e	**Mother**				
	Less than 26	4	12	18	20
	26 or older	21	13	7	5
	$\chi^{2*} = 24.96$, df $= 3$, p < 0.0001.				
	Father				
	Less than 26	1	5	7	12
	26 or older	24	20	18	13
	$\chi^2 = 13.39$, df $= 3$, p < 0.005.				
E d u c a t i o n a l / Q u a l i f i c a t i o n s	**Mother**				
	No qualifications	4	6	16	17
	CSE or above	21	19	9	7
	$\chi^2 = 23.14$, df $= 3$, p < 0.0001.				
	Father				
	No qualifications	2	8	22	23
	CSE or above	23	17	3	2
	$\chi^2 = 52.48$, df $= 3$, p < 0.0001.				

*Throughout this book statistical comparisons between groups are made by the χ^2 (chi-squared) measure. This tests whether the differences between groups (i.e. social class groups) on a particular measure (i.e. age) are greater than might be expected by chance. The less the likelihood of a result due to chance, the smaller the probability value (e.g. where p < 0.0001 we can assume that there is a less than one in ten thousand likelihood that this pattern of results has arisen by chance).

The third reason why this sample cannot be described as a random one lies in the fact that I decided to discard unmarried fathers and to include only members of the indigenous population. While recent figures show that more than 10 per cent of children born in the UK today are illegitimate (Finer 1974) – to use a term that is perhaps out of date – I excluded unmarried men for two reasons. Firstly, recent research shows that unmarried fathers of young babies are not a homogeneous group. Vincent (1979) found that the fathers of illegitimate new-borns ranged from the 16 per cent who had no contact with them at all to the 32 per cent who were cohabiting with the mother. Vincent's findings suggested that the inclusion of unmarried fathers in this sample may well have made comparisons between types of men difficult. Secondly, unmarried fathers were excluded because my time was limited; these men may have been living away from their children and would have been difficult to trace.

When planning the study I decided to exclude first and second generation immigrant families from the sample, since previous studies at the Child Development Research Unit had shown that these groups employ different child rearing styles which merit special attention (Dosanjh, 1976; Grace, 1983). In fact all the fathers selected were Caucasian and had been born in Britain.

Making Contact and Collecting Data

Rationale: interviewing in retrospect at the child's first birthday
In Chapter 1 I criticized the 'transition to parenthood' studies because they appeared not to consider the father's point of view. The present research, like other recent British work (McKee and O'Brien 1982a), set out to examine early family life from that perspective. There are many ways of examining a parent's perceptions of the arrival of the first or second child. Each gives a picture of family life as valid as the next, but none is without problems. Even living with a family for an extended period raises problems of interpretation for the researcher (Golden 1975).

As was mentioned in Chapter 1, studies of the transition to parenthood have come increasingly to use longitudinal designs, in which men and women are interviewed at set intervals both before and after delivery. There is no doubt that this type of method adds greatly to our understanding of events, particularly in the way parents' attitudes and relationships change over the period. However, this approach is not problem-free. It is very costly, in research time and money, to make frequent visits to families and then to analyse the resulting data. This has a tendency to make researchers either rely upon psychological scales, which elicit a restricted amount of information, or limit their samples to small numbers.

Two more complex issues also arise. Firstly, it is difficult to assess any possible effect that frequent contact may have upon the relationship between researcher and researched, and upon the subsequent findings. This issue was considered by Rapoport (1964: 71), who interviewed married couples over a five-month period:

> As we were dealing with concurrent processual material obtained by repeated contacts (approximately 12 interviews over a period of five months), there was the possibility that we might actually change some of the phenomena under study. In such a situation it was felt that the continued contact might set up expectations (counter-transference) in the interviewer that might effect this eliciting of subsequent data.

The interviewer – respondent relationship not only influences the researcher; it is also possible that frequent contact will alter the interviewee's perceptions of topics under discussion. Oakley (1979) found that 73 per cent of the mothers in her study felt that their perceptions had been influenced by the research process.

The second issue arising from longitudinal studies of this period stems from the nature of the transition itself. As indicated in Chapter 1, studies have shown that the arrival of a child may be a difficult experience. It has been suggested that parents may be reluctant to discuss their 'inner feelings' while they are coping in the first few weeks of the child's life. Certainly this was the experience of one recent research project, which attempted to run and evaluate courses for new parents:

> The early weeks and months of parenthood, as reflected in the groups, overwhelmingly featured the relationship between mother and baby. Only later on (and after the first four months of the baby's life) were there occasional references to changes in marriage. This suggested that such change, as more than a temporary phenomenon, became apparent later rather than earlier, and that it could only be acknowledged retrospectively. In relation to anxieties about surviving the baby and the baby surviving and in common with a pattern evident in the pre-natal period, worries tend to be referred to only when a crisis was past.
>
> (Clulow 1982: 102)

While these comments do not undermine the validity of the longitudinal approach they suggest that other methods might also be used in constructing a picture of early family development. As mentioned earlier, the present study adopted the approach favoured by the Newsons (Newson and Newson 1963). Fathers were contacted a year post-partum and interviewed once only, the aim being to reconstruct a history of each father's relationship with his child. This method, like others, has built-in strengths and weaknesses. On the debit side, it does not enable matters to be discussed in as much depth as possible in a longitudinal study. Furthermore, there is the danger that in one visit the interviewer and interviewee will not build up a rapport or the amount of trust necessary for a fruitful discussion. On the credit side, this methodology may reduce the impact of the researcher's own beliefs upon respondents' answers and likewise the 'threat' that might arise from repeated visits.

The fathers in this study knew they were to see me only once. Many admitted afterwards that they had discussed aspects of their personal lives which they might have found difficult had they not known I was a stranger whom they would not see again. In addition, this methodology allowed me to interview a relatively sizeable sample and to cut the number of losses to a minimum.

Designing the interview
The fathers' interview schedule was designed to enable men to describe the transition to parenthood as a whole and as a historical progression. It was based upon a much modified version of Newson and Newson's (1963) original interview. Leaning heavily upon the Newsons' schedule had distinct advantages. They have tried and tested important features of the semi-structured interview. For example, they have paid close attention to the ordering of topics so that questions flow smoothly from one to another. Like the Newsons, I found that interviewees often answered questions before the interviewer came to them, such was their natural progression.

The Newsons also worked hard on evaluating the wording of particular questions, and many of these were copied to avoid such problems as leading respondents or discouraging them from saying what they felt. These techniques are discussed by the Newsons (1963: 21–3), and I will not reiterate them in full here. They include the placing of specific prompts after a general question, so that interviewers can discuss a topic from numerous perspectives and thus be more confident that they are arriving at a valid conclusion. I phrased some questions to allow what might be regarded as 'deviant' parents to admit their deviance. For example, instead of asking, 'Do you punish your child?' I asked, 'How do you punish him/her when he/she's naughty?' – thus accepting the view that one-year-olds may be legitimately described as 'naughty' and eligible for punishment.

The interview was designed to focus upon the child, or at least on the man's perception of his one-year-old, and to make reference to the father himself in the context of this discussion about the child. Specific events in the child's life were cited to clarify his account. Like the Newsons, I considered that an interest in the child would give parents a focal point around which to construct their accounts of parenthood. The literature on men and masculinity, considered in Chapter 1, suggested that discussion about fathers' feelings and emotions would be difficult, if not impossible. However, as the forthcoming chapters will reveal, fathers seemed more than willing to discuss their feelings about their children, themselves and their marriages.

Making contact
Fathers' names were selected from the child-health records when the children were within two weeks of their first birthday. They were contacted by a letter from the directors of the Child Development Research Unit, at the University of Nottingham – a research unit that has a local reputation. The letter stated that the research unit had long been interested in obtaining parents' points of view, but had thus far neglected fathers. It informed the father that his name had been selected because he had a one-year-old, and that I would be calling at 7.30 p.m. on a specified date, usually on the next-but-one weekday.

This initial contact is an important part of the research process. It is bound to colour a person's impressions of the aims of the research, and of course his willingness to participate. The letter was purposefully simple so that my request neither put fathers off nor gave them any wrong impressions about the nature of the research. When I knocked on the door I met a variety of responses. A few men needed persuading that my interests and motives were honest, but all except a handful accepted my arrival as if a visit from an interviewer from a university is a commonplace event in a parent's life. Indeed, three fathers who had not received the letter let me cross the threshold with the minimum of discussion. Only the six refusers 'challenged' my right to impose upon them.

I got the impression that the initial letter did not have much of an impact on fathers. Many had to be reminded that they had received it. Others were out when I called, and many of these stated later that they had forgotten about the letter, even though it had arrived a day or two before. In these cases I left a note saying that I had called and would call again. I would return to these households on the next available occasion when I failed to obtain an interview. 191 visits were needed to secure 100 interviews.

While in terms of losses from the sample this means of obtaining participation is very successful, it relies totally upon the compliance of parents. However, compliance does not mean support or co-operation, and before the start of each interview I often needed to spend time discussing the validity of this sort of research.

The interview procedure
Research interviews are designed to take on a ritual-like uniformity. Ideally, respondents are asked the same questions in similar contexts with the minimum interference from others. To a certain extent the interviewers met this aim. For example, as was mentioned above, parents seemed to ask the same questions before it began. Fathers often took two stances. They either exclaimed that they were willing to help but did not have much to say about their babies – their wives being the experts – or else greeted me as an ally in the campaign to take more notice of fathers. It's about time someone asked fathers was a comment made by many men.

During the preliminary discussion I extended some of the points made in the initial letter: my connections with the 'impartial' institution of the university, the general concern held by the members of the Child Development Research Unit that parents' views are important, the role of the unit in imparting these views to members of the 'helping professions', and also the fact that their names had been selected at random simply because they had a child who was one year of age.

The interviews were 'uniform' in the sense that all the men seemed interested in the questions and, once the ice was broken, to regard the venture as a valid one. No father refused to answer a question or failed to treat a point seriously. Interviews are commonplace events on television and radio, and many men commented that they had enjoyed being part of the discussion rather than a detached outsider. After the interviews most parents again raised the same issues – for example, they did not realize that there was so much to discuss about fatherhood or that they knew so much about their children and their own roles as parents.

While the interviewer hopes to maintain an atmosphere in which the respondent imparts his or her views, the research act is never so cut and dried. In two important respects these interviews failed to meet the objective standards set in planning the project. In the first place it was hoped that I could interview fathers alone, so that they would not be influenced by the presence of others, and we would not be distracted from our joint task. This preference had been clearly stated in the letter of introduction. However, as Lorna McKee (1979) found in her study, it was not always possible to interview husbands alone. In some cases there was only one warm room in the home and/or no space for me to interview the father alone. In others the wives wanted to attend, if only for part of the discussion, and I considered that it would cause too much friction if I pressed my claim to exclude them. In fact I felt that it could have spoilt some interviews to have done this. So, as Table 2.5 shows, the husband was alone throughout in 56 interviews, and the wife was present to witness

Table 2.5   Who was present at the interview?

Personnel	Frequency
Husband only	56
Husband mainly alone (wife for less half the time)	12
Wife mainly present (wife for more than half the time)	8
Husband and wife together	24
Total:	100

all the proceedings on 24 occasions; in the rest, the wife was present for at least part.

The second reason why my contact with the interviewees was not uniform lies in the nature of the research process itself. While a good interview schedule, which aims to compare respondents' views, must be designed with the utmost care in order to make data collection as reliable and comparable as possible, the process of collecting data is different on each occasion when it occurs. As O'Brien and McKee (1982: 3) write: 'the talk and interactions that take place in interview settings have their own degree of autonomy; interviews themselves are social constructs, as are our reading of them'. The interviews with these fathers produced a variety of areas of discussion, as indeed the schedule intended. Every father was asked the same questions, but their responses necessarily led to an interaction of an unique nature. This is demonstrated in the variations in the length of interviews. Some lasted for little more than 1½ hours, while the longest went on for over 4 hours.

There are three ways in which interviews can be seen to be idiosyncratic. Firstly, however much the interviewer attempts to take a neutral stance, complete disinterest is impossible. Thus I cannot help but admit to have been influenced by my feelings towards fathers' responses. In one, interview for example, the father made it known early in the conversation that he was a supporter of an extreme political party whose attitudes I abhor. While I attempted to 'accept' his viewpoint, it would be untrue to suggest that my inner feelings, however well concealed, did not impinge upon the interview.

Secondly, fathers themselves varied in the ways they tackled the interview, or parts of it. The reasons for the variation between them are many. Some appeared to be generally tongue-tied, while others used the occasion to leap on a particular hobby-horse; for example, one man gave vent to his hostility towards his wife's domiciliary midwife throughout his interview. Another father appeared to be very withdrawn or shy at the start of the interview but warmed up dramatically towards the end, when he admitted that he had been recovering from a dental anaesthetic when I arrived. Other men, particularly those working on early shifts, became noticeably tired towards the end of the interview, and on two occasions I agreed to return on another evening to finish. Each interview had an individual quality to it, as the examples I have provided should demonstrate.

The third factor that gave each interview its individuality stems from the 'interactions' to which O'Brien and McKee (1982) refer in the quotation above. Interviews are dynamic and reciprocal affairs, and involve a constant negotiation over both fine points and broad areas of understanding. This process is one finely balanced between leading respondents on the one hand and not saying enough to interest or focus their attention on the other. No interviewer can claim to succeed at steering the course between these two pitfalls at all times.

When the men's wives were present the discussion became even more complex. In the following extract a husband and wife express different views about their baby's initial feeding routine and, having disagreed, continue to argue their point of view.

> *Father:* She was fed at certain times –
> *Mother* (interrupts): No, she was demand-fed.
> *Interviewer:* When?
> *Mother:* Before three months.
> *Father:* Before three months old.
> *Mother:* We used to feed her when she woke, but kept it to the four feeds.
> *Father:* Yeah, but she used to have it at a certain time.
> *Mother:* Not really, she was a demand-feed.
> *Father* (interrupts): I wouldn't say that! I think she woke up at a routine for her bottles
> *Mother:* Well, she woke up every four hours, but it wasn't at twelve o'clock, say.
> *Father:* Oh no, I'd say she woke up every . . .
> *Interviewer:* She really chose the time? . . . And they just happened to be . . . ?
> *Mother:* No, she woke up every four hours, but we never went and woke her up for a bottle.
> *Interviewer:* Right!
>
> (Barreller and his wife, a housewife)

Wives who were present at the interview did tend to join in, even though I directed my questions to their husbands. They often did more than 'correct' fathers who made 'inaccurate' statements. In some cases the interview became an arena for marital conflict, where wives used the occasion to tell me that their husbands did not 'do enough to help' and where husbands reciprocated by justifying their minimal involvement, or by accusing their wives of nagging. In other interviews the presence of the wife as a support clearly helped to jog fathers' memories and focus their ideas.

Interviews vary according to the personnel involved. For example, Newson and Newson (1963) found that mothers' accounts to health visitors and university researchers differed over some issues. I thus compared the results obtained from the 'wife present' and 'father alone' sub-samples and found that the men interviewed alone consistently mentioned the negative aspects of parenthood, particularly upon their marriages, more than those interviewed with their wives present. In one case the difference was statistically significant; 80 per cent of the 'father alone' group felt that parenthood divided a couple in some way, while only 58 per cent of those of the 'wife present' group considered that this was the case for them ($\chi^2 = 5.41$, df = 1, $p < 0.05$). There are many possible reasons why this result was obtained. It might be that the presence of their wives and fathers' answers to this question both have the same cause – in that 'close' couples could have taken steps to be interviewed together.

An interview of this kind ebbs and flows in terms of the ground of shared understanding covered, and there is always a danger that misunderstandings may occur. For example, the interviewer asks questions that might also be asked by a member of the helping professions, particularly doctors, which may never crop up in a father's conversation with friends and family. As a result there is a danger that the interviewee might perceive the interviewer as a representative of these professions. Thus, despite my reassurances at the start of the interview, fathers often made reference to my role as if I was representative of a particular group. One father justified his wife's decision to bottle-feed their baby with the following statement: 'I mean, I don't know what you people in the hospital see as advantages in particular, but I don't think any of my nieces and nephews have been breast-fed and there's nothing wrong with any of them. That's as good a test as any' (panel beater). Nowhere had I mentioned to this father any connection with 'the hospital' or any preference for breast-feeding. He simply assumed that, as a representative of 'professionals', I would hold these views.

The small sample
The one hundred fathers comprised the main sample in this study, and their accounts serve as the major focus of attention in the forthcoming chapters. However, taken by themselves, their descriptions of their roles would tell only one side of a complex and detailed story. As a result, part-way through the study, when funds were made available, it was decided that a sub-sample of wives would be interviewed specifically about the same issues discussed with fathers. Comparing mothers' and fathers' accounts would, firstly, corroborate men's assessments of the extent of their practical involvement with the child and, secondly, broaden our conceptual framework for understanding fathers' responses.

We had funds available for interviews with thirty mothers, and it was agreed that these would best be done by a woman, since we suspected that a male interviewer might not be very effective at discussing fathers' roles with mothers. Thus at the end of an interview at which only the father had been present I asked him if his wife would like to take part as well, explaining that a colleague of mine would like to talk to some wives about fathering. All the potential 'candidates' were asked, until thirty had agreed. Four women refused; one said she was too shy, one had had an argument with her husband and I decided not to press the question too hard, and two changed their minds after I had left the household, having initially agreed to participate.

The 'small sample' consisted of the wives of fifteen middle- and fifteen working-class men. The middle-class group was balanced between

professional and clerical workers. Since many skilled manual workers had
been interviewed before I started recruiting this sub-sample, the wives of
unskilled workers outnumbered them by ten to five in the working-class
group of mothers.

As discussion in the coming chapters will show, I compared the
30 mothers' and 30 fathers' accounts only to set the 100 fathers' comments
into context. There are many reasons why the wives' interviews play a
secondary function. The primary focus of this study is on fathers. At the
same time, more detailed comparisons of mothers' and fathers' accounts
would need a clearer understanding of how the research process influenced
the results of the study. For example, it would have to consider the effect
of the styles the two interviewers used for each sample and the procedural
consequences of talking to fathers (who did not know that their wives were
also going to be approached) before mothers (who knew that their husbands
had already been interviewed).

Analysis of parents' accounts
The fathers' interview schedule consisted of 193 questions, with numerous
prompts and points of classification. These gave rise to many answers by
which the one hundred men's experiences and attitudes could be compared.
These varied from the factual (e.g. the man's social class or the number
of children in his family) to the impressionistic (e.g. the man's attitude
towards breast-feeding).

The coding of responses was carried out with the aid of tape-recordings
of the interviews. The 193 questions gave me a massive amount of numerical
data – 235 items per interview – since the prompts themselves were
sometimes coded. These data could therefore have been analysed in a variety
of ways. In order to impose some structure I carried out the analysis in
three stages. Firstly, I examined the responses to each question among
various types of father. The research was designed so that fathers of first
and second children and from the four social class groups could be
compared. In addition, certain issues arose from the literature, and I
compared men according to the sex of the child, their wives' employment
status and the hours they themselves spent at work. Secondly, I compared
the responses of the thirty mothers with those of their husbands to examine
the similarities and differences between the accounts. Finally I carried out
single analyses that merited examinatioin.

Upon these numerical bones I collected lengthy excerpts of the interviews
to flesh out mothers' and fathers' accounts of the paternal role. While the
numerical data provide us with an impression of fathers' attitudes, the
extracts from interviews help to make them more concrete and
understandable. As a result the following discussion relies heavily upon
a balance of the quantitative and the qualitative. In order to present fathers'
points of view clearly, there is a great temptation to polish up extracts of

commentary. Interviews are often disjointed affairs with long pauses, frequent repetitions and many fragmented and ungrammatical sentences. In the transcript material I quote I have attempted to leave untouched almost all of the discourse, because changing just a few words can alter the meaning of a person's statement.

Conclusion

This chapter has outlined the methods and procedures used in the study. While the research act is an 'artefact', as Clulow (1982) suggests, I have described the steps taken to make the results of the study as valid as possible.

The following discussion will present numerical and idiographic data in tandem. The accounts of the one hundred fathers will be the central focus of concern, but in addition I will refer to the mothers who were interviewed. This latter group of thirty, together with their husbands, will be referred to as the 'small sample'.

Part Two
From Man to Father

3   *Expectant Fatherhood*

Introduction

This chapter and the next will examine the events leading up to the arrival of a baby. Men's reactions to pregnancy and delivery provide a good starting-point for this study, not only because they chart the origins of paternal identification with the child, but also because they reveal some of the complexities of the father's role.

In almost all societies the arrival of a child is greeted by changes in the parents' lives, which are marked out by prescribed rituals and practices (Paige and Paige 1981). As Ann Oakley writes:

> Having a baby is a cultural act. In bearing a child, a woman reproduces the species and performs an 'animal function'. Yet human childbirth is accomplished in and shaped by culture, both in a general sense and in the particular sense of the varying definitions of reproduction offered by different cultures.
>
> (1980: 5)

There are many 'definitions of reproduction' in western culture. On the one hand, those who regard pregnancy as a medical event tend to focus upon the woman's changing physiology. In contrast, proponents of 'natural childbirth' emphasize the influence of social factors on our understanding. Such a contrast in views is clearly reflected in the literature on both women and their husbands during pregnancy.

The vast bulk of literature discusses pregnancy in purely physiological terms and concentrates upon its potential disorders and complications (Breen 1975). As a result, fathers are not usually even considered. They receive attention only when they react pathologically to their wives' pregnancies (Arnstein 1972, Beail 1982, Coley and James 1976, Einzig 1980, Fein 1978a,

31

Trethowan 1972). Trethowan (1972) found that more than 10 per cent of expectant fathers experience acute physical symptoms, which often mimic those of pregnancy; nausea, stomach cramps and sickness are the most common. These comprise what he calls the 'couvade syndrome'.

However, in recent years there has been an increasing number of accounts which regard pregnancy from a social perspective. These publications come in the main from medical sociology, and stress the social influences upon the woman's passage through childbirth. They suggest that the experience of pregnancy is influenced by factors like the amount a baby is planned (Miller 1973) and also the nature of contact between the woman and the professionals who guide her through pregnancy (Macintyre 1976, Oakley 1980).

Similar moves have occurred in the literature on fathers. While some isolated examples of psychological research have regarded expectant fatherhood as a period of normal 'development' (Jessner *et al.* 1970) or have attempted to categorize the different types of approach that men might take to their wives' pregnancies (McCorkel 1964), the only concerted attempt to understand men's perceptions again comes from medical sociology (see for example, Brown 1982, McKee 1980, Richman 1982, Richman and Goldthorp 1978, Richman *et al.* 1975). By showing that expectant fatherhood stimulates psychological changes in men and in their relationship with their wives, these studies underline the importance of a model of pregnancy that goes beyond the physiological changes in the expectant mother.

Most notable is the research of Joel Richman and his colleagues. Richman's central thesis is that men are culturally separated from the process of child-bearing, firstly because their roles are ill-defined and secondly because the medical profession, the agency which determines how pregnancy should be perceived and experienced in our culture, actively works to exclude them:

> the father still remains the sleeping partner in the cultural conspiracy against fatherhood. . . . Fathers can be said to be alienated from the process of reproduction. They have a long way to go in developing their rights and consciousness about childbirth.
> (Richman *et al.*, 1975: 145)

> Birth provides the justification for initiating a series of new practices. The woman's status passage to birth is biologically and culturally visible. Men's pregnancy careers are primarily opaque, often more diffuse, but are still capable of producing attachment to the child-to-be.
> (Richman and Goldthorp 1978: 164)

As a result of their 'opaque' social status, Richman, like McCorkel (1964) before him, suggests that men may pursue a variety of possible 'careers'. At one extreme, they may deny that their wives are pregnant; at the other, some appear to take the experience over from their wives, by identifying with the foetus.

This chapter takes up many of the issues raised by Richman. Like him, I found that men are kept somewhat at arm's length from the events which mark out pregnancy, and that men experience the many changes in a variety of ways. However, fathers themselves suggest that a full understanding of men's pregnancy careers must take into account their relationship with the mother-to-be.

Preparation for Parenthood: the Man's 'Opaque' Role

A brief examination of some landmarks before the conception of their first child shows how and why men become secondary figures in family life. It is tempting to assume that males are kept at a distance from the process which socializes women to become ready for parenthood, or alternatively to think that men cut themselves off from such unmasculine activities. Both these assumptions have some grounding in fact, but the picture is more complex.

Experience before marriage
Before becoming parents themselves males are unlikely to have had much contact with babies or young children. Fifty-four of the fathers in this sample had hardly touched a baby before they were married. Only eighteen had taken regular responsibility for young children, and these were significantly more likely to have a sibling some years younger than themselves. However, such patterns are not peculiar to males. A comparison of the couples in the small sample showed no differences between mothers and fathers in their experience; nearly half (43 per cent) of the women had not cared for a baby before their own.

On some measures fathers and mothers do differ. For example, males are far less likely to have attended or wished to participate in classes instructing teenagers in the skills of parentcraft. Only one father (of the hundred) had had any such lessons at school, while 23 per cent of the mothers had attended them. When asked whether they would, in retrospect, have liked such classes, mothers were far more likely to profess an interest (73 per cent vs 17 per cent; $\chi^2 = 17.24$, df = 1, p < 0.0001).

The large difference between fathers' and mothers' (*post hoc*) feelings about parentcraft education matches the results of studies carried out with teenagers and young adults about the same issues. These show that, while girls seem keen that courses should be laid on to teach the skills of parenting, boys, teachers and parents give this topic very low priority (Balding 1977).

Again, it is tempting to conclude from these findings that males are simply less interested in the prospect of parenting than their female peers, but this may well be a false assumption. It has been repeatedly found that schools' courses themselves are 'dominated by home economics teachers' (Clark 1981) and as a result to be aimed at *girls* in low-ability groups (Cowley and Daniels 1981, Heron 1981, Smith 1985). On a more practical level, the way that courses are presented in schools, and the formal and informal pressures upon them to take 'male' options like woodwork, may well make males appear to be less child-centred than they really are. Indeed, discussion about their plans to have children suggests that this is a more valid interpretation of their accounts.

However little they have prepared themselves for parenthood, young adults seem to accept the cultural prescription that they will have children (Busfield 1974). Both young men (Long 1978) and women (Hubert 1974) express such beliefs. When asked to reflect back upon their desire to become parents, twenty-four of the fathers in the study claimed to have had no idea about having children of their own.

> I must admit I wasn't bothered either way. We planned for James, he wasn't a mistake, but if the wife had been in the same mind I don't think we'd have had any children.
>
> (Goods representative)

> I didn't have any ideas about getting married, to be honest. I wasn't really interested. . . . In fact I didn't really like children.
>
> (Civil servant 1)

However, the remaining seventy-six men recalled having assumed that they would become parents. Forty-four of these had definite plans about the number of children they would have; one, for example, had signed a Friends of the Earth declaration to limit the size of his family to two children. This group contained significantly more middle-class men (54 per cent vs 34 per cent working-class; $\chi^2 = 4.1$, df = 1, p < 0.05).

> Yeah, I only wanted two no matter what they were. [Prompt: 'Were you very definite about it?'] I did, but the wife wanted four, like. [Prompt: 'Can you say what made you decide?'] Well . . . the money and the way things are now I thought I could bring two up but I don't think it would be fair to bring any more up and the first two'd have to suffer. [Prompt: 'In what way?'] Well, clothes, food, keeping. Well . . . general.]
>
> (Fork-lift-truck driver)

The 'decision' to have a child; negotiation or 'drift'?
'Education for Parenthood' is a fashionable discussion topic these days, so the data on men's preparation for fatherhood might be regarded as crucial. However, these interviews with fathers suggest two other factors showing a reduced likelihood that men do prepare themselves

psychologically for the arrival of their first child. These are chance, and the man's secondary biological role in the parturition process. I will turn to these issues in turn.

In theory, with so many effective birth-control methods available a couple can plan a family with clinical precision. In practice, many parents report that the onset of pregnancy is a more muddled affair. The decision to try for a child is often very hard. Surveys like that of Cartwright (1976) suggest that just under half of pregnancies are 'unintended'. When questioned about the discussion that took place before conception, forty-five of the fathers in the study admitted that they had not seriously discussed the matter with their wives. Interestingly, there was no difference between first- and second-time fathers on this matter. An even higher proportion of mothers (60 per cent) felt that the topic was not considered.

The fifty-five fathers who had discussed the prospect of having a child were by no means a homogeneous group. Some couples were clear about how many children they were planning. Many of these made a definite plan to conceive, usually by abandoning birth-control methods, but in an important sense such couples may be said to 'drift' into pregnancy. As La Rossa (1977) suggests, newly pregnant couples have little mental conception of what parenthood entails. One woman, a 'planner' in that she stopped using birth-control methods, described her feelings at the start of her pregnancy:

> Pleased, but very apprehensive at the same time, 'cos we never planned . . . I mean, I ran out of . . . 'cos we moved to Nottingham and um . . . I ran out of pills and I'd only just got into work and Anthony [husband] wasn't working then, but we *knew* . . . I mean, if you don't have pills, you'll end up being pregnant. So it was choice, but it wasn't really planned as people *do* sit back and say, 'Right, this is it.'
> (Full-time housewife, whose husband is a factory labourer)

For others, an unplanned pregnancy which ended in a miscarriage or even a delayed period suddenly crystallized each partner's feelings into a joint decision to attempt to conceive:

> When it came to it she thought she was pregnant and she wasn't. But we were both upset, having got used to the idea. I don't think we would've ever consciously said to ourselves, 'We can now afford children', but then once we thought Sue was pregnant and she wasn't we were rather disappointed so we thought, 'In that case we may as well have some!' – having got used to the idea.
> (Deputy headmaster of a primary school)

However much couples drift into pregnancy, the move to have a child comes from wives much more than husbands. The wife was three times more likely to bring the subject up, and many commented that if the husband raised the issue he tended to make light of the topic.

There seemed to be two reasons why men accounted for their reluctance to initiate discussion about having children. Firstly, in keeping with a cultural stereotype about men, fathers tended to stress that the pressure to provide for the family was imposed more on them than their wives:

> We didn't quite plan it as clinically as . . . we did [plan] Simon . . . but I think it was a 'let's see how we go on with one' . . . we'd agreed on that. . . . Well, I think how it started was I'd got at that time . . . (I'm a little bit better now) . . . pressures with me mortgage and with one or two other things. It's not that I didn't want him but I had to get one or two things straight first. So then, as Helen [wife] pointed out, you can go on for ever feeling like that and you'll never have any children. So we agreed eventually to, um, have 'im. I think it was persuasion from Helen in the end.
>
> (Warehouse labourer)

A few husbands contend that child-rearing and the decision to parent are outside their frame of reference and interest. These admit their minimal role:

> I met Annette in the January and we married in the August, so . . . you know, it never . . . and then Annette fell for Heather [older child] about three, four months later. . . . So we never actually *talked* about it. Heather came along and it's as simple as that. [Prompt: 'So would you say you *never* discussed it?'] No, I don't think we ever discussed it, thinking back. You tend to discuss it *after* the fact. You know . . . once there's a baby on the way then that's the topic of conversation for the nine months.
>
> (Carpet salesman)

> Well, it was a fluctuating state, really. I *think* that Cathy probably always reckoned that two was the number that she was going to have and didn't always acquaint me with the fact. [Prompt: 'And how about yourself?'] I think probably there was a seven-year gap, or thereabouts, between the two and I probably reached the conclusion that we weren't going to have any more . . . without any great discussion.
>
> (Managing director)

These types of account were few in number, but they reveal something general about the detached stance many men take when they discuss the prospect of having children. Some may be totally uninterested, but a large majority feel they should defer to their wives on this matter. The biological difference between a man and woman makes them re-create the social difference between them; child-bearing and child-rearing seem to coexist naturally with one another in the minds of most fathers:

> It's wrong for me to sort of say, 'I want another child', because Jane has got total responsibility for bearing it and having it and bringing

it up . . . although I'm here to sort of help basically, whereas, you know, she's got the . . . the whole lot, hasn't she really?

(Journalist)

These sentiments tie in with those expressed by men in a study of involuntarily childless couples (Owens 1982). Owens found that however much men wanted children their main concern, when attending an infertility clinic, was to provide a child for their wives, whose social status very much depended upon their role as mother. This view – a direct contrast to the patriarchal notion that the woman should provide an heir for her husband – seemed to underlie many of the comments of fathers in the sample.

While Cartwright (1976: chapter 3) found that 9 per cent of women felt that the pressure to produce another child came from their husband, these fathers, like those interviewed by Jackson (1984), tended to place great stress upon their respect for their wives' responsibility for child-bearing. In only one case did a man 'persuade' his girl-friend to have a child, and that was by pleading with her not to have an abortion – she had 'caught' by accident. Another father summed up his attempts to 'conceal' his own feelings about having a child:

> I got it into me mind that I'd like one child. . . . Then when we got married we weren't going to have none 'cos Lindsay didn't want one, [Prompt: 'So you changed your mind then, did you?'] Well, I didn't want to push her. No use having one if she don't want none, you see . . . but she changed her mind. . . . I was putting a bit of pressure on her at the time but then I found that the best thing was to leave it alone and say nothing about it. . . . Then one day she just mentioned it to me . . . and that was it'.

(Records clerk)

The apparent contradiction between Cartwright's study of women and the men in this study is explained in part by the fact that each study represents the opinions of one of the sexes; but it does seem that men attempt to conceal their desires. Some of the wives in the study were unaware of their husbands' aspirations about parenthood, and not one of those who planned the baby felt that her husband was compelling her to have a child. For example, one woman, who originally did not want children, had been uncertain about her husband's feelings:

> [Interviewer: 'Were you in agreement, you and John, about not having a child?'] I don't know. John's quiet. He was willing to accept the fact that I'd never have a child when I married, because I told him before we got married and he was willing to accept that as part of me . . . you know, it was accepting my way. But I don't know whether he, he, you know . . . underneath he wanted children or not. He never showed any affection for children *ever*, but was it just for consideration for me? I couldn't tell you: . . . He's a very deep person. I know when I got pregnant he was *extremely* pleased, very frightened

about it in a way, but . . . oh, he was a changed person. . . . You know, his character softened a lot and, er, I think after about four months of pregnancy I realized just how *much* it meant to him, so I mean obviously he wanted one.

(Full-time housewife, whose husband is a legal executive)

This quotation reflects two themes which recurred in fathers' accounts. Firstly, the decision to become pregnant is often the responsibility of the wife, if a decision is made. Secondly, although men and women report having roughly similar desires to have or not to have children (there seemed to be great variation within both groups), the husband is often *seen* as being uninterested in the possibility, usually because he is concerned not to force his wife to comply with his wishes.

Public detachment from pregnancy

In terms of planning the child, therefore, a large proportion of men seem to take a secondary role. The same patterns continue during pregnancy. Sociological studies, discussed earlier, have shown that fathers have only minimal contact with the official 'socializing agents of this period – the clinics, classes and parents' evenings (Brown 1982, McKee 1980, Richman 1982, Richman and Goldthorp 1978). Table 3.1 shows that few of these fathers took part in such activities.

Joel Richman (1982) emphasized how medical procedures have the effect of keeping men at arm's length while their wives learn about the changes occurring within their bodies. Certainly this is true for the antenatal clinics, but when discussing the classes and tours round the hospital many fathers reveal that they prefer to withdraw from such public displays of their involvement in the pregnancy.

Table 3.1 Fathers' attendance at official procedures in pregnancy

Procedure	Description	Attendance (%)
Antenatal clinics	Medical check-ups that occur with increasing frequency as the pregnancy progresses	32 (1 participant)
Parentcraft and relaxation classes	Basic psychoprophylaxis and child care (usually a six-week course)	6
Parents' evenings	Tours round the hospital labour 'suite' and obstetric ward, often with a film of a delivery (usually a two-week course)	23

Antenatal clinics

Like Richman and Goldthorp (1978), I found that a sizeable proportion of fathers (32 per cent) take their wives to at least one antenatal clinic, especially near the end of pregnancy when they are less mobile. Yet only one man got beyond the waiting-room. His presence during examination was 'excused' because his wife was disabled and needed carrying from cubicle to cubicle. Some, particularly first-timers, are bewildered by the fact that the staff ignore them:

> None of 'em ever spoke. . . . [Prompt: 'How did you feel there?']
> I felt uneasy, you know, 'cos I didn't know what were going off and nobody spoke to you. . . . I think that husbands should be allowed to go in with their wives.
>
> (Coal-miner)

For the vast majority of fathers antenatal clinics are not as welcoming as the initiate might hope, and the nature of obstetric practice in these clinics puts experienced men and women off the idea of fathers attending:

> No, I certainly wouldn't. I think gynae, and antenatal clinics are a disaster in any hospital. They're a horrible sort of cattle-market.
>
> (Doctor)

> No, they weren't allowed past the waiting-room either at Peel Street [local maternity hospital] or at the doctor's. . . . [Prompt: 'Would he have got anything out of it?'] Not really. . . . You're pushed around . . . they don't treat you like people.
>
> (Part-time cleaner, whose husband is a factory labourer)

Antenatal classes

As Table 3.1 shows, only six of the fathers attended parentcraft classes of any sort. There are three main reasons why this figure is so low. To begin with, almost half of the wives (41 per cent) did not attend. Non-attenders tended to be second-timers (46 per cent vs 36 per cent first-timers; $\chi^2 = 7.7$, df = 1, $p < 0.01$). Class attendance was also clearly related to social class membership – see Table 3.2. Working-class men were far more likely to express animosity towards hospitals, professionals and the contemporary belief that parents need to be educated for their role. As one father commented:

> I think they used to manage in times gone by without all this . . . so I don't feel that there's any need for it myself. . . . Just a check-up to see that everything's all right, that's adequate.
>
> (Textile foreman)

Secondly, most classes take place during the day, when a majority of men cannot take time off work to participate. This might lead some to

Table 3.2   Mothers' attendance at antenatal classes

Social class	No attendance	Attended at least 1 class
III	5	20
III (w.c.)	9	16
III (m.)	11	14
V	16	9

$\chi^2 = 10.47$, df = 3, p < 0.02.

assume that men are kep at bay as a result. However, further discussion revealed a third reason for their non-attendance. Like the clinics, classes are events which reveal the cultural segregation of men's and women's spheres. A man's presence at relaxation class would embarrass all concerned, unless he were a doctor. Both husbands and wives agree on this matter:

> Certainly never went to any of those parent evenings . . . parent-craft . . . whatever they were supposed to be . . . probably because taken on hearsay . . . some of the people that we have known that had babies and some of them . . . and some of the experiences I've had of those things – they're all sort of common-sense things – that I *presumed* I already *knew* and I felt that really it didn't warrant the time which I spent there. They apparently did some silly things like lying on the floor and groaning like you were in labour. That sort of thing is OK, fine, but it seems such a waste. I don't know whether it is or not, we seem to have got through quite well, more than well, without participating in that so I didn't actually go to that. There were six, I think.
>
> (Sales representative)

> We weren't particularly encouraged, men weren't, to the actual relaxation classes because its just mainly all women there anyway. [Wife interjects: 'I wasn't all that keen on him going anyway, because, you know' (laughs) 'because, you know . . . I mean the demonstrations, "come on, push, push!"'] And it's not very nice, you know, it's *all* women there, not just your wife, you know. I mean it's a bit *basic*.
>
> (Unemployed sales representative and his wife, a housewife)

Parents' evenings

The low number of attenders at parents' evenings (23 per cent) is perhaps surprising. These are designed so that fathers can participate, and many hospital now call them 'fathers' evenings'. However, men see them in the same light as classes. They recoil in horror at the prospect of having to change a doll's nappy in the presence of others, for example. So despite pressure from their wives many will not attend.

Attenders do not all sing the praises of these evenings, nor do most claim to learn much from them. However, visits to the hospital allay their fears about taking their wives to the wrong place during advanced labour; they make events and the father's presence at delivery less embarrassing, and many comment that the visit provides them with their first encounter with a new-born baby:

> We went to some film shows and . . . it was very enlightening, yeah. . . . They showed us all the wards . . . where we would go, and that was nice to know. . . . I didn't want to go at first, but when I did finally get there, you know . . . I'm glad I went. . . . [Prompt: 'For any particular reasons?'] Yeah, I found out what the nurses were like and what goes on there and it all seemed very nice . . . that reassures you a bit. As I say, they shows us the delivery rooms and they looked nice. . . . And that's another thing . . . knowing what to do instead of making a fool of yourself when you're in there.
>
> (Central-heating mechanic)

> Did I go to any? . . . Yes I did, em . . . either once or twice I think. Once to see a film and I think a subsequent time to see a baby being bathed and nappies being folded and things like that. [Prompt: 'What did you get out of those two?'] Well, I think the baby being bathed was very interesting because I'd never seen such a tiny baby. . . . It was . . . this was probably the first time . . . a new-born child . . . it was a couple of days old, or perhaps even just a day old, so I found that very entertaining . . . well, very instructive anyway . . . but, um, the film . . . moderately instructive . . . the talk the midwives gave and so on not so instructive, but it was all right. [Prompt: 'But it was worth going to, was it?'] Oh, definitely . . . even though I'd heard it all before, it was worth going to see it, yes.
>
> (Engineering lecturer)

Reading about pregnancy

Even the least imposing or threatening of the sources of official 'knowledge' and involvement in pregnancy – the many leaflets which are distributed to women – seemed not to take up the interest or involvement of men. This is partly explained by the fact that many second-timers read nothing (77 per cent vs 33 per cent first-timers read nothing; $\chi^2 = 15.16$, df $= 1$, $p < 0.0002$).

Irrespective of their previous parental status, the 'reading' done by these fathers was, on the whole, cursory to say the least. Twenty-five read nothing, while twenty-three skimmed through the material without being very impressed by anything apart from the pictorial representations of foetal growth. The vast majority of fathers, including some of the thirty that read popular books on the subject, felt confused and isolated by the information provided, and many of their wives agreed with them.

Yeah, what they gave you in a vanity bag. [Prompt: 'Were there any that stuck in your mind at all?'] No, no, I don't . . . only . . . well, personally I think they're a load of rubbish actually, 'cos, you know . . . I don't . . . [Wife: 'We had two books the same, one of Robert and one of Louise, and they both said difference things, yet they were both the same publisher and everything.'] Yes, in my opinion you should bring up your kids in your own way. Other people's ways . . . all right . . . their children are different to what mine are. [Prompt: 'So you found them not very useful after all?'] No, not really.

(Disabled labourer and his wife, a housewife)

During the mid-1970s, when the new cult of father involvement was gaining popularity, it was assumed by many that men read little because publications represented a picture of parenthood that was mother-centred (De Frain 1977). Recent years have witnessed an increasing number of popular books on pregnancy and parenthood for fathers (Bitman and Zalk 1978, Fenwick and Fenwick 1978, Grad *et al.* 1981, Little and Ralston 1981, Parsons, 1975/81, Schaeffer 1964/72) and men receive frequent attention in general books and magazines on child care. Yet even in the United States, where the number of publications aimed at men is daunting, the small amount of evidence which exists seems to suggest that a very small proportion of those reading this material are men (Clarke-Stewart 1978a).

There seem to be two main aspects of the new father-centred publications which are likely to discourage men from reading them. Firstly, they tend to focus upon the pathological reactions of men, which are paramount in the psychological literature. Parsons's book, for example, is subtitled 'a guide for the anxious male'. As I shall suggest later in this chapter, while many men experience feelings of acute stress they also attempt to deny that these feelings exist, so they are unlikely to preoccupy themselves with reading about them. Secondly, many of these publications attempt to communicate with expectant fathers by making light of pregnancy, and their chatty and condescending style often pokes fun at the 'pregnant man'. Little and Ralston (1981), for example, depict the reactions of men in absurd cartoons.

The reading material for fathers that is distributed in clinics and maternity hospitals is more traditional in its orientation and portrays the man as being somewhat removed from the child-bearing process. At one Nottingham hospital, parents were given two leaflets. One, entitled *Advice for Father*, is a lengthy description of the types of condom supplied by a particular company. The other attempts to be more constructive by offering practical advice about the effect that parenthood might have upon his life. Yet it treats the father as a jealous hedonist, whose main preoccupation after the delivery of the child is the resumption of his sexual relationship with his wife. For example, on the topic of feeding the baby, it states:

In our society we have tended to regard the breast as primarily of sexual importance rather than a functional part of the body, intricately formed to feed babies. Because of this sexual rather than functional bias, some men look upon their wife's breasts as their 'domain'. They relish the sensual pleasures of feeling, stroking and sucking them – they are part of love making. They do not take kindly to a little infant coming in on the act – and who can blame them? Fathers who feel this may be cheered by some research that has shown that women who breast feed their babies are more likely to resume sexual activity quicker than their bottle feeding sisters! Also, many women find that they are more sexually active during the time they are breast feeding than at any other time in their lives.

> (From the Wyeth Laboratories publication,
> *It's Your Baby Too*, for fathers)

Summary
When expectant fathers are studied simply in terms of their contact with the medical agencies which process women through pregnancy, it is no wonder that their role is described as 'opaque'. Their involvement is limited by three interacting factors. Firstly, the medical authorities dissuade them from attending 'official' activities like the antenatal clinics. Secondly, there is a more general cultural expectation that some aspects of the pregnancy are not open to male participation. Thirdly, they are reluctant to be seen to transgress this norm, even when official activities are especially provided for them.

Private Involvement in Pregnancy: the Marital Relationship

Pregnancy for married couples is not simply a series of events whereby women are processed through educational and clinical procedures. It is a time when couples perceive great changes in themselves and in their social and marital relationships. The most central of these stems from the ideal of marital symmetry. The arrival of a baby is seen as a high point in marriage, and as a result parents describe the experience as a joint one.

Both parents strive to 'forge' a relationship with the foetus, as Richman and Goldthorp (1978) put it. However, we have to use two meanings of the verb 'forge' to understand psychological change in the expectant father. On the one hand, he strives with his wife to involve himself in shared parenting; on the other, he is not pregnant, so his psychological investment often seems false, contried or even counterfeit.

The experience shared
Married couples tend to describe expectant parenthood as a joint venture – in what the psychoanalyst Deutscher (1970) terms the 'alliance' of

pregnancy. There are many possible influences upon the way events unfold. These include whether a baby is planned, the couple's relationship and a variety of other factors. At first both partners have to come to terms with the fact that the woman is expecting, and this can influence each of them differently:

> Mixed feelings, really . . . I planned her and I caught almost straight away, so I was pleased in a lot of ways . . . but I also thought, 'Oh dear, I've done it now', you know. I mean, it wasn't a rush decision . . . we'd discussed it for a long time. It was just – it seemed a bit final, because I didn't go to the doctor straight away, I did one of those predictor tests and . . . I did it about five o'clock in the morning because you have to be in for two hours and I looked at it and there was this little brown ring and I went flying in to Keith and he was still asleep in bed, and told him . . . and it was a bit of an anticlimax in a way, because there was nothing to *show*. I just knew I was pregnant. I would say I was pleased, yeah.
>
> (Housewife, whose husband is the civil servant quoted above)

After an initial period of getting used to the pregnancy or plain disbelief, both expectant parents rely upon physical signs to make the experience real. Feeling the foetus move for the first time helps them appreciate that the child really exists. It is often recalled as a momentous event for both prospective parents, although men necessarily gain this assurance much later than expectant mothers and as part of a shared experience. Once the pregnancy becomes a 'reality' to them, fathers describe the unfolding of stages, in the same way that women do (Miller 1973). Events are explained in social as well as physical terms. The second trimester (between the third and sixth months of the pregnancy) is perceived as being a time for activity and preparation, while the final weeks are characterized by anticipation and boredom. One father summed up some of these stages:

> Well, you see, pregnancy takes a long time. Um, it seems to go on and on and sometimes you wonder if it'll ever come to an end. It's very hard to imagine at first. Although one is told, 'You are expecting a baby', there's no immediate sign of it, and it takes a long time before you see any evidence of it. So I suppose we were a bit sceptical for quite a while. . . . I mean, not that I didn't believe that she was pregnant, I couldn't imagine anything was going to change very much in the early stages. Later on that was replaced by impatience . . . hoping it was going to be over.
>
> (Engineering lecturer)

Apart from simply interpreting physiological 'growth' in their wives, pregnancy stimulates a number of changes for husbands that are purely social in their origins. The married couples in this and other studies (Bobak 1977, Dodendorf 1978) suggest that pregnancy stimulates a number of practical rearrangements in their lives, which depend very much upon their circumstances. They jointly perform 'nest-building' activities. For some first-time parents this means getting married, setting up home together and even getting to know one another:

> Just before we got married, when she was having a baby, we sort of got closer to each other. We sort of bonded each other, you know. [Prompt: 'Was there anything particular about the bond?'] I think it was the birth, you know, actually knowing she was pregnant, it sort of joined us together. You see, before Sharon was being born we didn't used to find out much about each other . . . just a casual relationship . . . and when we found out she was pregnant we got to know each other better.
>
> (Unemployed labourer)

Most parents preoccupy themselves with joint expeditions to Mothercare shops and decorating the baby's room. This sharing of experiences contributes to the closeness which, as I shall discuss later, couples claim to feel during pregnancy:

> I think they get closer if anything. . . . [Prompt: 'For any particular reason?'] Yeah, I think because you're both more . . . yeah, you've got something to share, and you're deciding together what to get for the children, or child, you know . . . what decorations, what sort of prams.
>
> (Disabled labourer)

So, while the stages unfold, couples work together to protect and nourish their offspring. Studies over the past thirty years (e.g. Landis 1950) show that expectant parents abstain early on in the pregnancy from their usual sexual activities, even though they may be advised that it will do no harm to the baby. Fathers often state the belief that they can nourish their offspring through caring for their wives:

> I probably took a much more protective attitude towards her . . . and I've got a theory, which may be right and may be wrong . . . in fact, it's probably wrong 'cos there's no basis for it and it's not at all scientific . . . which is that the sort of general physical and mental state of the baby starts, you know, virtually at conception, or very shortly thereafter, and is very heavily dependent on the mental and physical state of the mum throughout pregnancy. Not just the physical condition, which is obvious, but the sort of contentment, you know. So I've made a particular job of trying to ensure that Nancy had a happy, comfortable, if you like relaxed pregnancy, one that was completely free, as far as I could make it, of any sort of traumas, you know. I might be right and I might be wrong, but I don't think I'm wrong somehow.
>
> (House-husband and part-time photo-journalist)

Table 3.3 Fathers' reports of their wives' initial reaction to pregnancy

	Some negative feelings	All positive
Social class		
III	5	20
III (w.c.)	5	20
III (m.)	8	17
V	13	12
Totals:	31	69

$\chi^2 = 7.99$, df = 3, p < 0.05.

While joint activities are common to all, it is clear that couples' pregnancy 'careers' are influenced by factors like their current parental status and their social class position. For example, the initial reaction of both partners was more likely to have been reported as problematic lower down the class scale. Table 3.3 shows how fathers described their wives' initial reaction to the pregnancy.

On the surface it seems that these differences arise because pregnancy for working-class people tends to be less planned than for their middle-class counterparts. The journalist cited above described his and his wife's feelings at the outset:

> We had six years of marriage in which we'd done everything. . . . We'd built our . . . sort of . . . we've got a nice house together. We'd got cars and we had holidays and we dec— It's all economics these days. [Prompt: 'So how did you feel?'] Oh, quite excited I think, really. . . . It was all planned. It was all sort of . . . we. . . . It was all very deliberate, actually, because um . . . we planned to have . . . what we said was we'd sort of plan to have – if everything worked out all right – giving it two or three months from trying for a family so that Iona would be born round about March–April time, but the way it works . . . it just happened straight away.

A response not atypical of half the working-class respondents was:

> I was . . . well, I thought at first, I thought, 'Oh God, a kid already.' You know, we've got a lot of debt on and I thought we'd never afford it. . . . We hadn't got much stuff for her and we started getting a lot together, you know. We had a lot of stuff on HP so we thought, 'Oh God, we'll have to do summat.' . . . But the money just seemed to come. [Prompt: 'How did you feel at the end of the pregnancy?'] I thought, 'We've got everything', so I was happy.
>
> (Scrap-yard labourer)

As the earlier discussion suggests, the decision to have a child is not usually clear-cut, so it would be foolish to distinguish between working- and middle-class couples simply in terms of the planning of their pregnancies. However, middle-class parents seem to have the material resources available, firstly to feel able to afford to have children (and therefore to discuss and come to a decision about when to have them). Secondly, when the woman becomes pregnant, they usually feel confident that they can make the necessary domestic readjustments to provide for the baby in a culturally acceptable way. Interestingly, first- and second-time parents appear to have reacted in similar ways, and working-class couples are more likely to perceive the start of either pregnancy as an upsetting time.

While there was a class difference in fathers' recollections of both their own and their wives' initial reactions, as the pregnancy developed each social group tended to recall becoming equally positive about the pending arrival. Nevertheless they describe their preparation in different ways. Typically, working-class parents, like the scrap-yard labourer, discuss later pregnancy in terms of preparing materially for the child. Middle-class expectant parents describe their psychological 'developments'.

Complementary changes
Despite the similarities in the 'careers' of expectant mothers and fathers, the physiological changes in the woman necessarily make the ideal of 'sharing' the experience impossible. As Richman and his colleagues (1975: 144) have written: 'The wife is obviously chief authority on the progress of her pregnancy, relaying critical medical information. She can point to her *visible* biological condition to explain 'changed' behaviour.' Most married men recognize that their wives possess this authority and respect their ability to give physiological events a social meaning. Their own reluctance to participate in the 'public' events of pregnancy are in part a mark of their respect for the woman's right to this knowledge. While many men *appear* to take little notice of the official procedures during pregnancy, they take a great interest in their wives' interpretations of the events which they do not attend themselves. Often wives will give a 'blow-by-blow' account of clinic visits or parentcraft classes. In the study, twenty-four men, who did not attend any of these sessions, helped or watched their wives do their exercises.

At the same time, expectant parents perform complementary changes in their roles outside marriage. Like the scrap-yard and warehouse labourers quoted above, some fathers make additional financial efforts, particularly if their wives are giving up work, or if they have not been fulfilling the traditionally supportive role of a husband:

> before she told me, I was out of work for about nine months. . . .
> Soon as she told me . . . since then I've been in full-time work.

[Prompt: 'So you got a job?'] Yeah . . . it made me realize my responsibilities as well . . . it made me grow up as well, you could say.

(General labourer)

As well as coming to understand the pregnancy through his wife and taking on the responsibilities of bread-winning, the husband is perceived in an important emotional role by both himself and his wife. Both partners described complementary psychological changes in themselves and their spouse; characteristically they described the husband as the stabilizing factor.

Table 3.4 outlines the fathers' descriptions of psychological change in themselves and in their wives during pregnancy. Some (27 per cent) saw pregnancy as a period when women 'bloom', are healthy or more attractive. These men, who tend to have planned the pregnancy, usualy experienced the same feelings of euphoria as their wives. A larger number (48 per cent) perceived their wives' psychological state in very different terms. This group, which includes significantly more second-time fathers (39 per cent first-timers vs 66 per cent second-timers recalling some negative change in wife; $\chi^2 = 6.64$, df = 1, p < 0.01), felt that pregnancy made their wives 'ratty', 'moody' or 'depressed'. A similar proportion of the wives agree with this assessment. One commented on how pregnancy influences women:

I think their emotions are a bit mixed. . . . Little things used to bother me. I semed to be forever having rows with Rachel [older child] and . . . you know, things she did annoyed me much more than they needed to.
(Full-time housewife, whose husband is a general studies lecturer)

Conversely, men and women feel that fathers react to the pregnancy in very different ways. A comparison of the two columns in Table 3.4, coupled with the verbatim accounts, suggest that expectant fathers often pursue what has been termed the 'sturdy oak' ideal (Benson 1968, Hacker 1957, McKee 1980). The largest group of men (46 per cent) perceived no change in themselves; and all those who experienced negative feelings

Table 3.4   Fathers' perceptions of psychological change in their wives and themselves during pregnancy

Response category	Frequency	
	Wife	Husband
Only negative	14	4
Mixed, mainly negative	34	7
No change/neutral	25	46
Positive	27	43
Total:	100	100

(11 per cent) often commented that they did so because they had to grin and bear their wives' moodiness.

Since more second-time mothers were reported to have changed for the worse during the pregnancy, more second-time fathers claimed to adopt the 'sturdy oak' role. One father in the sample, whose wife was expecting a second child a week after the interview, described his reaction to her 'rattiness':

> [Prompt: 'Do her moods have any effect on you?'] Well, I can feel it sometimes threatening to, but I try not to let it, you know. . . . If I start to react to it it's not going to get us anywhere so . . . [I] turn a deaf ear when she starts ranting on.
>
> (Chemical plant operator)

A large number (43 per cent) of men felt the pregnancy made them change for the better, saying, for example, that they 'matured' or 'grew up'. Some even gained social recognition as a result of being expectant fathers:

> It was nice. I enjoyed her being pregnant. It seems a stupid thing to say but . . . [Prompt: 'In what way?'] I don't know, I was beginning to feel . . . like proud. It's a difficult thing to put into words . . . your feelings . . . but I was glad when she was pregnant. . . . People tend to ask you how your wife is. Friends . . . obviously all the time, it was always there. . . . It was 'Is she all right?' . . . 'Is she putting on weight?' It was always in the conversation.
>
> (Carpet salesman)

When discussing the similarities between expectant fathers' and mothers' pregnancy careers, I mentioned that the sharing of events often brought couples together. Questions about their relationship showed that the vast majority of fathers perceived pregnancy as a time when it continued to flourish (17 per cent) or when they got closer (67 per cent), and their wives agreed with them. However, the shared aspects of pregnancy do not by themselves account for these perceptions. Within the group who became closer during pregnancy were many couples in which the wife had been reported to have become more 'ratty' or moody. For example, the general studies lecturer, whose wife was quoted above, described how his wife and he changed:

> It probably depends very much upon the woman . . . *and* on the family, I suppose. I think they tend to get more susceptible to their emotions, I suppose . . . more prone to them. . . . It's very up and down, isn't it, particularly the second time, when you've got another kiddie as well. [Prompt: 'So did her emotional change effect you?'] Yes, I suppose it did . . . it does affect you in that you've got to take account of it and be sympathetic towards it. Sometimes it isn't always easy to do that dependent on what sort of problems you've had at work and so on which are totally divorced to the family situation. . . . And

as far as the mother is concerned those problems don't really enter into her thinking when she's pregnant. [Prompt: 'So would you say that it's made you a less emotional person?'] I'm not a very emotional person anyhow, but, er, it probably does, yeah. The father's got to be the steadying influence in the family, I think.

Like this lecturer, many men saw themselves as a steadying influence. These husbands commented that they felt closer to their wives simply because they adhere to the 'sickness' model of pregnancy, which explains psychological change purely in terms of physiological events:

I'm sure you're more aware of her, probably take a bit more care – but only because, yeah, only because she's pregnant, and you know she gets tired easily and you know that she's. . . . But you'd treat her like that even if she'd just come out of hospital from some other illness. . . . I don't think I viewed it as permanent.

(Doctor)

As La Rossa (1977) shows, being labelled as 'ill' often allows women to gain power in the marital relationship. For example, some persuade their husbands to do more household chores.

Adjusting to their wives' moodiness and 'illness' are only two ways in which men assumed the 'sturdy oak' identity, although they are the two most commonly reported ones. Other couples, particularly those where both partners reported that the pregnancy caused positive change in themselves, described the time as one of special closeness between them. In these cases the 'oak' was more comfortable to rest upon, even if the husband was reluctant to admit it:

Well, I think I became more caring and, er, more protective towards her during that time, you know. . . . Really I suppose what sort of changes came over me . . . and actually Margaret remarked on it some time after the baby was born, er, she did say something about, er, 'You was all loving and caring when I was having him . . . you've changed now' [Laughs]. . . . Not that we've gone the other way [laughs].

(Computer clerk)

He was softer. . . . [Prompt: 'Was he?'] Yes, yes . . . we used to sit and cuddle a lot [laughs]. He made an effort anyway to sit with me a lot more than when I was . . . 'cos normally he's pottering around doing something.

(Foster-mother, whose husband is an assistant caretaker)

These quotations summarize an important aspect of the man's pregnancy 'career'. The sturdy male oak supports his wife, often not admitting that he is more cuddly. A pregnant wife may express her feeling of dependence.

The expectant father often uses instrumental terms – ones which make him appear detached from the experience.

Another man, for example, compared pregnancy to 'waiting for a new car'. While this may be interpreted to mean that he lacks feelings that his wife may have, his account also conveys more than an air of detachment:

> You tend to start looking at children – that's the first thing. I mean, you walk down the street and you see children – you wouldn't notice them. Before you'd think, 'Ugh, kids.' . . . But 'Children,' you say, 'I'm going to have one of them.' I suppose it's like waiting for a new car. . . . And also you tend to notice pregnant women more. . . . I think you become more aware, more aware of what's going on about you. I've noticed also that you become more safety-conscious.
>
> (Product-development officer)

Unforeseen Effects of the Supportive Role

For most men the adoption of an instrumental or supportive role seems to create few problems and to serve a useful function in protecting the pregnant women through a difficult period. Pregnancy appears to be a time when couples maintain a balance between their similarities (sharing the pregnancy) and complementarities (men supporting their 'sick' wives). Yet this picture is far too simplistic and incomplete, for the 'sturdy oak' role may have unforeseen effects. This role has the potential to lead to marital tension and psychological anxiety.

Firstly, although not too commonly as far as this married sample was concerned, the man may appear to be too unperturbed and unsupportive to his wife by not sharing the experience as he 'ought'. Those couples who felt that the woman changed for the worse, and that their relationship suffered during pregnancy, gave the impression that the man's aloofness did little to enhance their circumstances. It is impossible to judge from this retrospective study why a few men appear to be unsupportive at a time when their involvement seems (judging by the consistency of most fathers' accounts of the process) to be culturally prescribed; but some adhere too closely for their wives' comfort to the ideal of unflappable masculinity. Richman's (1982) work and the accounts of couples in this study suggest that a minority of expectant fathers appear to perceive the pregnancy as 'nothing unusual' and attempt to play down the changes in their wives. One wife, for example, described the differences in her marital relationship thus:

> I was ever so mardy [Nottingham dialect term meaning 'grizzly']. It didn't take a lot to have me in tears, especially towards the end. . . . He used to think I was making something out of nothing

or . . . he was . . . sometimes he was pretty good, like. . . . We had central heating put in . . . about a month before I had him we decorated the baby's room and all these things, right? And they drilled and there was filth and dust everywhere and I just . . . and all day long I seemed to just be crying and he used to come home and I used to say, 'Oh, Ron, all the baby's room's filthy.' . . . And he used to . . . to him it was funny. He used to put his arm round me and he used to laugh and say, 'Never mind', and, er . . . I don't think he really . . . I don't think he really *understood*.

(Part-time nursing assistant, whose husband is a
goods representative)

The accounts of men who fail to sympathise with or who make light of their wives' distress certainly need closer examination, yet in some respects they are hard to distinguish from the bulk of contemporary expectant fathers who take on the role as sturdy but supportive oaks. In order to be supportive most men become at least slightly detached. This may be a defensive pose for some expectant fathers, however, who might otherwise have a tendency to become acutely distressed by the experience.

As was mentioned earlier, the bulk of psychological research on pregnancy and men has concentrated upon a tiny minority who react in bizarre and pathological ways to pregnancy – the 'couvade syndrome' (see Lewis 1982b for a review). So I consciously avoided asking direct questions about whether fathers had experienced psychological symptoms while their wives were expecting. Nevertheless it became apparent in both men's and women's accounts of the pregnancy that the experience is often distressing for them both. Without being asked, forty-two men said that their wives had had consistent fears for themselves or the baby, and twenty admitted such feelings in themselves. One father, for example, described these as you know, the obvious. Indeed, the impression gained from some small-scale longitudinal studies of the period suggests further that these worries might be ubiquitous (Marquart 1976, McKee 1980). A study which compared parents at this time found that the husband experienced more stress than his wife (Miller and Sollie 1980).

In some men the anxieties evoked by pregnancy are particularly intense. Six expectant fathers experienced neurotic symptoms ranging from stomach pains and claustrophobia to a complete nervous breakdown during a previous pregnancy, which had resulted in the man being in a psychiatric hospital for six months and still considered unfit for work three years later. One of those with relatively mild symptoms described his expriences:

Pretty rough . . . [Prompt: 'Pretty rough at first?'] Well, they say it, like, that the man don't go through the woman's symptoms, but I *did* with Shaun. [Prompt: 'Which ones did you get?'] Er . . . everything, actually . . . from morning sickness to headaches to backache . . . everything. [Prompt: 'So it lasted all the way through the pregnancy?'] No, only a certain period of the pregnancy and then it died off and then when she was more or less nine months gone, it started again. [Prompt: 'So it was right at the beginning and right at the end? So did you have these feelings more or less at the same *time* as Pat, or didn't she have them?'] She didn't have them, it was just *me* who had them. [Prompt: 'Do you think there was any reason why you got them and she didn't?'] Er . . . no, not really, 'cos I went to the doctor's, right, and he says . . . well, you know, he just explained to me it's just natural, like, and I says, 'Well, can I cop a week off work, like, see how I feel' you know. I had time off work and I told my mates and they all laughed, know what I mean? . . . And I says, 'Well, you'll have your time to come.'

(Unemployed construction labourer)

Why, then, do some expectant fathers cut themselves off from their wives and others develop 'pathological' symptoms? Given that so many men report having been preoccupied by fears during the pregnancy it seems reasonable to assume that the intense reactions of a small number are extreme examples of a more typical reaction of married expectant fathers to pregnancy. Even in highly technological societies the possibility of disaster is present, particularly near the end of pregnancy. Psychological theories of these extreme reactions tend to neglect the very real dangers and attribute them to untestable dynamic causes, like 'womb envy' (Bettleheim 1955), or to weakly defined psychological constructs, like 'cross-sex identity' (Monroe and Monroe 1971).

Fathers themselves suggest much simpler and more understandable explanations based upon the conflict between their psychological involvement in an experience which is 'shared', in the sense that they are partners in 'symmetrical' relationships, and the very nature of the experience, which cannot be shared in the way that contemporary ideals suggest. Worries about the risks of pregnancy and birth begin to prey on them and their wives. Men firstly feel helpless about, and partly responsible for, the possible dangers which face both mother and child. In addition their wives have the constant physical reminder that they are pregnant and are more able to show their moodiness and fears. Fathers, adopting a 'sturdy oak' role, feel they cannot express their own worries unless their relationship allows them to do so. In only a few couples was it reported that the wife acted as a support when the man attempted to understand the changes that were taking place:

I tend to think that a lot of people say that the women during the pregnancy need the men. I think it's the man needs the woman a lot more. . . . [Prompt: 'Can you say in what ways you needed Catherine?'] I think it was, er, again it was a traumatic experience for me and I tended to lean on Catherine through this traumatic experience as a stablizing influence, because, er, Catherine knew the physical changes that she was going through and I was just sort of sat back watching it . . . er, you know, [I] just needed that little bit of calming down, I think. [Prompt: 'Do you know why you needed it?'] Well, yeah, it's something that you've got no control over. Your wife is there with this, er, you know, foetus growing inside of her and, er . . . you have no control over it. . . . All you can do is make sure that the conditions that your wife exists in, as it were, are best for her, but apart from that you've got no control over what's happening. [Prompt: 'So what sort of effect does that have?'] Again, er . . . it's a mild state of panic and then again Catherine's [the] stabilizing influence, because it was sort of, er . . . a specific example's where Catherine'd sort of sit down, particularly in the later stages, where the baby'd jump and I'd keep saying, 'Well, what's it doing that for?' and Catherine would say, 'Yeah, it's perfectly all right, it's been doing that all day, moving and turning.' [Prompt: 'So she calmed you down?'] Yeah, oh aye.

(Industrial relations officer)

A larger proportion of expectant fathers become trapped between their identification with the pregnancy on an emotional level and their publicly expected role as sturdy, instrumental providers on another level. Thus a comparison of husbands' and wives' accounts of the changes in the husband during pregnancy reveals that significantly more men mentioned having had these fears than their wives attributed to them (40 per cent of husbands vs 17 per cent of wives mentioning fears in fathers; $\chi^2 = 4.02$, df $= 1$, $p < 0.05$). Feeling under pressure to appear cool, calm and collected can make expectant fathers susceptible to these types of reaction.

Conclusion

The accounts of fathers presented in this chapter show that there are big individual differences in the patterns of emotional dependency which may exist between men and women in marriage. Whatever front they may exhibit to the outside world, some men are highly dependent upon their wives. Pregnancy is an experience which highlights this aspect of a marital relationship, since it brings about changes in the wife, both in appearance and mood, which a husband might find particularly difficult to cope with. His anxieties may be compounded by a number of additional factors. These include the cultural expectation that the father should appear pleased when his wife becomes pregnant and the implication that the changes in his wife may last beyond the pregnancy – and thus prevent their relationship from providing an emotional outlet for him. In addition, her physical symptoms constantly remind him that they are approaching an event which is deemed to be so dangerous and painful that hospitalization is thought to be essential. It is on this event that the next chapter will focus.

4 Giving Birth: Fathers at Delivery

This chapter divides into two parts. The second half will examine how men feel about taking part in the delivery of their children. Before this, it is necessary to consider why men have been accepted as normal attendants in the hospital delivery room.

The Historical Content of Contemporary Birth Practices

The lost father in the childbirth literature
On the question of fathers and birth-attendance, a typical newspaper story (from the *Sunday Times*) reads:

> Nobody was actually astonished that Prince Charles was there for *the* birth. It's remarkable how the climate has changed over the past decade: even ten years ago fathers weren't allowed into the delivery room, and were considered bizarre if they suggested it. Prince Charles's father didn't see any of his children being born. 'Chaps simply weren't around,' says my father. No question about it – far too indelicate. If it was a home birth one was dispatched elsewhere . . . the whole process was nothing to do with the male sex.
>
> (Moggach 1982: 34)

The beliefs implicit in this statement reveal much about our perceptions of recent 'history'.

Moggach is correct that hospitals now expect fathers to attend their wives' confinements whereas many excluded them during the 1960s. In keeping with her assertions, more serious accounts of pregnancy suggest, for example, that 'In 1960 men almost never entertained the thought of witnessing the birth of their own children' (Entwisle and Doering 1981: 2). Yet the clear-cut distinction between today's attendant father and the non-participant man of twenty years ago is by no means grounded in fact. There is good evidence to show that, contrary to this current belief, men's involvement in childbirth is by no means a new phenomenon in industrial societies. While twenty years ago the Newsons found that no spectators attended delivery in hospital, 60 per cent of births took place at home

55

(Newson and Newson 1963). Of these, 13 per cent were witnessed by fathers (8 per cent of all births), and a further 15 per cent of women in labour were accompanied by another woman – their mother, sister or neighbour. So the 'chap' *was* included as one of a restricted circle of possible birth companions twenty years ago. Even in the United States, where hospitalized birth took over much earlier than in the UK (Mehl 1978), and where some studies selected hospitals at which no attendants witnessed delivery (e.g. Shareshefsky and Yarrow 1973), there is evidence to show that men attended deliveries more than is realized (e.g. Bradley 1962, Goetsch 1963, International Childbirth Education Association 1965, Miller 1966, Moore and Bridenbaugh 1964, Thoms and Karloosky 1954).

Misconceptions about the numbers of men at childbirth over the past twenty years are far less important than the simple claims made about the reasons for including fathers in the delivery room. The rapid change in hospital policies is sadly lacking in documentation, and many possible explanations for the inclusion of fathers have been offered without clear substantiation. Followers of the natural childbirth movement, for example, have claimed the 'credit' for the change since they have been campaigning for father participation for fifty years (Dick-Read 1934). Yet fathers have been included at hospital delivery at the same time that birth has become increasingly 'unnatural', so their claims cannot by themselves be justified.

Similarly, there are those who assume that the rise of feminism accounts for the change in events. Moggach (1982: 34), for example, simply accepts the view of one father that 'If women's lib did anything, it made us feel guilty about staying away.' Yet the evidence from one of the earliest studies of men and delivery showed that fathers who attended the birth of their children did not have any particular 'ideological rapport with feminism' (Richman *et al.* 1975). Indeed fewer birth-attenders supported the concept of women's liberation than those who were present for the first stages of labour only. So if feminism influenced the change in practice it did not do so by raising the consciousness of expectant fathers.

Reports in contemporary literature (Riley 1968) and recollections of childbirth practices as they moved into hospital (Rich 1977) do show that many women deeply resented the isolation caused by what Rich terms 'alienated labour'. Similarly, recent studies of women in pregnancy have suggested that pressure to include fathers at the delivery appears to come more from the expectant mother than from the father (Graham and McKee 1980, Oakley 1979), but their evidence does not necessarily account for the *establishment* of the new emphasis on sharing this special event as a 'couple experience' – as husband-attended delivery has been termed (Soule 1974).

While there is a need for a more detailed social history of birth practices over the past few decades, the evidence which has surfaced seems to suggest that the pressure to change them as they have become technological has not come simply from the consumers, or their husbands. In 1961, when hospitals were taking over increasing numbers of deliveries, an obstetrician carried out a survey among 776 patients who passed through his hands (Matthews 1961). Half the mothers and fathers disagreed with the idea of including men at either labour or the birth. A few parents were in favour of the father's presence; and it is interesting to note that, contrary to more recent evidence and the claims of the 'feminist' argument, men wished to attend (22 per cent) more than their wives wanted them to (17 per cent). However, Matthew's overall impression was that these fathers were not clamouring at the labour-room door to assist their spouses.

Medical attitudes towards fathers and childbirth

(1) 'Conservative' obstetricians and the exclusion of men

Matthews's study was carried out to resolve a furious battle within the medical profession which closely resembles the differentiation – emergent debate discussed in Chapter 1. While doctors were taking control of delivery by institutionalizing hospital practice and cutting down the responsibilities of domiciliary midwives (see Oakley 1980 for a discussion), they were deeply divided about the 'social' (rather than biological) aspects of their area of authority. Some were adamant about preserving the mothers', and perhaps more importantly their own, dignity, and there is much in their writing to suggest that they were also keen to protect their new territory and their power within it. For example, in the United States opponents of the move to include fathers feared that it would result in a dramatic increase in 'malpractice suits' (e.g. Morton 1966).

The sort of argument raised against the presence of men is represented in the following two *British Medical Journal* letters, and in the conclusion to an article on natural childbirth and the inclusion of fathers from the US journal *Medical Times*. These 'conservative' obstetricians assumed that the clear differentiation of adult sex roles made it unnatural to suggest that men should witness delivery:

> Sir – The normal father would run a mile if asked to witness his wife's delivery. The normal mother would 'see him further', to use the local idiom. With the notorious exception of the male seahorse, who incubates and then gives birth in an alarming explosion (serves him right), the sires of the animal kingdom, including *Homo sapiens*, tend to keep well out of the way when parturition is in progress. Let us not pander to morbid curiosity and sensationalism, nor to those featherbrains who wish to be in the van of a new fashion, by encouraging a highly unnatural trend with the mumbo-jumbo of pseudo-psychology. The proper place for the father, if not at work, is the local, whither instinct will usually guide him.
>
> (Patterson 1961: 594)

> Shorn of its ideological aura, the actual process of birth is a pretty
> unglamorous affair . . . the public exposure of parts usually described
> as private do not make an edifying spectable. . . . Most obstetricians
> and midwives feel hampered by the presence of the father at delivery.
> They regard it as sadistic and unnatural curiosity and are constantly
> afraid that his reaction to a possible abrupt complication might hinder
> their work.
>
> (Davis 1961: 594)

> A fantastic scheme has been perpetrated upon the gullibility of the
> unsuspecting layman which has resulted in the breakdown of hospital
> techniques which have been perfected since the time of Semmelweiss,
> and produced an orgy of sadism and masochism into the sacred
> privilege of motherhood.
>
> (Stewart 1963: 1068)

To most people today these views seem to be extreme, even absurd. Yet
they appear to have represented a majority of contemporary opinion in
the medical profession. A 'round table' conference at the British Medical
Association in 1958, for example, met to discuss the rights of the father
and divided into two main groups: those who felt fathers should be excluded
altogether and those who felt they should be allowed to stay with their wives
during the first stages of labour and then excluded.

(2) 'Progressive' obstetricians and the inclusion of fathers

While this 'conservative' faction within the medical profession was keeping
men out of the delivery room it did so because an increasingly powerful
group was espousing a different philosophy which took many of its ideas
from Dick Read. In the words of Ann Oakley (1980: 36), 'in its origins
and type of cultural accommodation over the last thirty years, natural
childbirth has been colonized by medicine itself'. 'Progressive' obstetricians
promoted causes which reflected a new ideology, including a belief in
'emergent' or involved fatherhood. At home the birth companion might
have been one of a number of people (Newson and Newson 1963), but
the medical profession focused only upon the issue of the husband's presence
in their hospital delivery room.

Matthews's (1961) study reflects this new ideal. He asked no questions
about which person the mother preferred to have present with her.
Disregarding tradition, proponents of the new ideology asserted:

> The father seems the only person to assist his wife at this time in a
> way in which no midwife is able to do. . . . The husband is there at
> the marriage and he should be there at the birth of his children. . . .
> Why does he appear sheepishly with a bunch of flowers when it is all
> over? Because he feels terrific guilt at being absent in a crisis concerning
> them both.
>
> (Burne 1961: 594)

The aims of these obstetricians were not simply humanitarian. Implicit in their philosophy was a belief that fathers ideally ought to play a more central role in the family. Burne continues:

> In short, fatherhood as an ideal has to be reinstated and put back on its pedestal. The pathetic, chain-smoking, restless and flower-offering expectant father should be a figure of the past. The paternal instinct is as strong as the maternal and should not be frustrated.

As well as asserting that fathers had rights and 'instincts', the progressive obstetricians adhered to (or generated) a belief that the experience of birth, if shared, may have dramatic effects upon the couple's relationship:

> The birth of a child is the creative climax of the physical relationship between husband and wife, a time of intense emotional significance for them both. Rightly used, it can draw them together and provide the background of security so essential for a healthy childhood.
>
> (Hill 1961: 430)

> The manifestations of tenderness and joy exchanged between husband and wife immediately at birth are heart-warming. They seem to contribute to the solidity of family ties.
>
> (Bradley 1962: 474)

This ideology of couple-centred delivery, which is closely related to the more recent notion of father–infant 'bonding' (to be discussed in Chapter 7), became increasingly popular in the 1960s, and 'husband-coached childbirth' (Bradley 1965) has been readily accepted by the medical fraternity. The change in hospital practice has been exceptionally rapid, especially in light of the resistance of the conservative faction twenty years ago. The fact is that many doctors still find it hard dealing with a conscious 'anomaly' in the clinical atmosphere of the hospital delivery room (Brown 1982). As Brown shows, medical attitudes towards fathers still maintain aspects of the conservative ideology, and this often gives the impression that the profession as a whole is more intent on institutionalizing technological innovations than on recognizing the psychological and emotional needs of its clients.

However, the evidence presented above does show that the progressive view – that fathers should be included at delivery – was being promoted in medical circles *before* it gained widespread support from the press or expectant parents. This is witnessed by the fact that the two popular books promoting the move to include fathers, Bradley's *Husband-Coached Childbirth* (1965) and Schaeffer's *Expectant Father* (1964), never reached a mass market. More recent texts (e.g. Phillips and Anzalone 1978) started selling in small numbers long after many hospitals had already started to include men at birth. The message communicated at 'fathers' evenings' in maternity hospitals is that fathers *should* be there. Both the discussions presented by the medical staff and the films (e.g. *The Waiting Game*, Farley's Ltd, 1976) depict delivery as an event that is psychologically important. The reasons that are given to encourage fathers' attendance closely resemble those presented by the 'progressive' obstetricians during the past twenty years.

Father-attended delivery: a modern couvade ritual?

Father-attended delivery is one of a number of recent medical changes. Procedures within the labour room have become standardized. Women are encouraged to adopt the same posture (Mehl 1978). Medication and foetal heart monitoring are the rule rather than an exception. So too have fathers become an essential ingredient. As a result of all these changes, procedures have become ritualized and have taken on new meanings.

Father-attended delivery is not restricted to industrial cultures. In many societies couples perform 'couvade' rituals – a term given to customs which are carried out in order to 'brood' over or 'hatch' the baby. In these, men may 'labour' alongside their wives, for example. Anthropological accounts of these practices suggest that they enable the father to identify with the child (Frazer 1910, Tylor 1865). They have come increasingly to argue that men become involved in the 'drama' of birth, in societies where critical socio-political issues (about who 'owns' the child and how property is inherited) remain unsolved by more straightforward institutional means (Fock 1967, Paige and Paige 1981). Mary Douglas (1975) claims that couvade practices have to be understood on a number of different levels. Since contemporary birth practice has been standardized, I shall discuss each of her levels with reference to our own practices.

The three explanatory levels used by Douglas (1975) have relevance to both the statements made by the obstetricians above and the accounts of fathers which I shall discuss in the rest of this chapter. Firstly, she maintains that the couvade reflects much about the beliefs of the particular society. It is clear that in our own culture (see the 'conservative' letters above) the presence of men in the delivery room reflects a recent shift not only in medical practice but also in social customs, like our attitudes towards sexual modesty. The taboo against the exposure of 'private parts' has to some extent been lifted, although it has not completely disappeared.

Secondly, in their potentially dangerous outcome, Douglas maintains that couvade rituals 'are the occasions for arousing emotion and fastening it on social values: the propositions they make are general consensus-producing statements about the essential nature of society' (1975: 65). In contemporary practice father-attended delivery is a 'consensus-making statement' about family togetherness. Men now share in the labour process. One obstetrician has even developed a 'bonding manoeuvre' on the baby for fathers to make during a breech delivery (Scott 1981). Mothers and fathers repeatedly report that the birth brings a new family together. However, it is not coincidental that such claims are made at a time when the 'traditional' nuclear family appears to be under threat, given such a large number of single-parent households and a high divorce rate. As Craven and his colleagues (1982) point out, the family has become a major focus of political and social concern particularly among those sections of the population that strive to maintain the political status quo.

Thirdly, Douglas points out that couvade rituals enable participants to 'manipulate other people' (1975: 61), for example by laying 'claim to a special relation' (1975: 63). Such interpersonal manipulation is evident in recent comments on delivery. 'Progressive' obstetricians like Burne (quoted above) made it plain that men had a 'right' to attend and to re-establish themselves on the pedestal of fatherhood. Many maternity hospitals refuse to allow anyone other than the father into the delivery room. Men and women can thus use the occasion of birth to define or redefine the amount of domestic power they have. For example, the man's presence signifies that he is the father, demonstrating that he has rights over and duties towards the child. Indeed, for unmarried couples this may be the first time a man acknowledges his involvement. On a more psychological level, the man's presence at delivery gives 'power' to the mother, since witnessing her going through such pain and danger is thought to increase the father's respect for her (Graham and McKee 1980, Oakley, 1979).

When fathers discuss delivery, three themes recur. In the first place they are often cajoled into participating by the masters of ceremonies – the medical staff. Secondly, medical delivery unfolds in a standard, ritualized way. Thirdly, delivery has profound emotional effects on the participants, just as the initiators of the ritual intended.

Fathers' Impressions of Birth

The decision to attend: a conflict between the father's private and public roles?

As I indicated earlier, in 1960, 60 per cent of Nottingham births were at home, and fathers attended 13 per cent of these deliveries (8 per cent of all births). Twenty years later, at the time of this study, only 2 per cent of births took place at home, and 84 per cent of fathers attended their wives' labour, with 67 per cent staying right through for delivery – see Table 4.1. Although the composition of the samples of these two studies was slightly different, the contrast between them is sufficiently striking to show that father attendance, like delivery itself, has become institutionalized. In fact, research throughout the British Isles (Beail 1980 and 1982, Bell *et al.* 1983) and the United States (e.g. Entwisle and Doering 1981) show that the number of men present in this study is, if anything, *lower* than the norm.

On the surface it seems as if fathers, in keeping with the enthusiasm of local medical authorities, are keen to be present in the delivery room.

Table 4.1   Fathers' attendance at birth

Father attended	Frequency
(a) Neither labour nor delivery	15
(b) Early stages of labour (not delivery)	18
(c) Later stages of labour and delivery	2
(d) All labour and delivery	65
Total:	100

Table 4.2   Who wanted father in the delivery room?

Response category	Frequency
(a) Mother and father	66
(b) Mother, not father	14
(c) Neither mother nor father	14
(d) Planned Caesarian deliveries at which it was known that the father would be refused entry	6
Total:	100

Table 4.2 shows that 66 of the sample had agreed to be present with their wives throughout the labour and delivery. Nevertheless, discussion about the fathers' *reasons* for attending and the time at which they agreed to participate suggests that the decision is not always clear-cut. The dividing line between many fathers who 'chose' to attend and those who in the last analysis were persuaded is often very thin. Some clearly are committed to the new ideology, and like the following second-time father were keen to witness the birth of their child:

> I wanted to be there. We were quite young when we had John [aged eight], and it wasn't really encouraged at that time, and I've always thought I've missed something. [Prompt: 'So you didn't even consider going in for his birth or . . . ?'] I didn't somehow, no! It was never mentioned all the way through, so I just did as I was told. But this time things have changed, and they seemed to assume that you'd want to be there, and you tell them if you don't want to be; and *I* wanted to be! [Prompt: 'So you just walked in casually and they accepted you!'] Yeah, they were great, they were really good. And Gill had some trouble, and they had to deliver Ruth using forceps, and I've heard that they often throw you out in that case, but the doctor just

said, 'It could be messy but you can stay if you want to!' . . . And so I did.

(Accountant/auditor)

These 'committed' fathers represent only a minority of attenders at birth. For the majority the question of their presence in the labour room raises a dilemma. Delivery is one of many public events which they have skilfully avoided thus far, and they are reluctant to risk exposing their emotions in front of others. Yet the experience is labelled as being of 'private' importance to the marital and parental relationship, and fathers feel they should be there, especially as their wives are often keen that they should stay. As it turned out, six of the fathers refused to attend, claiming that the event would be embarrassing or would make them faint. Fourteen needed to be persuaded by their wives to accompany them. The accounts of those who agreed to be there showed just how many factors might influence their decision. Some, having weathered the storm of the 'explicit' film at the parents' evening, felt confident enough to attend (although others used this as an excuse not to do so):

> Beforehand I thought there's no way I'll be there because I'm squeamish and I don't like any . . . even spiders, that sort of thing. But we went to the parents' classes beforehand and saw the films and what-have-you and (I) decided to go.
>
> (Bank clerk)

In their study of the transition to parenthood in the United States, Entwisle and Doering (1981) found that half the fathers in their sample had talked to a friend about whether they should attend. In this study, men also claimed that their families, their wives and hearsay all helped them to make their decision:

> My wife wanted me to go. . . . *I* wasn't too keen . . . not because I'm squeamish, I think the only point that put me off was possibly seeing my wife in pain . . . but she really wanted me to go. I think because it was our little lad that was coming adds another factor that made me want to see it. . . . My brother-in-law had seen his two and he said . . . quite a few people said it was quite a sight . . . you've got to go and see it, it's worth it . . . you know, all those factors.
>
> (Goods representative)

So the majority of those who 'agreed' to attend had to a large extent been persuaded to do so. Some of these did not make the decision until the eleventh hour:

> I'd no intentions initially of being present at the birth. . . . [Prompt: 'Then what happened?'] I think my wife was in, sort of, a state of panic . . . 'cos my wife is disabled. She was in a considerable amount of pain and she was frightened . . . it was her first child. . . .

So I just stopped there . . . and the birth happened and I was there.

(Finance company representative)

We . . . sort of . . . I was asked earlier on whether I wanted to be and I said, 'I don't particularly know.' I said, 'I'd rather sort of see how the circumstances develop and if it is of benefit to Jane, I'll be there.' Or, 'If I feel as if I want to be, I'll be there', but . . . umm . . . I took Jane in during the night, and they said, 'Do you want to stay with your wife?' and this sort of thing and . . . I think it was – at the time it was of benefit to Jane that I was . . . so I did.

(Journalist)

A lot of men, having carried out their instrumental role of getting their wives to the right part of the hospital, and on time, find themselves in a state of 'drift', not knowing whether to go or stay. Richman and his colleagues (1975) compared the man's status in the hospital to that of the boy who enters the school staff-room; he is treated as the lowest of the low. Yet, some years later, this research suggests that hospitals now exert an important influence in keeping men with their wives during labour and delivery. One respondent, for example, had not made up his mind when he brough this wife to the hospital:

Oh they were very good. As soon as I walked into the labour suite they sort of put a gown on me; there was no 'Are you stopping?' or 'Aren't you stopping?' It was sort of a foregone conclusion I *was* stopping.

(Floor layer)

Similarly, another husband, who had decided to sit it out in the waiting-room, described the attitudes of the staff:

Well, they came and fetched me. . . . They said that she was a bit, um, getting a bit upset, you see . . . so they were rather pleased that I went in.'

(Plasterer's labourer)

Labour, delivery and the channelling of emotions
Whatever the reasons for their attendance at labour, fathers' accounts of their role in the delivery room, and to a lesser extent their psychological reactions to the proceedings, bear a very strong resemblance to one another. The same themes recur in interviews, and perhaps it is not surprising that they do. Medical procedures have not only become regular discussion topics in the media and between experienced and prospective fathers, they have also become so standardized that events are much the same for most couples (Lomas 1964 and 1978).

Men's and women's accounts of the procedures during labour suggest that the father becomes part of the medical team, whereby his role is both to keep his wife company and to assist the medical staff with the many technological aspects of modern birth. While fathers have been incorporated into the team for psychological reasons, the staffing on maternity units is such that labouring women cannot be given constant attention and so a lay helper is often as necessary as at a home delivery. This has the potential to make him feel centrally involved:

> I think the good part about it was when she was connected up to the machine and we could see where the contractions were and the baby's heartbeat and all this, you know. . . . You knew there was something *there* then.
>
> (Floor layer)

At least some duties given to the father are organized by the medical staff to 'give him something to do' (Brown 1982). However, it is likely, given the similarities in fathers' accounts, that the father is often of genuine assistance, particularly on busy days in understaffed maternity wards:

> Well, she was induced, and she was there for about twelve hours. [Prompt: 'And in labour for twelve hours?'] No, she was on an epidural. . . . That was one of my jobs, you see, watching the epidural chart . . . and her saying, 'I think I've got a contraction' . . . 'Oh, that's right, yes,' I said. I was just confirming that it was time for her. [Prompt: 'So you found yourself fairly helpful in this capacity, did you?'] Yeah, and also, you know . . . really it must have been really boring for her. She was just lying . . . she could hardly move, 'cos she'd got these wires all over the place, and, er, she just needed someone to talk to. . . . I think the hospital staff encourage it because the father can be there, and it means the nurses have got more time to go to the other patients and do other things, whatever they want to do, and at least somebody's in with the patient all the time and they're not just lying there for twelve hours by themselves getting bored to tears.
>
> (Factory manager 1)

Negative effects
While technological innovation has attempted to make childbirth an equally controlled experience for all women, the actual unfolding of 'standard' events varies, and fathers tend to be much influenced by their perceptions of their wives' pain and danger. Table 4.3 shows that 60 per cent of the attenders (40 fathers) reported that the labour and delivery were at least partly distressing. As I intend to show, the fathers' accounts reveal that most experience acute fears during the process.

Ten men recalled that the procedure was either completely upsetting or completely worrying. Two claimed it was 'nothing special', and over a quarter of the attenders felt that it brought mixed blessings.

Table 4.3   Husbands' recollections of the birth

Response category	Frequency
Negative/neutral	12
Mixed	28
Only positive aspects discussed	27
Not present at delivery	33
Total:	100

The sociological literature (Brown 1982, McKee 1980, Richman and Goldthorp 1978) suggests that men's experiences may be adversely affected by their contact with the medical staff. Some of these fathers expressed similar sentiments. Aspects of the 'conservative' ideology still remain; without realizing the consequences of their actions, medical professionals appear seriously to disturb some fathers, usually without intending to. For example, some fail to realize that medical terminology is both foreign and frightening to the layman, particularly if a problem arises:

> [I was] nervous because they told us . . . the doctors were very secretive on this, er – what do they call it? – ostrio antigene? . . . Well, to me that sounds something terrible, and I couldn't get a decent explanation as to what it was. . . . 'Oh, it'll be all right, no need to worry', that sort of thing. And so when I was sitting in the waiting-room and the woman came to me and said, 'Now we might have a few difficulties, and we might have to use forceps', well, of course I knew nothing about birth and had never been interested in it until that time, and I was . . . 'Forceps! What's going on!' you know, and so I was worried when I went in . . . probably for no reason.
>
> (Warehouse labourer)

This father had been excluded from the labour for a 'routine examination'. The practice is carried out in order to protect the modesty of the mother and both the embarrassment and professional integrity of the doctors and midwives. At the same time, as Richman and Goldthorp state, it underlines the father's low status, as a removable part of the proceedings. In a few instances it has dramatic effects. One father, for example, could not face returning to the delivery room, having been sent out for one of these examinatioins:

> She was in that much pain but . . . it's a funny thing to explain really, you know. I didn't like to see all that suffering. While I was out the room I wanted to go back in, but . . . I was all right, you know, I could've . . . I *was* upset, but I could've sat there if they hadn't told me to go out, you know, for the examination. . . . I'd've stopped . . .

but with them saying, you know . . . 'Go out', and then having to go back in again . . . 'cos I'd built myself up for it'.

(Plant operator)

While a few are undoubtedly influenced adversely by medical terminology and procedures, most husbands simply comply with any request that is made of them, since their main preoccupation concerns their wives' health and safety. And it is this aspect of the delivery which leaves a more lasting effect upon them. Seeing their wife in pain is the most frequently repeated reason for the experience being remembered by fathers as partly or wholly disturbing.

Witnessing such pain and distress in his wife reveals just how thin the veneer of marital symmetry is, and the husband is often left with very mixed feelings about the delivery. On the surface, men are unlikely to admit to such feelings. Yet only a little probing unearthed many negative reactions. Only twelve fathers continued to describe the experience in completely glowing terms. Men often commented that they could remember this suffering far more vividly than their wives could, and the difference between mothers' and fathers' responses in the small sample showed a trend in this direction (although not a statistically significant one):

Well, she was in labour for a long time. . . . She thought it was a bad experience at the time, but she seemed to forget about it straight away. [Prompt: 'So how does she look back on it now?'] Ah, she can't remember it as a bad experience now.

(Bricklayer)

Well, I wouldn't have liked to have done it, to be quite honest. . . . She was in a lot of pain . . . most women are. . . . Thank goodness she didn't have it for very long. . . . I suppose it was the *worst* occasion for her having a baby pain-wise. I mean afterwards *OK*, fine. At the time . . . [sighs].

(Sales manager)

The extent to which men find delivery disturbing is evidenced in some cases when either they leave the delivery room or are excluded. Six men conveniently withdrew at the crucial moment to get air or to take a break. While they all mentioned that the events were distressing, only one of these suggested this as the reason for withdrawing:

I was there until it started and I couldn't stand it any more, so I went out. . . . I wouldn't like to have seen the blood and everything and also I wouldn't like to see my wife in pain, so I walked out of the room. I thought I was going to faint. I was *going* to stop there.

(Builder's labourer)

The intensity of these emotions can have lasting effects on fathers. One man, for example, was very concerned that his wife should not go through the experience of childbirth again and was contesting her desire to have a second child. In keeping with Richman and Goldthorp's (1978) findings, the group of fathers who experienced most distress were those who were excluded at the last stage of labour as a result of a 'medical' complication. Having gone through labour with their wives, these men were very upset when it became apparent, from the activities of the medical staff, that a complication had arisen. In addition, their exclusion might have caused serious disturbance. Clearly their main concern was that mother or child was in danger, but their accounts also suggest that they missed out on an important event in the development of their family:

> I'll be honest, I was in . . . I rang up Viv's mother . . . and I couldn't say anything, I was so choked. I just burst into tears . . . and I said, 'It's a girl', and Mum thought there was something wrong . . . and it started it off and then I was all right. . . . It's just the fact that I'd wanted . . . [Prompt: 'You'd wanted to be there?'] Well, you help to conceive it; you're the father. Um . . . the earlier you see your child, it sarts the relationship. . . . In fact, it's the fathers that suffer. Against what a lot of people say – a lot of people sort of say, 'It's the mothers every time that suffer during the labour and everything.' But I think it's the father who actually gets it worse; he's got more stress, because he's not going through the physical side. His is all mental.
>
> (Primary schoolteacher 1)

Positive effects
Table 4.3 shows that those fathers who remained with their wives throughout delivery tended to describe the experience as a positive one overall. However, these men described it very much like a trial-by-fire, which is well worth going through as long as all remains well. Even the twenty-seven men who considered that they had had entirely postive feelings in the delivery room concurred with Richman's (1982) assertion that the father's main feeling after delivery was of relief that everything had passed without upset – an admission which suggests that the delivery is commonly more anxiety-provoking than fathers readily admit.

> You've waited there for twelve hours or so and then all of a sudden you get this . . . at the end of the wait . . . well, not only the twelve hours but the nine months before. You know, you get the baby at the end of it and, you know, that's what you've been looking forward to for nine months. It's a wonderful feeling, but, you know, the question I would think 99 per cent of the couples ask is, 'Is he all right?' or 'Is she – is the baby OK?' They don't care what sex it is, you know. 'Is the baby all right?' And as soon as you hear, 'Yes, no problems', fine everything's right . . . marvellous, wonderful. . . . It's just a relief and, er . . . it's a *good* relief.
>
> (Factory manager 1)

The delivery is the culmination of parents' pregnancy 'careers' and it perhaps comes as no surprize that it should serve as a cathartic outlet of all the worries that have been preying on the minds of sturdy male oaks. Yet relief is not the only feeling men recall when discussing the significance of the birth. The cathartic feeling is also caused by the fact that delivery marks the end of the 'transition' to first- or second-time parenthood; couples perceived the event as a shared landmark in their marriage.

Technological intervention in childbirth has meant that many women find it less painful. Yet this has the effect of making the process more difficult both to 'feel' and to recall. Consequently, many couples recognized that the father became an essential source of knowledge about what was happening. When the wives were asked about their labour they frequently mentioned that their memories were vague and that their husbands knew more about events than themselves:

> I think I had too much trouble of it. They gave me so many drugs I really didn't know anything about it. I was in a haze.
> (Housewife, whose husband is civil servant 2)

> He held me hand and, er . . . took great delight in looking at the equip-ment, you know, for the heartbeat and the contractions . . . and . . . he can remember . . . he told me a lot more than I can remember.
> (Housewife, whose husband is a floor layer)

One couple described the effects of anaesthesia upon the wife's memory:

> She don't remember owt. [Wife: 'No . . . I don't remember an awful lot actually 'cos he was there, 'cos half the things I had to ask him afterwards . . . I just didn't remember. They kept giving me pethidine.'
> (HGV driver and wife, a part-time nursing assistant)

Husbands not only have a grandstand view from which they can take in information to recall at a later date. Their accounts of the delivery also suggest that, while few espouse the philosophy of husband-coached childbirth, many recalled being involved in attempting to communicate the midwife's instruction through the 'haze' to their wives, and some felt they 'took over' the experience altogether:

> Well, having this epidural she didn't really know a lot about it. But it was *me* as had it. She couldn't breathe properly, she couldn't push. I was doing it all for her.
>
> (Lorry driver)

Most fathers do not identify with their wives as much as this man, although medicated childbirth certainly makes it possible to even out the differences between their experiences and their control over events. The descriptions of most parents suggest a great deal about what the childbirth means to them as a couple, and they both tend to refer to it as a shared experience where each has a part to play. Only the excerpts from the transcripts can suffice to demonstrate this point; both partners feel that the husband labours and should labour alongside his wife:

> He rubbed my back and when it came to the second stage he . . . [was] kneeling on bended knee and mopping my face and really encouraging me. I think he was more exhausted than I was at the end of it. He was shattered. He went through it – he really did.
>
> (Housewife, whose husband is civil servant 1)

> I found it hard work and much more traumatic than I thought it would be . . . um . . . certainly felt as if I'd done a very full day's work at the end of it. I was quite exhausted, but, um . . . [Prompt: 'What was it that made you exhausted?'] Well, just . . . I don't know really . . . I passed the time by sort of playing with all the electronic instruments that were moved up to her and, er . . . helping her . . . helping her to have gas and air and this sort of thing. . . . I felt by the end of the experience that I'd done a full day's work and was absolutely washed out, but nevertheless I wouldn't miss being there a second time. . . . I don't think one could put one's wife through such an experience without being there.
>
> (Engineering lecturer)

Conclusion

It is clear from the explicit statements of nearly half the attendant fathers that labour and delivery can be a traumatic time for many men, since on top of the fact that they are thrust into a strange environment they are also acutely worried for their wives' safety. This concern usually overrides the effects of their low status in the medical 'team' and the threat of having their emotions 'exposed' publicly, in an event which has considerable personal and private significance to them. The genuine anxiety felt by men is perhaps best attested to by the fact that the vast majority mention a distinct feeling of relief after delivery, even though 40 per cent of attenders do not mention the stressful aspects in their accounts of labour and delivery.

Despite this anxiety, the majority of couples who do not have severe medical complications recall the event in glowing terms as if it is all worth struggling for. The effect is expressed very much in terms which echo the writings of the 'progressive' obstetricians twenty or so years ago. A shared delivery is perceived as a landmark which heralds a new phase of the family life-cycle, and the quality of the experience seems to be similar for both first- and second-time fathers. Couples frequently mentioned that the birth brought them closer together, just as the shared pregnancy had done; and as I shall outline in the Chapter 7, fathers feel closer to the child as a result.

In short, birth is the symbolic climax of a shared pregnancy in married couples, and this is recognized by all attenders and even by some of those who missed out on the experience. The following father described the mixture of emotions which well up at the time of delivery, and his testimony perhaps serves as a most succinct summary of the event in both its positive and negative aspects:

> Oh, marvellous . . . um . . . people often ask you now, friends and things. You can't put it into words; I don't think so. . . . You tend to get lost for words [swallow]. . . . Tremendous, I can't think of anything you could compare it with at all. . . . Friends that have had babies since, you know, I've always tried to say, 'Ooh, you must be there.' Fantastic . . . also I think you're at a little bit of a loose end as well, 'cos you're not really part of it, I don't think, in that respect. [Prompt: 'So what was it like to be at a loose end?'] That was awful, particularly when it got painful, 'cos there was nothing you could do or anything . . . but when the actual birth took place that was great, 'cos you were back into it again, you know, they make you a part of it, you sort of have an arm or a leg to hold, you know. . . . I took a lot of interest beforehand in the breathing exercises and, you know, encouragement that way. . . . I really enjoyed it . . . very essential, you know. At the end you feel a bit of a fool, tears running down your face, but it is tremendous. . . . Yeah, at that moment you are definitely together, you know, all three of you. That is . . . probably it's the beginning, you know, I don't know . . . it made a tremendous difference to the two of us. . . . I think before we had Marilyn, I don't think you're married, quite honestly. Like you're still best friends or whatever except you're living in the same place. But the home is only a sort of hotel 'cos you're never in it that long, you know. So I think it's a big difference.
>
> (Hairdresser)

5   Patterns Are Established: the Baby Comes Home

The 'transition to parenthood' takes longer than just the pregnancy and delivery, and great practical and psychological changes occur in the early weeks of the child's life. The three sections of this chapter examine different aspects of paternal involvement during this period: firstly, the man's role during his wife's stay in hospital; secondly, the domestic division of labour when mother and baby return home; thirdly, the couple's psychological adjustment to coping for a new baby. The patterns of 'paternal' involvement during pregnancy and delivery continue and become more clearly defined.

Mother and Baby in Hospital:
Awaiting the Home-coming

Nowhere are the roles and behaviour of parents more clearly culturally patterned than in the early post-partum period. Ethnographic evidence shows that the vast majority of societies – 82.9 per cent in the Paiges' (1981) review – segregate the mother and child from their kin and other social networks; and most of these also enforce ritual avoidance and/or food taboos. In western society the 'cultural' influences upon the activities of young mothers are no less apparent. There appear to be good medical reasons for segregating women away from their families, but hospitalization has more than just medical implications. Clearly new mothers have to fit in with the hospital regime, often without due consideration of their individual needs and regardless of the support they may have at home. There are some exceptions but these do little more than show us the pervasiveness of the social norm. For example, Princess Diana was allowed to return home only twenty-four hours after the birth of her children. This breach of standard policy after the arrival of Prince William was quickly explained by the honorary secretary of the Royal College of Obstetricians and Gynaecologists: 'Those who want people to run back to their home environment after a birth will say that if the Princess of Wales can do it, so can Mrs Thing from Rochdale – except Mrs Thing is not going back to the same circumstances at all as the princess' (*Guardian*, 23 June 1982: 1).

The 'social' effects of the hospitalization of childbirth are numerous. For our purposes it is important to consider the amount of time that hospitals allow fathers and other visitors to be with their wives and babies. The mother's relationship with the outside world is controlled by the hospital, even if its rules are not always strictly enforced. Medical institutions still restrict visiting hours (usually to two brief periods during the day), the number of visitors per 'patient' and even the categories of people encouraged to visit. For example, many hospitals allow only the father to enter on the evening after delivery. Lomas, in a paper on the social significance of the isolation of mothers, comments on the effect that this 'exclusion' (i.e. segregation) can have upon fathers:

> In hospital this exclusion extends into the post-partum period, the husband – but not his children – being permitted to visit his wife, in circumstances of constraint, now and again. During this time the husband has little or no influence over the affairs of his wife and baby. He is patronised by the hospital staff who, in the same way as the general public, humorously assume him to be in a state of incompetent dither, best out of the way since liable to be a nuisance, and he accepts this practice.
>
> (1964: 13)

The hospitalization of mother and baby automatically puts father at a disadvantage. Firstly, as fathers often commented, all eyes turned on them when they entered the hospital ward, and this inhibited many from touching the baby as much as they wanted.

> I had to handle him delicate, you know. I picked him up, but it didn't feel right, because I was in hospital. You see there's *married* women who's had one or two kids and they watch to see if you're doing it right. [Prompt: 'So it's an embarrassing time, is it?'] Not really embarrassing. It's just you can feel them looking at you, that's all.
>
> (General labourer)

In contrast to home delivery, at which members of the family are left to care for both mother and child soon after birth, hospitals have taken away the necessity for a skilled attendant (a role traditionally reserved for women themselves who have their own offspring) to be present to nurse the new mother. Hospitals also determine when a family may be reunited. The standard practice today is for first-time mothers to stay in for a minimum of five days, with 'experienced' women being let out after two, as long as all is well. The first-timers stayed a significantly longer time in hospital, but many second-timers stayed at least three days (73 per cent of first-timers stayed more than three days vs 45 per cent of second-timers; $\chi^2 = 8.18$, df = 7, p < 0.005). Before we consider this return home, we should thus examine what happens to fathers while they await the release of their wives and children from their confinement.

'Fathering' in the very early days

While their wives are confined to hospital, the activities of husbands are influenced by norms and customs as well as by the official hospital policy of keeping them at arm's length. Men's descriptions of the way they spent their time often strongly resembled one another. Their accounts usually contain three themes, each of which can be seen in both practical and symbolic terms.

Firstly, they announce the arrival of the child in a number of ways. As their wives are segregated and they are not, all but a handful are delegated to contact friends and relations as soon as the baby is born. This procedure is lengthy and occurs in a set order. The father first gets in touch with the new maternal grandmother, then his own mother, followed by other close relatives and finally good friends. One father summed up this order of procedure when describing his role as communicator immediately after an early-morning delivery:

> When I left there, at half-past four – quarter to five – I left there and I went straight to her mother and father's, like, and knocked them up . . . and I sat there drinking tea wi' them. And I left their home, went straight up to me mother and father's, knocked them up . . . had another cup of tea at their home. Then shot up and see me sister . . . and everybody was awake!
>
> (Lorry driver)

After the initial telephone calls or visits to family members, fathers continue to mark the arrival of the child. Many placed announcements in the local newspaper, or registered the child's birth. A majority remembered to 'wet the baby's head', celebrating the arrival with family or friends over one or more drinks.

Secondly, fathers often mentioned that they spent a considerable time making last-minute preparations for the home-coming. Many completed decorating the child's bedroom, as they often ran out of time before the delivery. One father, for example, spent most of the night before his wife's return laying a new carpet. If they have completed the new decorations fathers still find jobs to do, cleaning the house in preparation for the arrival or fetching important pieces of equipment. For example, superstition prevents some expectant couples from fetching the cot or pram until after the child's safe delivery.

Thirdly, married fathers spend much of their time organizing their brief visits to their wives. Apart from spending time with mother and baby, men are often called upon to transport other relatives to and from the hospital. Only seven fathers visited their wives less than daily. The reasons they gave for not doing so were either that the birth was a Caesarian, and the wife was in for up to ten days, or because there was an older child to look after. Sixty-five men visited their wives at least daily in hospital.

Table 5.1　Social class trends in the frequency of
fathers visiting their wives in hospital

Social class	Daily or less	On average more than daily
I/II	2	22
III (w.c.)	7	17
III (m.)	11	14
V	13	12

Linear trend: $\chi^2 = 12.07$, df $= 3$, p<0.008.

Table 5.1 shows that this group contained more middle- than working-class fathers.

Middle-class men appear to visit their wives more than daily for two reasons. Firstly, they are more likely to have cars (the Nottingham hospitals at the time were both notoriously inaccessible). Secondly, they are more able to be given time off work (for example, late lunch hours or working flexible hours).

In recent years it has become customary for men to take time off from work after the delivery of their children. As we shall see in the next section, married men usually take some time off once their wives are home from hospital. However, a third of this sample started their leave at the time of delivery. The first-timers in this group tended to be those who need to make final preparations, while second-timers often had to be at home to look after the older child. A quarter of this latter group of fathers cared for the older child single-handed. In addition, 35 per cent of them shared the responsibility for such care either with another relative or by arranging their routine to fit in with the time the child was at school.

Taken together, the activities described by fathers in the period between the child's arrival and home-coming make them very busy, particularly if they continue to work. Even if there are few preparations to make, many find a need to fill in time, having been through the experience of delivery and missing their wives. Typical accounts by fathers sum up this feeling of urgency:

> I went round to get the birth certificate, put it in evening paper, tell people, fetch the pram – no, fetch the cot – could have been the pram, I can't remember. . . . Just mad, rushing round like mad.
>
> (Police constable 1)

The Family Reunited at Home

The cast of characters

Recent studies indicate that a majority of fathers take time off work after the arrival of the baby (Bell *et al.* 1983, Daniel 1980). As Table 5.2 shows,

Table 5.2   Amount of time taken off Work by fathers
after the arrival of the child

Number of working days off	Frequency
(a) None (subtotal = 18)	
(i) no change in work time	15
(ii) altered shifts to suit family	3
(b) Seven days or less (subtotal = 43)	
(i) 1–3 days	14
(ii) 1–7 days	29
(c) Eight days or more	30
(d) No need to take time off (subtotal = 9)	
(i) unemployed	6
(ii) disabled	2
(iii) teacher on school holiday	1
Total:	100

eighteen men in the study carried on with their normal patterns of work.
Most took some time off, and one-third of those in work spent two working
weeks at home.

In some countries, like Sweden, 'paternity leave', which allows men time
off from work to be with their families after the delivery, is institutionalized
and funded by the government (Lamb and Levine 1983). In the UK no
such state provision exists, and moves to initiate similar schemes here have
been deliberately opposed. A Private Member's Bill brought before
Parliament in 1979, which attempted to introduce state provision for seven
days' paternity leave, failed at its first reading, having been described on
the floor of the House as 'grotesque' and 'an incitement to a population
explosion' (Equal Opportunities Commission 1982). The number of firms
known to provide paid leave is only about sixty, and most of these permit
men five or ten days off, but often at reduced levels of pay (Bell *et al.* 1983,
Equal Opportunities Commission 1980). While Daniel (1980) found that
13 per cent of fathers received special paid leave, in this study not one man
admitted to having benefitted from such a scheme, though an employee
of the National Coal Board was allowed a few days' 'compassionate' (not
paternity) leave. All of the rest took part, or all, of their annual paid holiday
during this period, and it is clear that many of those who took no leave
at this time simply could not afford to stop working.

There appears to be a related class difference in the amount of leave
taken at this time. Non-professional white-collar workers – class III
(w.c.) – were more likely to take four or more days off during this period
than men from all the other class groups (83 per cent class III (w.c.) vs
58 per cent classes I/II, III (m.) and V; $\chi^2 = 4.89$, df = 1, $p < 0.05$).

In the absence of any institutional provision to enable them to take time off, some men have to take unusual steps to be with their wives, particularly if they have already used up their holiday decorating the baby's room. Two labourers said that they had asked to be made redundant just so that they could be on hand. One of them commented:

> [Interviewer: 'Did you take any time off work?'] No, because I couldn't. . . . Wait a minute, I *did*. I *was* out of work. It was the fact that I couldn't afford to have a holiday, but we'd got nobody to look after Karen [wife] and the baby when it was born. So just before Christmas I asked the foreman on the building site I was working if he could make me redundant, and he made me redundant.
>
> (Factory labourer)

Others relied upon the goodwill of their local doctor to grant them some paid 'sick' leave – as it was necessary at the time of interviewing to obtain a certificate to be off work sick:

> Well, I had a week's holiday owing to me and I'd got to take it by the end of March. Now, we knew that the baby was due any time, so I had a week's holiday to be at home, you know, in case anything happened. Well, it happened on Tuesday and I went to the doctor's and told him, like, that my wife had just had a baby and I'd like to be off for two weeks, you know, sick. And he says, 'All right', straight away. . . . This doctor was good, see. If there's owt like that he'd help you out, only you get some at this place where they're just not bothered.
>
> (Plant operator)

Table 5.3 Who was present in the few days after mother and baby returned from hospital?

	Frequency
(a) Nobody	4
(b) Father only	50
(c) Father and others (subtotal = 27)	
(i) father and relative	24
(ii) father and friend	3
(d) Grandmother	12
(e) Other relative/s	3
(f) Other (subtotal = 4)	
(i) maternal grandmother and au pair	2
(ii) daily help and au pair	1
(iii) maternal grandmother and neighbour	1
Total:	100

Why do so many men take time off work after the birth of their children? Questions about the availability of other people to help in the home during this period show that in many households fathers are the only or the main assistant to their wives. Table 5.3 shows that in 50 per cent of the families fathers were the only people available, and they provided a significant part of the essential care in a further 27 families.

The number of fathers present during the week or so after the mother returns is striking when compared with the figures for two decades ago. The Newsons' data (1963) shows that only 30 per cent of men, in a comparable sample, helped their wives at all after a first or second birth in 1959; whereas, in 1979 – 80, 95 per cent of fathers were present at some time to help, and 77 per cent claimed to have played a part in the domestic division of labour.

A number of factors seem to have influenced this change. Men now have longer periods of paid holiday per annum (English Tourist Board 1979). Twenty years ago the mother's own mother or sister was often an important figure at the delivery and immediately afterwards. As I mentioned earlier, hospitals have taken the immediate, and perhaps crucial, responsibility away from the mother's own female relatives. Recent history has also resulted in changes in the employment patterns of older women. So, while the role of the domiciliary attendant is now less important at birth, women are also less available to assist once the mother returns home.

More middle- than working-class fathers took responsibility for part of the domestic routine (86 per cent middle-class vs 68 per cent working-class; $\chi^2 = 4.54$, df = 1, p < 0.05). While insufficient data was collected about why they took time off, fathers' accounts suggested that this class difference arises for two reasons. Firstly, working-class fathers have on average less holiday time available to them. Secondly, middle-class parents appear less likely to have, or to want to have, help from their own relatives.

The division of labour

In the few cases where fathers took very little or no time off, the general division of labour seemed to vary according to the needs of the mother and older child (if they had one) and the availability of help from others. Some, particularly working-class men, came to a suitable arrangement with their female relatives. The lorry driver quoted above, for example, sung the praises of his mother-in-law, whose presence enabled him to return to work after two days:

> Well, her mother's just like that, you know. If she can help, she'll help, sort of thing. . . . Sort of thing, at night time when I came home . . . 'cos I used to tell her mother to leave all the housework . . . at night, you see, I used to come home and I used to do everything what I could do. [Prompt: 'What sort of things?'] Well, in the morning I'd hoover . . . first thing in the morning. I was up

at seven and used to get the home hoovered out and while her mother used to do things like nappies and babies' bottles and suchlike during the day. At night I used to do the dusting and clean the windows and other things like, you know.

In contrast, many a father's accounts of the division of labour around this time suggest that, if both he and a female relative were present together at the same time of day, there was a potential for conflict. In a few cases couples took action and sent the traditional source of help packing. One man made no attempt to conceal his feelings about the help of his mother-in-law:

[Wife: 'She came during the day.'] She did to start with, and then she got . . . then she became a pain in the arse, so . . . so we sent her back again . . . when her services were fully rendered. [Prompt: 'So, what did you do at this time?'] Kept out the way of her! Well, I don't know . . . you get a lot of comments about mother-in-laws . . . 'cos they told us that . . . we both went there . . . what do you call them? . . . parentcraft. And the first thing they tell you is your parents are the worst advisers. And I think it's true; they base it on their own experience and that's it, full stop.

(Financial controller)

Another father described the tension between himself and his sister-in-law:

Well, actually, the idea was for her sister to come up. She was going to do this, she was going to do that. . . . Well, it ended up I didn't like it. I thought she was taking over, and anyway it was getting like one against one. She was doing this and I was feeling out of it and, er . . . well, anyway, she eased off a bit and I was doing nappies and everything. [Prompt: 'So you did absolutely everything?'] Yeah. [Prompt: 'And around the house, did the sister stop coming or did she ease off a bit?'] No. She stopped, and it was a prompt stop after we had a few words, and that upset Lindsay [wife] and . . . but she saw *my* point of view.

(Records clerk)

Of course the father's presence during this period does not necessarily imply that he plays a major role in running the household. Indeed, the amount and nature of men's contributions to housekeeping varied considerably. Table 5.4 gives a breakdown of both factors. The *nature* of father participation was divided into child care and housework. The *amount* a man participated in these activities was classified according to whether he perceived his role as 'major' (i.e. took on the main responsibility) or 'minor' (i.e. did less than some other member of the household).

Table 5.4 shows that a majority of married fathers now take over considerable responsibility for the running of the household during this period. The comments of the few who did not do some of the extra domestic

Table 5.4　The father's recalled part in the domestic
division of labour in the early days

Response category	Frequency
(a) None	5
(b) Helper (minor role) (subtotal = 49)	
(i) in the home only	22
(ii) with the baby only	7
(iii) in the home and with the baby	22
(c) Major responsibility (subtotal = 44)	
(i) all the housework	13
(ii) all the housework and some child care	18
(iii) all the housework and child care	2
(iv) looking after the older child and the house mainly (but also the new baby)	11
Total:	100

work often indicate that they 'should' have, which suggests that the pressures
to conform to this practice are ubiquitous:

> [Interviewer: 'What did you do during this time?'] Well, not a lot,
> I don't s'pose . . . but, you know, the odd chores . . . a cup of
> tea, wash the pots. . . . But it never works with me, you see. I'm . . .
> I'm just idle by nature. I go to work and that's me as far as I'm
> concerned. You know, I'm usually too tired to start playing about too
> much. . . . 'Eck well, it's hard to think. . . . What I had to do at
> first, like, I had to steady the baby while she washed her because she
> was always very nervous of holding her and, er . . . I had to feed the
> baby sometimes – you're bound to . . . and as I say, I've never been
> one for chores, you know; that's always been her province. Er, you
> see, when it came to it if there was any nappies or anything like that
> she would . . . she just had to do them herself. . . . I've never been
> the greatest cook, so I couldn't take on anything like that. I could
> probably help hoover up or something like that, you know, but that's
> about it.
>
> > (Plasterer's labourer, who took one week off work
> > to be the main attendant to his wife)

These non-participant men were few in number. Five admitted to having
done nothing, and only eight of the fifty who were the sole attendants played
a 'minor' (as opposed to a 'major') role. Most of the rest were highly active
in at least one aspect of the domestic routine.

    Within the variations of paternal involvement during this period, some
patterns are apparent. The amount fathers contributed was related to the

time they took off work; so those who took eight or more days off work were far more likely to play a 'major' role. At the same time non-professional white-collar workers – social class III (w.c.) – who took more time off during this period also claimed to assume more responsibility than members of other social groups (59 per cent class III (w.c.) vs 33 per cent classes I/II, III (m.) and V taking a major role; $\chi^2 = 5.41$, df = 1, p<0.02). Furthermore, the nature of the father's involvement seemed to be partly dictated by subcultural 'rules'. For example, thirty-five men who were present had nothing to do with the care of the baby. These tended to be working-class fathers. Indeed, skilled manual workers – class III (m.) – undertook significantly less child care than the other groups (66 per cent class III (m.) vs 33 per cent classes I/II, III (w.c.) and V taking a minor role; $\chi^2 = 5.56$, df = 1, p<0.02).

While Table 5.4 indicates that a majority of fathers did become involved in some child care, the extent of their involvement deserves closer scrutiny. The impression gained in *most* households was that the 'natural' division of labour was for fathers to take major responsibility for the housework while their wives mainly looked after the baby, even if the fathers did assist, at times, in child care. One father, who in Table 5.4 was reported to do all the housework and some child care (since he changed the occasional nappy), summed up his basic duty:

> Very much a sort of . . . er . . . becoming, I suppose, not a nurse . . . what would you call it? A skivvy, I suppose. I was very much . . . cleaning up after Carrie [wife], looking after that thing there [looks at the dog], looking after myself . . . cooking meals, etc. . . . . So generally being house-'man' I suppose, or house-'husband'. We are like a unit anyway, I suppose . . . whether we're fairly unique I don't know.
>
> (Sales representative)

The most frequently cited activities fathers mentioned doing were shopping, domestic chores and, in the case of second-timers, looking after the older child. Some men commented that they preferred to do the domestic chores because they were afraid of handling such a small baby – a common theme in studies of this sort (Cleary and Shepperdson 1981, McKee 1979, Oakley 1979). As I discussed above, many fathers are reluctant to be seen to hold their babies, during hospital visits. When their wives arrive home men are at a distinct disadvantage, since not only have they had less contact with their new-born babies, they also have not had the support and guidance of the hospital staff. The general labourer quoted above about handling his baby in front of the other women in the ward commented:

> It's a lot harder than you think it's going to be with a baby that young. [Prompt: 'In what way harder?'] Well, he was fragile and I just couldn't handle him proper. [Prompt: 'For how long?'] Well . . .

[it] took about four weeks to *hold* him and that, you know . . . properly without feeling nervous, 'cos he used to wriggle really bad.

Parents commented that their early experience as parents often made the mother's and father's perceptions differ. If mothers spend a long time in hospital their handling skills obviously increase. One woman, who had a Caesarian delivery, compared her husband's and her own experience:

> I suppose in a way it's a bit different, because I was in hospital a fortnight and by the time I came out I'd been used to bathing the baby and feeding. . . . The feeding was all right. I think we managed quite well. . . . It's just that I was exhausted all the time. I'd see to the baby and fall asleep. David [husband] did most of the housework. He had a week off, and me mother helped the next week.
>
> (Housewife, whose husband is the floor layer)

The Psychological Impact of Early Parenthood

Table 5.4 shows that most men do participate in the care of their offspring in the early days, even if they act as 'helpers' and may be afraid of doing so. Chapter 3 considered the paradoxical nature of men's roles in pregnancy. Their public front of 'detachment' appears to conceal an often intense involvement in the pregnancy. When the child is born the same apparent contradictions are present. While they usually have little contact with the baby they often share with their wives an intense interest in his or her daily progress.

It is tempting to speculate that fathers who fail to involve themselves in child care do so because their relationships with their offspring have not developed. However, more straightforward explanations are equally plausible. To begin with, mothers are much less mobile and they are often confined to the home, or the bedroom, for much of this period. In addition, those who are attempting to establish a breast-feeding routine, particularly one based upon demand feeding, need to be on hand when their baby awakes. Perhaps the most important reason for the clear division of labour is that nobody really expects fathers to play a major role in child care as long as their wives are capable of coping themselves. They simply accept the cultural prescription that the mother should take primary responsibility for the baby. At the same time this does not mean that they are uninvolved. They often regard their work as a contribution to the nurturance of the baby as well as the care of their wives.

Table 5.4 shows that two fathers took over total responsibility for the child as well as for the house. In both these cases the mother was ill enough to be physically incapable of sitting up, let alone looking after the baby. In three other families fathers took on a major role because their wives also were unwell. More generally, the mothers and fathers expressed a brief that the father *should* participate at this time, so that he could act as a substitute if the need arose. This feeling of 'being available' contributed to the reciprocity between parents. Fathers may play 'second fiddle' in the domestic set-up, but their availability to understudy compensates for their lesser status as care-givers.

While fathers have much less contact with the baby in most families, the majority of parents do not depict the early days as a period within the household division of labour was strictly demarcated. Indeed, they more typically give the impression that the early days after the arrival home are a period of family 'togetherness', when both parents share in their new responsibilities. They occupied themselves primarily in household chores, but men often took time off to 'be' with their wife and baby:

> Um, I suppose I did everything. . . . I shopped, cooked, um, washed . . . got up every time the baby cried. [Prompt: 'To do what?'] Um, well, er, Val had to feed him, but it was so novel for me that every time he wanted a feed I was quite happy to watch him, especially as I didn't have to go to work.
>
> (Accountancy lecturer)

Many of the wives expressed surprise at how involved and competent their husbands were. The participation by fathers in child care, however minimal, contrasts sharply with the stereotypical image of men and the fathers' self-presentation in the 'sturdy oak' role during pregnancy. About half a dozen mothers were surprised to find that their husbands were as adept as themselves:

> She was [a] marvellous baby but the first night she cried I said, 'I don't know what to do.' In fact Keith changed the first nappy because I didn't know what to do. I was quite helpless, really, because she seemed so tiny I didn't know what to do.
>
> (Housewife, whose husband is civil servant 1)

More common was the feeling of general surprise at their involvement:

> I think the most important thing is that we shared in it right from the start. I mean Patrick took *his* part. It surprised me really how much he *did* for her to start with, 'cos he always said that he liked . . . he liked children, but he was a bit frightened of babies. He's an only child . . . never had much to do with them, and he said, 'Well, don't expect me to take much interest for the first couple of years.' In fact he took one look at her and that was it!
>
> (Nursing sister, whose husband is a house-husband and part-time photo-journalist)

The arrival of a new baby does more than simply alter the domestic division of labour for a few weeks. Parents describe this period as one of upheaval, in more than their routine, and any understanding of it must take into account the emotional adjustments which this time demands. When I asked, 'Were you prepared for the first few weeks?' the responses vividly described a feeling of disruption or anxiety in at least half (33 out of 60) of the first-timers and even a few (7 out of 40) of the second-time couples (a difference that is statistically significant: $\chi^2 = 14.06$, df = 1, p<0.0005).

A majority of first-timers reflect back on the first few weeks as a period when emotional adjustments were far more preoccupying than any rearrangement in the division of labour. Oakley's (1979) and other studies of the early weeks have concluded that mothers find it exhausting getting up in the middle of the night and worrying whether the baby is healthy. While fathers have not been through delivery and do not have to cope with stitches, piles and other complications, their accounts also suggest that their psychological adjustment is potentially problematic. Two recent studies have noted that one-third of fathers report symptoms of depression in the first weeks similar to the 'blues' common to mothers in the post-partum period (Atkinson 1979, Zaslow *et al.* 1981).

In this sample numerous parents compared their experiences with the stereotype portrayed in the media:

> The first few weeks I had to get used to, you know, getting up in the middle of the night to feed her. [Wife interjects: 'Big anti-climax, really. Not how you see it on television . . . bouncing babies all smiling and everything. You know, nappies and things . . . and it came down to she's screaming for feeds at four o'clock in the morning.'] You know, it's a big adjustment.
>
> (Coal-miner and wife, a housewife)

At the same time, a large number of these parents felt that it is impossible to forewarn first-timers of the upset and exhaustion due to the arrival of the child. Ten of the sixteen who claimed to be totally unprepared for the first weeks (and a number of second-timers reflecting back to their first child's arrival) suggested that there is no way that you can fully anticipate the disruption of parenthood. They felt that, however parenthood is depicted, theory and practice do not begin to match one another:

> I don't think you *can* be prepared. . . . I didn't think until you've *had* the baby you can possibly envisage what it involves. I think we were quite lucky, as I say, in the first week, with the baby settling down . . . we more or less got back into routine. But I think that the first three or four weeks, your mind's just conditioned to the baby. You're thinking about the baby, and you're thinking, you know . . . we didn't get much sleep the first two nights and, um . . . – the wife – or the mother – at the time, I don't think is able to *cope* with it because she's been through an experience *like* that and I think she feels very tired and, um . . . I think it's an emotional time for the father as well,

and I didn't relish the prospect of having to sleep probably two hours per night. But as I say, it didn't last long.

(Assistant contracts officer)

So first- and, to a lesser extent, second-time parents describe the first few weeks as a period of muddling through in an attempt to set up a routine. Many have a less easy time than the above father. First-timers devise a number of coping strategies, which they often use jointly or to complement one another. Husbands 'do their bit' by looking after the home, and may also retain the 'sturdy oak' image. While many men felt that they were far less prepared than their wives, a recurrent theme in the mothers' interviews was that their husbands gave them emotional support at the right times.

Apart from giving each other moral support during this period, it is clear that numerous couples receive help of this kind from outside sources. Both mothers' and fathers' accounts were full of comments about the usefulness of the domiciliary midwives, maternal grandmothers, other relatives and in one case a counsellor from the National Childbirth Trust.

[Interviewer: 'What about the first few weeks, coping with the baby yourselves, do you feel you were properly prepared for that?'] Yeah, I think so. . . . A lot of helpful advice from her mother, you know. . . . [Prompt: 'So that helped you through, did it?'] Yeah . . . and the midwives were very good. . . . You get little problems and you tend to think, 'Oh my God, what do we do?' you know. Then they walk in when it's over; you know, you think, 'Well, why the hell were we worried about it?' [Prompt: 'Do you think you could have prepared yourselves for them, and not had to turn to them in the first place?'] Er . . . well, I think you can read as many books as you like, and every baby is different. So there's always going to be something to do which you can't really legislate for. . . . But the older they get the more confident you get with them, and now we can cope with more or less everything.

(Chemical plant operator)

I didn't think you can ever be prepared for that because it's so totally unpredictable. . . . We planned beforehand . . . we'd bought all the necessary implements to bath him, feed him, etc. But as to things like – which I think is where the mother-in-law comes into her own – things like the boiling of nappies, the sterilization of bottles . . . things like that have been even harder. [Prompt: '*Could* you have planned these things?'] No, not reading from books or anything because of the unpredictability of, you know, whatever you hear or anything . . . although I suppose they're all the same for the first few weeks. But, er, no, that sort of thing is never wrote about . . . the involvement you're going to have.

(Sales representative)

Perhaps the importance of moral support is best shown by the couple who were not visited by the midwife after the return from hospital:

> [Interviewer: 'What about the first few weeks coping with the baby yourselves – do you feel you were properly prepared for that?'] No, not at all. . . . Well, we never had a midwife, 'cos . . . no . . . not for the first day – over a day. [Wife: 'We came out in the morning and we were told that someone would come that day, an' it was midday the following day and we'd had to ring up and we'd had a whole night with her and she'd screamed all night.'] It *was* upsetting at the time thinking that there's a baby who wants something and we couldn't do anything for her. We probably could but we didn't know what to do.
>
> (Police constable 2 and his wife, a housewife)

While couples normally gained a great deal of help from these professionals and their own relatives, such help appeared to have the effect of limiting the father's practical role. As other studies suggest (e.g. Kerr and McKee 1981), both parents might be equally concerned about and involved with the child, but help is usually directed towards the mother. Midwives often include her alone, either because the father is out at work or doing chores, or because they feel that he is uninvolved in child care. The accountancy lecturer's typical description of a visit was: 'I opened the door, and she didn't say anything except, "Where's baby and mother?" – rather treating it as Val's work.' Similarly, the wives' mothers were reported to help their daughters but never their sons-in-law.

Conclusion

This chapter has charted the course of a very brief period in the development of a family. However, it is of interest because it highlights many important aspects of men's initiation into parenthood. From the start the father tends to be kept at a distance from his offspring. This is obvious while his wife is in hospital, but an examination of his role in the early days suggests that his status as a parent remains paradoxical. On the one hand he shares the trials and joys of adjusting to the new baby. For example, he gets up with his wife to watch her feed in order to give her moral support and also to be with his new offspring – a point that is returned to in the next chapter. At the same time, however, the father's status as parent is not the same as that of his wife. While she holds the centre of the stage, he acts as a household help and works around the mother–child pair – unless, that is, he has to return to work or is 'deviant' and 'shirks his duty'.

Here we can see distinct similarities between a father's role in pregnancy and in the early life of the child. The man's public uninvolvement often continues. For example, health-care professionals may treat him as an outsider. In many instances the father, not wishing to be seen as 'cack-handed' or clumsy with the baby, often avoids practical care-giving activities. Yet at the same time he usually demonstrates an intense interest in the baby, which may well surprise even his wife. The father's developing relationship with the child is examined in Chapter 7.

6   The Patterns Continue: Child Care and Housework during the First Year

Differentiation between Mothering and Fathering

During the very early days at home the differences between mothers' and fathers' roles become increasingly apparent. Other studies report a decrease in father involvement over the first three months (Berstein and Cyr 1957, Oakley 1979), with a slight increase between six and twelve months (Richards *et al.* 1977, Wandersman 1980). Whatever the absolute involvement of fathers, it is clear that in the vast majority of cases their daily commitment to both child care and housework becomes small in comparison to their wives' contribution (Beail 1982, Cowan and Cowan 1981, Entwisle and Doering 1981, Kotelchuck 1972, Moss 1981, Shereshefsky and Yarrow 1973).

As Oakley (1974) pointed out, the critical difference between parents lies in their responsibility for the child. Not only did the mothers in this sample undertake most of the child care, but in all but a few homes they also exclusively organized the minutiae of the child's daily routine. Fathers usually maintain a key interest in the child, but their practical and executive role is that of 'helper'. We see such patterns, for example, in parents' daily discussions about the child.

A young baby monopolizes attention even when he or she is asleep. Parents often find that they have to make efforts to stop talking about him or her, particularly in the early days. At a year, seventy-two couples still discussed the baby every day. Yet during this discourse the wife, as primary care-giver, is instrumental in informing the father about the child's daily antics and any changes in his or her routine. Rarely does the father contribute to the organization of the child's life.

> [Interviewer: 'How do you come to start something new in his routine?'] I think really it's left up to Denise [wife] . . . things like that. . . . She's got quite a few friends with young babies. They seem to talk about it a lot and I think they pick things up naturally that way.
>
> (Spring maker)

88

If I come in at night Jane [wife] will say, 'She's done this today' or 'She's done that today', and I tend to . . . Jane tends to come up with ideas on it, and then I'll sort of follow it on. . . . In sort of routine things, Jane will sort of decide, basically . . . there's no way I would sort of say, 'I think we ought to stop that and do that.'

(Journalist)

I think I rely upon her a bit more because she's with her during the day. But sometimes she'll kind of want reassuring about something and she just refers it to me and I say, 'Yeah, that sounds like a good idea', or offer my advice then. . . . But I think she makes most of the decisions herself . . . and on the odd occasion she just wants reassurance about some things.

(Assistant contracts officer)

Only eighteen men decided upon what the child should wear more than once a week. Even if a father dressed the child, his wife usually selected the clothes he or she should wear. Kerr and McKee (1981) suggest that fathers become involved only in 'major decisions' about the child. This holds for vaccinations; a majority (57 per cent) of couples decided together upon whether and when the child should be inoculated. However, the same does not apply to all major decisions. For example, fathers said their wives were responsible for potty-training in eighty-five families, even if they might discuss the topic or participate at first:

Elizabeth [wife] would certainly be the one who did it. . . . We would have discussed it before we started, and we would discuss progress daily. [Prompt: 'So Elizabeth would do it but you think . . .'] Probably I . . . when we started it we'd do it together. But it would be Elizabeth, being at home during the day, who'd organize it, and would be the one who'd actually get it going. But we'd have discussed it before we started it and the first one . . . I've actually said that I'd find it hilarious and I'd be there to see what happens.

(Doctor)

Even if they discuss such topics, the wife, by her very presence at home, is the executive of most changes in the child's routine. In an illuminating study of parenthood, Kathryn Backett (1982) showed how such changes in routine are not discussed by spouses, because they wish to sustain a belief in marital mutuality, where such parity obviously does not exist. Rather, new practices are legitimized by 'explanatory incidents . . . where a single experience or incident was often regarded as constituting sufficient evidence on which to base a whole set of beliefs about appropriate behaviour (Backett 1982: 62).

This clear division of responsibility between parents gives rise to a difference in the way each perceives their roles. So involved do mothers become in the child that the psychoanalyst Donald Winnicott coined the term 'primary maternal preoccupation to summarize their involvement. Ann Oakley has examined the development of these feelings:

> Three processes happen in the early months. In the first place, the mother learns how to take care of *her* baby, and the baby makes it plain, by sleeping better, crying less and eating more, that the mother is satisfying it – this in turn boosts maternal confidence. Secondly, the baby becomes more responsive, smiling and laughing and *rewarding* the mother for all her work. And, thirdly, the baby begins to demonstrate a dependence upon the mother, which makes the mother feel she is *necessary* to the baby.
>
> (1979: 244)

In contrast, Oakley feels that men experience the first months of parenthood differently:

> It is clear that birth produces a peak of masculine domesticity; many fathers may be quite heavily involved in the early days, but this level of participation falls off as babies become older, life becomes more routine-like and the novelty of fatherhood is eroded by time and sleepless nights.
>
> All the old dodges are dragged in: you do it better than me; we have different standards; I don't know how to do it; you go out and earn the money, then.
>
> (1979: 211, 219)

Oakley makes an important distinction between mothers and fathers. Some fathers certainly opt out of child care in a way no mother can – unless *she* can find alternative care. Few mothers can reflect upon their role in the following way:

> I'm not extremely . . . well, I shouldn't say this with the tape-recorder going, but I'm not extremely interested in babies as such. I like them when they're children rather than babies, and so I'm not so interested in giving bottles and so on.
>
> (General studies lecturer)

However, Oakley's description of fatherhood is a matricentric one. The vast majority of men do not simply opt out of child care.

The rest of this chapter will examine three features of men's involvement, which show that their participation is no unitary phenomenon. It is, firstly, subject to constant change over the first year because both the baby's needs and his or her mother's reaction to these do not remain constant. Secondly, there is great variation between different aspects of the father's involvement; he tends to be more participant in some areas of child care than in others. Thirdly, the variations between fathers are great. Paternal involvement is constantly negotiated by spouses (Backett 1982) and has to be understood by taking into account the changing needs of the child, the significance of parenthood to both mother and father and the influence of external factors, especially the world of work, upon the family.

The Changing Nature of Child Care: Fathers' Contributions to Feeding during the First Year

As we saw in the last chapter, during the first weeks the child becomes the responsibility of the mother: partly because she is expected to take care of the new baby, but also as she has been temporarily immobilized by the delivery and can more easily tend to the needs of the new-born than go shopping or do the housework. These 'forces' continue to operate after the early days. The tasks which I shall discuss show that a combination of factors all contribute to the man's relative withdrawal from domestic labour. He is not only expected to leave the home to his wife's attention; he is also at the disadvantage of keeping up with a rapidly changing role on a part-time basis. He is alongside a partner who has more practice and is attributed with more skill. The effects will be discovered at length here with reference to one aspect of care over the first year of the child's life: his or her feeding patterns.

The effects of physiological limitations: breast-feeding

The most direct limitation upon men is their inability to breast-feed. In pre-industrial cultures biological necessity greatly reduces the number of potential feeders. In western society early feeding patterns are more influenced by parents' subcultural values and practices. Whether or not a women breast-feeds her offspring to be most heavily influenced by her social class background (Martin 1978). Table 6.1 illustrates that even within this small sample there was a statistically significant linear decrease in breast-feeding down the social class scale, both among those who breast-feed at all and those still feeding at three months. Middle-class parents are far more likely to espouse the belief that 'breast is best'.

Table 6.1   Class differences in the numbers of mothers who breast-feed their babies

	Any breast-feeding?		Breast-feeding at 3 months?	
Social class	*No*	*Yes*	*No*	*Yes*
I/II	6	19	12	13
III (w.c.)	6	19	15	10
III (m.)	11	14	19	6
V	18	7	24	1

$\chi^2 = 15.99$, df = 3, $p < 0.002$. $\chi^2 = 15.4$, df = 3, $p < 0.001$.

Two decades ago the Newsons found that mothers tended to suggest that they had been physically incapable of breast-feeding, often in order to conceal their antipathy to what they regarded as a distasteful process (Newson and Newson 1963). Today fathers were more likely to mention their opposition to the principle of breast-feeding. Of the fifty-two mothers who did not breast-feed after the child was two weeks old, thirty-two husbands claimed that it was a 'revolting', 'disgusting' or 'embarrassing' way of feeding babies.

Just as they tried to hide their feelings during pregnancy, most fathers claimed they took a back seat in the decision as to whether their wives would breast-feed or not. Whatever their views, they claimed to keep any preference to themselves or to agree with their wives, since it was their lives that were influenced more by the decision. Some men realized that it was unfair to put 'pressure' on their wives by expressing a preference:

> I understood that breast-feeding had a lot of advantages and, er, you know, I didn't really want to . . . um . . . make a deep preference in case it proved too difficult for her to breast-feed and then she would have felt that she had failed in some way. [Prompt: 'So you played it fairly . . .'] Well, I played along the lines that, er, if she could breast-feed that would be great, but if she couldn't . . . well, you know, hundreds of babies around have survived without being breast-fed.
>
> (Primary schoolteacher 2)

Only ten men claimed to have influenced their wives in the decision to feed (six in favour of the breast and four towards bottle-feeding); none of these, nor their wives, felt that they had been a major influence.

Once started, the course of breast-feeding is variable. Some mothers feed the child exclusively for many months, while most introduce the bottle as an alternative to breast milk, before the child moves on to solid food. The child's birth order seems to influence mothers' persistence in breast-feeding. First-timers were more likely to be feeding their three-month-olds (38 per cent vs 17 per cent of second-timers; $\chi^2 = 4.96$, df = 1, $p < 0.05$).

Many men appear to play an important, if unseen, role in helping their wives to establish their feeding routine. This may take weeks, especially for those attempting to breast-feed. One recent study found that a woman's success at breast-feeding was associated with her perception of her husband's emotional support and favourable attitude towards breast-feeding (Switzky *et al.* 1979).

We asked the mothers whether their husbands had been encouraging, and found that most (thirteen out of nineteen women in the small sample who had breast-fed for more than two weeks) suggested that they had been helpful and supportive, even to the extent of enabling them to persist with feeding:

> He was very encouraging. I think it was only because of him that I carried on. The first few days, when I was very engorged, and she

had difficulty suckling then, he was the one . . . he said afterwards that he knew how much I wanted to do it and that's why he encouraged me. We did have some bottles in the house, just in case, and I said, 'It's no good, I'll have to stop', and he said, 'Keep persevering', and I did.

(Housewife, whose husband is civil servant 1)

At the same time, six mothers found their husbands to be 'neutral' or indifferent towards their breast-feeding. Some of their comments suggest that more support would have been welcome during this period, particularly in view of our cultural concern with the breast as a sex object:

He was a bit indifferent, really. He didn't mind one way or the other, you know. He said I've got to do it, so he left it up to me. I wish he had've been a bit more encouraging actually. [Prompt: 'Do you feel you would have gone on for longer?'] No, no, he just seemed a bit . . . mind you, he sometimes gives the impression that he's not bothered, but I don't think he *means* it. I just think it've been nice if he had said, 'Isn't it marvellous', you know. I used to say to him, 'It doesn't worry you, does it?' and he'd say, 'No, no, no.' He didn't find it off-putting or anything. I don't think he had any views on it at all, really.

(Housewife, whose husband is a floor layer)

Bottle-feeding: mother and father negotiate paternal involvement
Child care is a craft which continually changes during the first year. The left-hand column of Table 6.2 shows that different babies' routines vary considerably, at lest in terms of feeding. Some never have the bottle, while others start from birth. A comparison of both columns in the table reveals that men usually get in on the act soon after the child's first bottle.

However, the fact that men tend to bottle-feed their babies at an early age does not mean that fathers become totally involved or committed once

Table 6.2   Age at which the child was first bottle-fed and the father gave his first bottle

Age of child	Child started bottle-feeding at	Father started bottle-feeding child at
(Never had a bottle)	14	14
Less than 2 weeks	55	42
2–3 weeks	4	10
1–2 months	15	17
3–5 months	10	12
After 6 months	2	3
(Father has never fed child)	–	1

they have given their first bottle. Indeed, there is much evidence to suggest that, especially at first, their contribution is minimal or occasional. In the early months, it appears that they are also kept at a distance from the baby. Firstly, many retain their initial clumsiness in handling the child, which was discussed in Chapter 5. Often time does not erase these feelings because of the infrequency of their contact:

> I was quite reluctant to hold her at all for a long time and didn't get involved with 'handling' her, if you like, for quite some time. She looked too bloomin' fragile, you know.
>
> (House-husband and part-time photo-journalist)

The view expressed by this father cannot simply be dismissed as a 'dodge'. He was especially keen to become involved in the care of his child. Once he had overcome his fear he took on the major responsibility of caring for the child, while his wife went back to full-time employment.

Fear of the baby was only one reason why fathers did not actively participate both in the early months and later. While the baby's feeding routine was still unsettled fathers consciously allowed their wives, as full-time care-givers, time to get used to him or her and establish a pattern. However interested and supportive they were, husbands felt it was the mother's natural choice and territory:

> Well, it was just a matter of coming natural, like, which was best, like, 'cos I always left it up to Beryl [wife], 'cos, like, with her being the mother, like, she'd have more inclination of what to do. [Prompt: 'So you left it up to her?'] Yeah, I just left it up to Beryl and just followed on in me own way, like . . . picked it up from there.
>
> (Refuse collector)

One father, who wanted to become more involved, made it plain that it is possible to participate 'too much':

> At the beginning I used to interfere . . . I think that's perhaps the right word . . . *too much*. You know, if she wanted to do something such a way I'd say, 'I think this is a better way.' And I learned, through getting my fingers burnt, a little bit, that perhaps that wasn't the best way to go about it . . . with regard to feeding. After the first couple of weeks I was back at work, you know. . . . I hadn't got a say in it anyway, 'cos I wasn't here.
>
> (Hairdresser)

Clearly some mothers also felt ambivalent about the amount they wanted their husbands to contribute:

> [Interviewer: 'Were you keen for Ron to give James his bottle?'] No, I really wanted to do it myself this time, though I really felt he *ought* to. Just to show interest. I really contradicted myself a lot in my feelings

over that. I didn't want anybody else to feed him but me, but I used
to think he ought to.

(Part-time nursing auxiliary, whose husband
is a goods representative)

While their wives are becoming 'expert' in child care and, more
particularly, in catering to the idiosyncratic needs of their own baby, fathers
feel their role is diminished. So, when their participation conflicts with their
work schedules, as it does most obviously in the case of getting up to feed
the child at night, they are often prone to abdicate responsibility. As in
the early days, many fathers continue to work 'around' the mother–infant
pair. Thus, in the field of feeding, they often turn their attention to washing
and preparing the bottles. This activity enables fathers to do something
for the baby without coming into contact with him or her, and bottle
preparation is an activity which they feel suits the 'scientific' and practical
male temperament. While nine men hardly ever made up a bottle, and
thirteen did so sporadically, the majority (fifty-two) shared the chore,
or in ten cases (like that of this postman), made up more bottles than
their wives:

> [Interviewer: 'Did you used to get the bottle ready for a feed?'] More
> often than feeding because, if he's crying, I'd sooner be making a bottle
> than nursing him.

(Engineer's clerk)

> Yes, I made up his bottles for him. [Prompt: 'For how long?'] All
> the time. [Prompt: 'Till he was four months?'] No, right through,
> didn't I [to wife]? I made them up in the morning and put them in
> the fridge because I thought she was underfeeding him . . . made a
> mistake. . . . So I made them up myself, put them in the fridge, then
> heated them up again.

(Postman)

As the first year unfolds, patterns of bottle-feeding change. Fathers
become increasingly involved, once their wives establish a regime of mixed
foods (bottle and solids), and the status of the bottle-feeder is not so high.
While there are great differences in the frequency with which fathers feed,
fifty-eight did so on a daily basis at one time. There are many reasons why
they usually get involved. A few men, for example, take over from their
wives for a short while to enable them to cook the evening meal. Eighteen
fathers claimed to take over when their wives were fed up or asked them
to administer a particular feed.

Whatever their reasons for contributing to a feed, a large majority (64
of the 85 bottle-feeders) made special efforts to be available to give the child
the bottle, and they expressed great pleasure in having done so. Significantly
more professional workers (social class I/II) than members of the other social

groups recalled bottle-feeding on a daily basis (82 per cent of class I/II vs 54 per cent of other social classes; $\chi^2 = 4.61$, df = 1, p < 0.05).

> I find it relaxing. You can't do anything else while you are doing that! Especially when you've come home from work, you know . . . you sort of need to wind down a bit. It's one of the most relaxing things, I should imagine.
>
> > (Assistant contracts officer)

> He keeps in touch with him that way, especially on a night time . . . I mean, to give me a rest. Mark [son] still likes to be cuddled when he's fed on a bottle and we enjoy it even *now*. It settles him, so John will sit down with him.
>
> > (Housewife, whose husband is a legal executive)

Solid feeding

Most fathers come to take on more responsibility for bottle-feeding later on in the child's first year of life – that is, at a time when he or she is transferring to solid foods. When their child was one year old, far fewer men were involved in solid than in bottle-feeding, a finding which replicates that of Manion (1977) with younger children. Only twenty-six fathers participated in solid feeding on a daily basis, and twenty hardly ever did so. This latter group of fathers tended to cite all the 'dodges' mentioned by Oakley (1979). Some, unaware of the child's idiosyncrasies, attempt to become involved and end up with egg on their faces, or perhaps on the floor! Others attempt to participate but get impatient and withdraw. While their wives come increasingly to appear competent in all areas of child care, some fathers often maintain a fear of upsetting the child. Insecurity is felt even when it comes to cutting the food up for him or her:

> Like I say, I'm a bit weary now, frightened. I won't mash them up . . . might choke her. See, the wife knows what to give her. I don't mind bottles, 'cos they're basic, but I don't like trying to make meals for her . . . solid meals, 'cos she's still quite young, you know, small.
>
> > (Unemployed builder's labourer)

The fathers who become involved in feeding solids to their one-year-olds tend to do so for specific reasons. Some have to, since their wives go out to work before the child's evening mealtime. More typically, fathers act as assistants in the daily domestic routine, taking over if their wife is having problems, if the child is 'difficult' to feed, or while they are waiting for their own evening meal:

> Well, actually, in fact, I sort of start off giving it him, while Mary's [wife] preparing mine, and by the time he's half-way through it mine's sort of ready and she takes over.
>
> > (Factory porter)

[Interviewer: 'How often do you feed her?'] *Every meal.* Near enough every meal I feed her. . . . Well, we take it in turns, like, with the two of them at meals, one of them's doing Robert and one of them's doing Louise, like. [Prompt: 'So you feed her a whole meal or just . . .'] Well . . . we swap over about half-way, don't we [to wife]? . . . when she starts getting a bit . . . when she's not interested, you know.

(Disabled labourer)

That all but a few fathers are assistants, rather than partners, in the venture of child care is illustrated in the number of men who actively contribute towards the preparation of meals. While six did so on a regular daily basis, and twenty-eight did so more than weekly, most of the fathers were hardly ever involved in this activity. Indeed, almost a quarter (twenty-four) had never prepared any food for their child. So, as with the administration of bottles in the early days, at the age of one year solid feeding is labelled by many parents as the responsibility of the mother, because it is usually she who is evolving ways of dealing with the child and, as a result, is more aware of the child's individual needs than the father.

Child Care and Housework: Variation between Tasks

As with feeding, the father's contribution to each child-care activity fluctuates. At the same time a variation *between* tasks is also apparent at any age. As much previous research has shown, fathers tend to perform certain aspects of child care more than others (Newson and Newson 1963, Richards *et al.* 1977), and we shall examine these here.

In order to demonstrate the variation in paternal involvement between the different activities, I compared their participation in the 'tasks' represented in Table 6.3. In absolute terms, these are difficult to compare with one another, since one task (like nappy changing) might have to be done many times per day, while another (like getting up to the child at night) may need carrying out on a spasmodic basis, if at all. I therefore classified fathers' involvement in each task into three basic categories. Firstly, 'little or no involvement' meant that the father contributed very little to an activity. In most tasks, like nappy changing, this meant that a father would perform a chore on a less-than-weekly basis. In the case of tasks like 'night waking' he would go to the child much less than his wife. Secondly, 'some involvement' was attributed to a man if he participated in a task more than occasionally but less than his wife. He might change a nappy more than weekly, but not daily, for example. Thirdly, 'a lot of involvement' meant that a father participated as much as his wife in his available time at home. In order to be classified as a 'regular' contributor, a father would have to change a nappy more than once daily, or give the child at least half his or her baths, to name but two examples.

Table 6.3   Level of fathers' involvement in child-care tasks

Involvement	Activity							
	Bottle-feeding %	Solid feeding %	Meal prep. %	Putting to bed %	Night waking %	Bathing %	Nappy %	Look after alone %
Little or none	36	32	51	26	13	62	40	53
Some involvement (less than wife)	11	13	29	24	52	9	32	33
A lot (shared with wife when home)	53	55	20	48	35	29	28	14

Some patterns are discernible in Table 6.3. Many fathers appear to avoid almost completely tasks like bathing, looking after the child alone, nappy changing and meal preparation. At the other extreme, a substantial number of men become actively involved in putting their child to bed and feeding. In between these extremes many fathers seem to assist occasionally in 'night waking', getting up to the child if he or she wakes at night.

As child-care patterns develop during the first year, the father's contribution becomes channelled along certain lines. As we saw with feeding, mothers, as the main care-givers, are primarily responsible for the general care of babies, particularly when it comes to new or difficult tasks. On the other hand, if they are to participate at all, fathers actively have to be incorporated into a routine which fits in with the demands of the baby and the convenience of their wives. They appear to 'fill in' when their wives are unavailable or express a particular need for their help. As lower-status, secondary care-givers they are compensated in that to a certain extent they can choose the activities in which they become involved. As a result, fathers tend to participate in those tasks which might enhance their relationship with the child and which they can fit in at convenient times.

Low paternal involvement: bathing, nappy changing and single-handed care-giving

The activities to which few men contribute actively – bathing, nappy changing and taking (single-handed) care of the baby – are basic in two senses of the term. They are day-to-day, even mundane chores which 'have' to be done, but at the same time they are the hallmark of active responsible caretaking. As Davidoff (1976) points out, domestic chores can be regarded in a number of lights: as 'science' at the one extreme or sheer drudgery at the other. These child-care tasks are seen by parents from both perspectives at the same time. On the one hand, fathers claimed not to become involved in these activities because they had an aversion to them:

> Well, I *used* to change quite a lot but I haven't done recently. [Prompt: 'So how often did you used to?'] Oh, I used to every night, like. [Prompt: 'And is there any particular reason why you don't now?'] The *mess* [laughs], really, I'm not one for all that. [Prompt: 'So you wouldn't change her at all now?'] Well, I *would* change her, I *could* change her, but I couldn't go on scrapping it all off. I could do it if I had to. [Prompt: 'Would you change a wet one now?'] Oh yes, I'm not bothered 'bout that. . . . Well, it were all right, 'cos she was putting the nappies on a certain way. Then she changed them to a different style and I couldn't *do* um. [Prompt: 'You couldn't master them?'] *No*, I couldn't master it, so I gave it up as a bad job.
>
> (Plant operator)

Fathers like the above are obviously dodging nappy changing, but this does not tell the whole story. The mother's role as 'expert' contributes to her husband's lack of involvement. Together they construct a rationale for the disparity between the ideal of marital equality and the reality of the differences between them:

> *Interviewer:* How about changing him? Do you often change his nappies?
> *Father:* Don't think I've done that, have I [to wife]?
> *Wife:* In the first week when I weren't well.
> *Interviewer:* Is there any reason why you haven't?
> *Wife:* Only 'cos I've always been there. They don't bother me in the slightest, you know.
> *Father:* Nappies don't bother *me*, you know. If Jan [wife] turned round to me and said, 'Could you do it for me, then?' . . . Like I say, she's a very competent mother.
>
> (Barreller and wife, a housewife)

Bathing the child brings with it similar sentiments. Parents often mention the father's clumsiness, but at the same time both stress that the mother's expertise is a balance to the father's lack of skill and a source of prestige for the wife in the domestic division of power:

> [Interviewer: 'Is there any reason why you haven't (bathed him)?']
> I'm probably too clumsy. . . . I suppose it goes back to the original awkward feeling. . . . Um, I feel the way they are, how small they are . . . remarkably delicate. . . . And since I know I'm not going to do it full-time I might as well let the experts get on with it and leave the amateurs out.
>
> (Managing director)

> *Interviewer:* Have you ever bathed him?
> *Father:* Yes.
> *Wife:* Not alone, you haven't.
> *Father:* I've splashed him.
> *Wife:* I'm holding him . . . don't I? You only splash him.
> *Interviewer* (to husband): Is there any reason why you haven't bathed him yourself?
> *Wife:* I'd sooner trust myself. . . . It's not that I don't trust him. I'd sooner do it myself where water comes in.
> *Interviewer* (to husband): So you would rather trust Sandra [wife] than yourself?
> *Father:* No . . . I'd do it.
>
> (Grade-room worker and wife, a housewife)

There are understandable reasons why the parental division of labour becomes 'imbalanced', with the wife 'in charge' and husband as helper. For a start, the father's availability seems to be an important factor. For example, forty of the fathers were at home for two or less baths per week. Many mothers choose to bath in the morning, since it is the time when their children may need cleaning after night-time wetting, and it also seems to suit their schedules. This routine often prevents husbands from being involved. Indeed, it seems that the men who become active in these tasks usualy do so for pragmatic reasons. If the wife worked, the husband was significantly more likely to change nappies daily (63 per cent vs 26 per cent if wife did not work; $\chi^2 = 12.03$, fd = 1, p<0.001) and look after the child single-handed (69 per cent vs 31 per cent if wife did not work; $\chi^2 = 11.83$, df = 1, p<0.001).

Active paternal involvement: making contact with the child
Table 6.3 shows that fathers are relatively more involved in feeding their one-year-old children and putting them to bed than in the other activities listed. Feeding and putting the baby to bed are both activities which mark out the child's day, and the most obvious reason why men become involved is that they can be scheduled to occur at a time when the father is around. The relatively large number of fathers who share in putting-to-bed can be explained, in part, by the fact that some wives work on twilight shifts. At the same time, one-year-olds can be put 'down' at a time to suit their care-givers. This contrasts with a finding concerning older children; Jackson (1984) reported that 50 per cent of fathers of five-year-olds arrive home after they are in bed.

It was clear from the transcripts that these parents often adjusted their work routines so that the father could contribute. As the following mother suggests, the nightly ritual is often a special time at which the father can see his child:

> [Interviewer: 'who usually puts him to bed?'] Well, it varies. We usually do it together. You know, I bath and then Simon [husband] helps me dry him and put him to bed because otherwise he would be . . . Simon wouldn't see him. . . . This is what we decided . . . because by the time he gets home it's half-past five, so we're usually ready to bath him then.
>
> (Housewife, whose husband is factory manager 1)

Fathers and housework
The same variations in paternal involvement seen in child care are to be found in the division of housework between mother and father – see Table 6.4. Unlike with child care, which is explicitly shared between parents, a repeated theme in both the mothers' and the fathers' interviews was that couples regard the home as the woman's responsibility. This echoes previous studies (Clearly and Shepperdson 1979, Oakley 1974). So a woman will say that her husband *helps* with *her* housework. Similarly, any contribution by him is judged by her. Many qualifications about the amount the men participates are accompanied by statements like, 'He does *X* for *me*', and assessments of his (often minimal) performance as an assistant, such as, 'Oh, he's very good.'

He does tend to be very good. He doesn't do ironing very often but if I said to him, 'I just don't want to do this', he won't argue, he'll just do it for me.

(Schoolteacher, whose husband is
a finance company representative)

As other studies show (Cowan and Cowan 1981, Shereshefsky and Yarrow 1973), for many couples the arrival of the first child marks a significant shift in the division of labour. A 'traditional' role pattern occurs as a matter of course:

[Interviewer: And what about housework?] Very little . . . very little indeed, because Anne's [wife] . . . [Wife: 'If necessary'.] Yeah, if it . . . when she – Anne's not well or if she's been busy or something like that . . . hoovering around. . . . But I don't, I bet I don't do much more than once a week . . . hardly ever if you like that. [Prompt: 'About once a fortnight, something like that?'] Yeah, you know, we perhaps . . . well, as I say, he's in a reasonable routine in the mornings now. Anne finds the time to, while he's in bed, to come and do the housework in an hour or so, um . . . where before we were at work it used to be fifty-fifty, you know, either do a room or do set jobs apiece to get through it all. Anne does that as a matter of course now and I find I've very little to do.

(Police constable 2, whose wife is a housewife)

Table 6.4 shows that men are more likely to help with the shopping and dish-washing than with the other tasks. Both these activities appear to symbolize the man's support for the ideal of marital symmetry. Fathers often accompany their wives to the supermarket. However, many do this to act as chauffeur, and relatively few become involved in the shopping:

Well, we go to Asda and, er . . . we go there every Saturday and I'll take the kids to the toys section and let her get on with the

Table 6.4   Levels of fathers' involvement in housework

			Tasks			
Involvement	*Shopping* %	*Dish-washing* %	*Cooking* %	*Cleaning house* %	*Washing clothes* %	*Ironing* %
Little or none	25	14	48	68	76	75
Some	18	28	31	24	14	19
Regular (shared when home)	57	58	20	8	10	6

shopping. . . . And we'll load up and probably go to my mum's for the greens and veg and everything . . . and that's about it.

(Engineer's clerk)

Similarly, dish-washing, as Newson and Newson (1963) found more than twenty years ago, is considered a 'male' activity. There are good practical reasons why men might choose to indulge in it after the evening meal:

What usually happens is that at the end of a meal he'll have his nappy changed. Di [wife] will usually do that, because she'd rather do a nappy change than wash up. And I'd rather wash up than do a nappy change, and so it works out. . . . I probably wash up every evening.

(Legal executive)

[Interviewer: 'How often do you wash up?'] Oh, regular, [Wife: 'Always!'] No, not always, 'cos I'm not always here, but again I would . . . if you have a meal we usually do. . . . Depending if Louise's [one-year-old] playing up, me wife will go and see to her, 'cos she's better when she's playing up and I wash up. Or we wash up together, you know, and she [nods at older child] helps as well.

(Prison officer)

Table 6.4 also shows that many fathers do not involve themselves at all in activities like ironing, cleaning the house and washing clothes. Those men who occasionally helped wash the clothes usually commented that this involved little effort as they possessed an automatic machine for the purpose. A typical description of involvement in housework suggests that the man participates only minimally:

Washing isn't any problem. Fran [wife] does it most of the time. I'm quite happy to do it as well. It's an automatic washing-machine, it's just a question of stuffing it in . . . it's a doddle. I mean, nobody could have any objection to that. . . . I will *not* iron, I absolutely refuse to iron anything. I . . . I . . . I detest it. [Wife: 'Half an hour a shirt' (laughs).] It takes me ten times as long as it takes Frances anyway. I will not iron. If Fran's here and I need a shirt ironing . . . obviously . . . the . . . as a matter of course. I'll even drag her out of bed to iron a shirt. [Wife: 'If I'm not well he can cope.'] I can cope quite well, I run down to me mother's.

(Sales director and wife, a part-time physiotherapist)

Overall Father Participation: Variation between Fathers

Tables 6.3 and 6.4 show great differences *between* fathers on individual domestic tasks. It is therefore appropriate to examine whether 'participant' and 'non-participant' fathers can be distinguished and, if so, to attempt to discover some of the reasons why some men do considerably more than others. This can be done by aggregating the amount of involvement by men in a number of activities and developing a scale of their overall involvement.

This method is not without problems, because the nature of both parents' involvement with a child changes continuously (Lewis *et al.* 1982), and different measures suggest different amounts of paternal involvement (Cronenwett 1982). As McKee (1982) points out, there are no absolute guidelines about how we should, or can, construct an overall picture of father participation. Her criticisms were lodged against studies which attempted to gain an overall impression of father involvement based upon vague questions and measures, usually asked of mothers, not fathers. In this study, each activity was discussed in detail, a precise account of the father's involvement was taken and, as described in Chapter 2, the data from women's interviews were used to corroborate the men's accounts.

In this section I will examine a measure of participation based upon specific questions concerning child care. Table 6.5 gives a full breakdown of the items used to construct this scale. It shows that the child-care measure consisted of fathers' responses to specific questions concerning feeding, putting to bed, getting up in the morning, nappy changing and general care. A similar procedure was employed to construct a 'housework' scale, using all the items listed in Table 6.4. This will not be discussed here in any depth.

The frequency distribution of scores on the child-care scale was unimodally distributed, as figure 6.1 shows. In keeping with previous findings (Newson and Newson 1963, Pedersen and Robson 1969, Russell 1983), it demonstrates that, like each individual measure examined above, father involvement varies between total uninvolvement at home and active participation. Previous research suggests many possible correlates with the level of men's participation in the home. These can be divided into social factors (e.g. parents' social class status or employment patterns) and psychological influences (e.g. the effects of being present at delivery, the father's sex-role identity). Broadly, when the distribution of scores on this measure was analysed, social factors appeared to be more important.

Parental employment and paternal involvement

Two main factors appear to override the other potential influences on paternal involvement in child care and housework: maternal and paternal employment outside the home. Fathers' work patterns play a particularly important role. Moss (1980) reports that married men with young children are four times more likely to work longer hours and overtime than their older workmates. In this study, at the time of the child's first birthday only forty-eight fathers worked a basic 'normal' working week (of 37–45 hours). Thirty-nine worked shifts or 'long' hours (more than 45 hours per week) as a matter of course, and over half of this latter group (twenty-five worked

Table 6.5   Items used to construct the fathers' child-care scale

Questions and response types	*Score*
Qs. 81 and 82 Regularity of father feeding child solids throughout the week.	
Less than once a week	0
Once a week	1
More than once a week, but less than wife	2
Shared with wife in time available	3
Q. 83 'Do you ever prepare food for him? . . . How often?'	
Never	0
Less than weekly	1
1–3 meals per week	2
At least four meals per week	3
Q. 97 'Who usually puts child to bed?'	
Father once a week or less	0
Father 1–3 times per week	1
Shared father and mother (50–50)	2
Father more than mother	3
Q. 105 Fathers' morning role with child.	
Occasional (not regular)	0
Occasional caretaking/regular play	1
Regular caretaking (shared with wife)	2
Q. 110 'How often does father change child's nappies?	
Less than weekly	0
Less than daily	1
At least once daily	2
Q. 112 'Do you ever take care of child on your own?'	
Less than monthly	0
Less than weekly	1
1–3 times per week	2
4 or more times per week	3
Maximum possible score:	16

Figure 6.1   The frequency distribution of scores in the scale measuring fathers' participation in child care

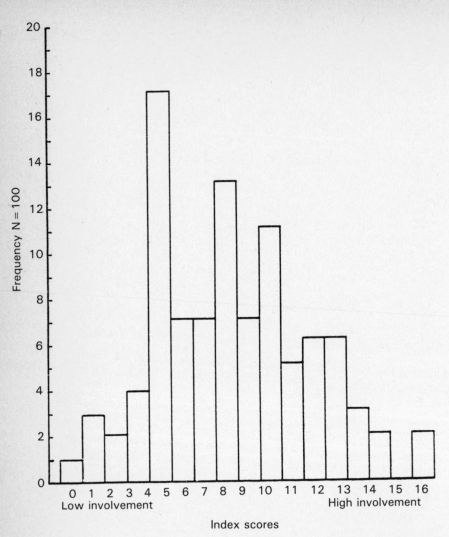

at weekends. Many more working- than middle-class men worked long hours or at weekends (44 per cent working-class vs 12 per cent middle-class men working long hours as a matter of course; $\chi^2 = 11.3$, df = 1, p < 0.001). However, as Moss (1980) points out, we cannot simply assume that middle-class men work less hard, since they are more likely to bring work home with them to do outside 'office' hours.

Table 6.6 gives a breakdown of employment patterns amongst these fathers, in terms of their 'normal' working week. As such it serves as a baseline, since all but twelve of those employed full-time did some overtime when it was available, but not necessarily every week. So, as other research shows (Moss 1980), and despite the difficult economic climate, many fathers with young babies still spent much of their waking life at work when this research was carried out in 1979–80. In contrast, thirty of their wives were in employment when the child was one, and nineteen of these worked less than 15 hours per week.

Large-scale surveys of parents' work patterns suggest that the father's involvement at home relates to the number of hours he is available there (Walker and Woods 1976). Judging by table 6.7, similar patterns were evident in this sample. The longer a man worked outside the home during the day, the less child care he reported doing. Shift-workers who do no overtime are more likely to be involved than those who work a 'normal' week or long hours. The eight unemployed or disabled men obtained higher scores than the norm, but we should remember that their involvement as a proportion of the time that they were at home was low. Four men stood out as taking a highly involved role, which aspires to the emergent view of fatherhood. All these had jobs, but arranged their work to fit in with their wives' employment. A newsagent, for example, worked mainly in the early mornings and evenings, and looked after his daughter during the day, while his wife was a community nurse.

Table 6.6 Basic working week of the fathers when the child was one year of age

Response category	*Frequency*
(a) Normal hours (37–45 hours per week)	48
(b) Shifts (subtotal = 12)	
(i) including nights	7
(ii) excluding nights	5
(c) 'Long hours' (more than 45 hours) (subtotal = 26)	
(i) including weekends	24
(ii) excluding weekends	1
(iii) on call at night	1
(d) Unemployed	7
(e) Disabled	2
(f) Other (subtotal = 4)	
(i) 25 hours per week	1
(ii) normal hours but including evenings and weekends	3
(missing 1)	
Total:	100

The impact of maternal employment upon husbands' involvement in child care has been much debated in recent years. General surveys suggest that fathers participate more if their wives have jobs (Berk and Berk 1979, Blood and Wolfe 1960, Eriksen *et al.* 1979, Pressman 1980). However, Russell (1983) noted that these tend to show an increase in the man's *relative* contribution, perhaps because his wife does less. Taking Russell's point into account, I analysed the amounts of paternal involvement in child care.

Table 6.7   Means scores on the child care scale for fathers according to their own employment patterns

Father works	Number	Mean score	Standard deviation
Long hours (more than 45 per week)	25	5.80	3.08
Normal hours (35–45 per week)	46	6.82	2.77
Shifts	12	8.08	3.25
Unemployed/ disabled	8	9.62	2.82
At home in day	4	14.50	1.73
Overall scores	95	7.27	3.05

Comparison between groups: $F_{(4,90)} = 7.75$, $p < 0.0001$.

Table 6.8   Mean scores on the child care scale for fathers according to the amount their wives were employed per week

Wife's employment status	Number	Mean score	Standard deviation
Not working	67	6.55	3.25
Less than 15 hours per week	18	8.06	3.28
More than 15 hours per week (but part-time)	6	8.80	2.56
Full-time	5	12.00	4.30
Overall scores	96	7.26	3.28

Comparison between groups: $F_{(3,92)} = 5.33$, $p < 0.05$.

As Table 6.8 shows, there was a positive, linear relationship between the wife's employment status and her husband's involvement, although one not strong enough to differentiate between each group. Thus, taken together, Table 6.7 and 6.8 show that the father's involvement appears to be influenced by the couple's working arrangement outside the home.

Social class
Since working-class men are more likely to spend long hours in outside employment, they might be expected to undertake less child care than their middle-class counterparts. However, the literature is unclear. Surveys of different types of family suggest that paternal involvement in the home increases down the class scale (Robinson 1977). In contrast, research on families with young children finds that working-class men do less (Cleary and Shepperdson 1981), particularly when it comes to housework (Oakley 1972). Such contradictory findings may well reflect either a difference in samples and methods used in the various studies, or that men's relative involvement varies according to the age of the children.

This analysis found no overall class differences in fathers' involvement with their young children, except a trend to suggest that non-professional white-collar workers – class III (w.c.) – are more involved in child care. Rather, class differences seem more apparent when individual child care measures are compared. For example, significantly more members of class III (w.c.) took part in child care on a weekday morning (72 per cent got their children up more than once a week vs 44 per cent of the other class groups; $\chi^2 = 4.82$, df = 1, p < 0.05). These men were far more likely to work on flexitime systems that enabled them to be participant. Men in professions put their children to bed less often (32 per cent did so three times per week vs 54 per cent of members of the other social classes; $\chi^2 = 3.87$, df = 1, p < 0.05) but were more likely to bottle-feed their children more often. Differences such as these suggest that we should consider what members of different social groups do with their children, as well as their overall contribution.

Psychological factors
In recent years numerous attempts have been made to attribute the amount of paternal involvement to deeper psychological causes. For example, some studies have suggested that men who are more involved in child care tend to identify with an 'androgynous' sex role, with both 'masculine' and 'feminine' qualities (Russell 1978). Russell points out that associations like these fail to distinguish cause and effect, nor are they conistently found (Alter 1978, Russell 1983).

Similarly, some authors have argued that fathers who participate highly in the care of their children do so because they themselves had warm, nurturant and inolved fathers (Herzog 1982, Kelly and Worrell 1976,

Keylor 1978, Manion 1977). The measures used in this study revealed a statistically significant association between a man's recall of his father's practical involvement in child care and his own participation (own father 'highly' involved vs 'little' involved: $F_{(1,90)} = 5.007$, $p < 0.05$). However, we cannot conclude that identification is the main cause of involved fatherhood. Other research finds no such significant relationship (Blendis 1982), and at the same time the opposite case has been put; some highly involved fathers in non-traditional families claim to participate more than typical men because their own fathers were aloof or rejecting (Eiduson *et al.* 1982).

Some studies have found correlations between two other 'psychological' factors and paternal involvement, which failed to be replicated in these data on either the child care scale outlined above or any of the individual measures within the scale. In the mid-1970s it was found that highly involved men were more likely to have attended the delivery of their children (Manion 1977, Richards *et al.* 1977). Despite a groundswell of opinion at the time, which predicted that father-attended delivery would increase a man's bond and hence his participation with his offspring (Klaus and Kennell 1976, Lind 1974), Richards was at pains to stress that there may not be a causal link between the two correlates. The data from this study do not show a significant correlation between birth attendance and later involvement. This supports the belief that attenders in the early 1970s may well have been highly committed to parenting before the arrival of their offspring. Today a much higher proportion of fathers attend delivery, and this seems to have little or no effect on their practical involvement with the baby.

Pressman (1980) found, in a sample of forty men, that father participation is greater in younger fathers. However, she did not distinguish between older fathers and those with older children; the men in her study had children at any age below ten. This analysis, where the age of the child was restricted, failed to find a correlation between the father's age and his contribution to child care. Pressman also found that men with children under two years old participated more than other men. So perhaps this latter correlation is the more important, as older children need less necessary care and attention.

Conclusion

This chapter has attempted to build upon the discussion in Chapter 5, to show just how involved men become in child care during the first year of the baby's life. Just as the needs of the child change during this period, so too does his or her father's practical involvement with him or her. Men appear to 'dodge' their responsibilities, and when it comes to unpleasant chores it is clear that men are less involved than they might be. However, a full understanding of contemporary fathers' participation in child care has to look beyond any reluctance on their part.

Fathers' and mothers' accounts suggest that father participation is clearly delimited within physiological and cultural guidelines, which are sanctioned by both parents. Fathers, as secondary care-givers, settle for an 'incompetent' role, and this of course enables them to evade certain tasks. As primary care-givers, mothers have to perform these chores, but by way of compensation they are conceded the role of 'experts' in the domestic sphere. The house and, to a lesser extent, the child are 'theirs'; fathers 'help' them to keep both in working order. While there are differences in the amounts fathers involve themselves with the domestic routine, in comparison to their wives' contributions to the upkeep of the family men perform a minor role.

I have spelled out in detail the practical contact which a father has with his child, partly because this aspect of the father–child relationship has hitherto been neglected by psychologists. The chapter turns to examine the more traditional focus of these researchers: the father–child relationship. However, the nature of this relationship must be considered in terms of the total contact between parent and child, and so many of the points raised in the past two chapters will serve as an important backcloth for the following discussion, particularly in Chapter 7.

7   The Father-Child Relationship

Introduction

This chapter examines how the father–child relationship develops during the first year. Given their diminished practical involvement we might expect men to be somewhat detached from their children. However, research has long shown (Newson and Newson 1963, Scaffer and Emerson 1964) that fathers form close 'attachments' even with their young offspring. Recent observational studies have reiterated the two points that children under the age of two develop close relationships with their fathers and that men take on the role as 'playmate', specializing in particular types of boisterous interaction (e.g. Lamb 1981b, Pedersen 1980a). As Lamb (1981b: 478) writes: 'fathers are associated with playful – often vigorously stimulating – social interaction, whereas mothers are associated with caretaking'.

While many scores of observational studies have examined the father–child relationship, there is surprisingly little discussion about the origins of differences between parents. As I have indicated elsewhere, these researchers usually assume that they have biological causes (Lewis 1982a). Such a position seems unlikely, since these parental roles are not ubiquitous. For example, men in Fiji (Katz and Konner 1981) and Sweden (Lamb *et al.* 1983) do not appear to play in a vigorous way. Object-relations theorists have argued that the differences between parents derive from their own perceptions, as children, of clearly differentiated roles in their parents (Chodorow 1978). While this view is appealing, it is hard to prove such direct links between early and later experiences.

Much of the interview in the present study was concerned with attempting to gain some insight into how father–infant relationships develop. Questions about parents' perceptions of the child and the closeness of their 'attachments' were set into discussion about their practical involvement through the first year. The discussion will fall into two main sections. The first part will examine the father–infant relationship in its developmental context, and will assess how the man's early practical role influences the way he relates to the baby. The second part compares the father–child relationship with that of mother and baby. Mothers and fathers appear

112

to interact with their infants in different ways, particularly as they perform dissimilar domestic roles. As a result they mean different things to the child him/herself and they perceive the child in ways which derive from their daily contact with him or her.

Building a Relationship with the Baby

Love at a distance: the early days

Nowhere is the biological model of parental behaviour expressed as often and with as much force as at the time of the baby's arrival. Researchers and clinicians have described the time after the delivery of a child as one when parents form 'bonds' with their offspring (Bowlby 1969, Klaus and Kennel 1976). Klaus and Kennel in particular have suggested that the contact between parents and the new-born child has beneficial and long-term effects upon the parent–infant relationship and also upon the child's development. The 'progressive' obstetricians and paediatricians, cited in Chapter 4, have accepted many of these ideas to justify the inclusion of men at delivery and have also speculated about bonding in fathers. Greenberg and Morris (1974), in an oft cited study, interviewed men shortly after delivery and found them to be 'elated' or 'engrossed' with their offspring. They suggested that this feeling of 'engrossment' is an innate and unconscious reaction akin to those in parents of other species, which arise during 'critical periods'.

While this theoretical perspective has become popular among practitioners, its validity has been increasingly criticized by researchers (Sluckin *et al.* 1983). Theories about the 'engrossment' of fathers can be neither substantiated nor refuted. The arrival of a baby does not occur in a cultural vacuum, and our understanding of the reactions of parents to their new-born children must take into account their perceptions and expectations.

Fathers' descriptions of the time around the delivery suggest that this period is far more complex than 'bonding' theorists argue. Apparent contradictions in fathers' roles during pregnancy and in early care-giving patterns are reflected in the developing father–child relationship. In some respects, fathers *do* become centrally involved with or attached to their new-born babies. Yet at the same time they often find themselves to be psychologically distanced from their offspring. So again, the father's involvement has to be considered on a number of apparently contradictory levels, the two most opposing of which I shall outline here.

On one level these fathers report having experienced the sort of feelings described by Greenberg and Morris (1974). Their accounts of delivery, for example, suggest that the event has a profound effect on their attitude towards children:

[Interviewer: 'Some parents say they are surprised by some of the emotions they feel. Have you found that?'] I think when he . . . when he was born, yes. I don't think it . . . I never realized that I'd feel so emotional about it. [Prompt: 'So how did it strike you?'] I feel quite elated, I suppose. [Prompt: 'And did that sort of persist or was it for that brief moment, then?'] Er, no, I think it lingers on, to be quite honest, quite a degree. [Prompt: 'Had you expected that?'] No, as I say, I didn't really . . . I didn't know what to expect. I'd heard people, you know, that . . . So I s'pose yes, but you can't kind of think yourself into it . . . I think a lot if it is, see, you're very concerned, right, there's a baby inside and you don't honestly know what it's gonna come out like, or anything . . . so when it does come out, you know, it's a tremendous outlet of relief, yeah. [Prompt: 'And so how does the relief persist?'] Er, I think it's the baby itself, you see . . . something so perfect, it's quite a miracle.

(Building-society trainee)

That fathers' accounts demonstrate an involvement or 'engrossment' with the new-born infant and a general feeling that something magical occurs at delivery is perhaps hardly surprising. Like their wives, they have awaited the child's arrival for months and expect to feel elated, particularly after the worries of pregnancy and delivery are over.

At the same time, on another level, it is clear that many simply do not expect to become involved, and other fathers become alienated psychologically during the early life of the child as a result of their diminished practical role. This can start very early on. For example, Angela Brown (1982) found that many men greet their babies in the delivery room by saying, 'Hello, I'm your dad.' Mothers, in contrast, tended to act as if they already knew their new-borns. For most men the initial euphoria or engrossment is not all they feel. Indeed, half of the fathers perceived the initial contact with the baby as an 'odd' experience – a group which included significantly more first-timers (62 per cent first- vs 32 per cent second-timers; $\chi^2 = 8.2$, df = 1, p < 0.005).

In Chapter 5 I mentioned that the practice of segregating mothers from their families in the immediate post-partum period has an effect upon fathers, particularly with regard to the contact they have with their new offspring. Many men's feelings of oddness are exacerbated by the events of the early days. For example, in the delivery room they often feel more out of place after the delivery than during labour, when at least they are given jobs to do. Handling new-born babies is outside their range of experience; and a variety of factors may inhibit a father's 'engrossment' in the baby, as the following father describes:

[Interviewer: 'When did you first hold him?'] Straight away . . . well, no, it was't, sorry [wife: 'He daren't.] . . . because he was *there* all of sudden, you know. The nurses were joking with you. I mean, for a forceps delivery they had to hold her legs up and they said, 'catch the baby', and it is literally 'catch the baby' . . . and he's away, and they were going to suck his mouth out and that . . . wrap him up and put him in the cot. And the first thing . . . the nurse turns round and says, 'Go on, then, he's yours' . . . and I went up to have a look and I wanted to pick him up . . . and he's so tiny . . . I sort of thought [gulps], 'I'll leave it', you know [laughs] . . . 'I'll leave it for a while.' And it wasn't until the next sort of day in actual fact that I picked him up then . . . I think that after all that time and all the, you know, the strains of the long day, the birth and . . . it just looked so fragile, I thought, 'I daren't . . . am I going to drop him?' . . . 'Cos I'd love to have picked him up . . . I wanted to.

(Police constable 2)

While mothers also often feel odd or simply not interested in the baby just after delivery (Oakley 1979, Robson and Kumar 1980), fathers suggest that their initial strangeness may linger on. They may perform a central practical role in the early days and take time to 'share' experiences with their wives, but their relationships with the new borns themselves are not so straightforward. Many men claim to feel 'left out' in the period after delivery:

Thinking of the first few weeks with Barbara, you feel left out . . . well, I did . . . you know, especially when she's there being cuddled something like that . . . you know, the love side of it.

(Grade-room worker)

He was a sort of small little bundle. I mean, 'odd' is a strange word to use, but perhaps, yeah. I don't think this 'maternal' thing comes out straight away in you . . . um . . . I certainly didn't feel entirely maternal towards him because he was so sort of helpless and there was *nothing* I could do for him . . . you know . . . and probably the first three months all I could do was to sort of help Carrie change him, etc. I never did become *that* involved with him until he became six or seven weeks old.

(Sales representative)

Even if the father tries to become psychologically involved he can find himself in danger of being excluded:

Well, I think the situation is that, er . . . you know, the child's first formative weeks and months . . . he gets to recognize his mother . . . you know, sees her as a symbol for food and such to do . . . it's comfort . . . probably more so than the father in the early weeks . . . er, probably dad is often a sort of face that peeps in from now and then . . . although, you know, I tried to avoid that situation with Michael and Ruth [older child] really. . . . Really, I tried to handle them as much as I could and, er . . . you know, to try and make sure that they did recognize me . . . fairly early.

(Computer clerk)

So in the early months the father's 'bond' with the new baby is not as simple and straightforward as some attachment theorists suggest. Some men continue to perceive the child as totally unresponsive or fragile and they avoid any contact with him or her if possible. At the same time, it is clear that they are expected to demonstrate their affection towards the baby:

> We had everything ready. . . . There was only one thing . . . dropping him, thinking about them things what worried me, like . . . in case I pick him up and drop him. [Prompt: 'Did that prevent you picking him up?'] No . . . no . . . I kept picking him up, like, but careful, like. . . . I didn't like to say to Judith, 'I'm not picking him up in case I drop him', 'cos when you say it a couple of times it looked like you didn't want to hold him.
>
> (Scrap-yard labourer)

These ambiguous feelings towards the child often persist. Men usually attempt to build a special relationship with their offspring in the time they have available to them. Some develop specific 'paternal' skills. For example, they become expert at 'winding' or getting the baby to sleep immediately after a feed. Most men, however, have to content themselves with being involved from a distance. These tend to do this by sharing with their wives an almost fanatical concern for the health and safety of the child. In the early days many will leap up at the first noise over the 'baby alarm' or check the baby is well at regular intervals during the first few days and nights.

> We [were] never really asleep, like, because we were that worried about him. We'd never pass without walking into the bedroom to see if he was OK, like, you know. [Prompt: 'So was he actually awake or was it just your worry that kept you awake?'] It was just my worry . . . case anything happened to him during the night.
>
> (Dye-house labourer)

While mothers become concerned with the daily care of the baby and build up their relationship during this frequent contact, fathers, as secondary care-givers, have a far less routine and continuous role. Thus, as the above quotations suggest, much 'fathering behaviour' occurs around the baby, ensuring that he or she is safe. His feelings of 'attachment' are often mediated through the mother. Indeed, the one study which has monitored direct contact between fathers and babies on a regular daily basis, using continuous tape-recording for twenty-four hours at a time, found that US Middle-Class men interacted on average less than three times per day with their babies in the first three months, for an average period of 37.7 seconds per day (Rebelsky and Hanks 1971). A recent UK replication of this research found similar patterns of father–baby contact (Korman and Lewis, in preparation).

Father as friend and playmate:
the relationship develops

As the first year unfolds men tend to become psychologically more involved with their children, for two reasons in particular. Firstly, the child is awake more when his or her father is at home. Secondly, he or she is more active, alert and responsive. Stereotypes of 'good fathering' depict men as benign playmates (see, for example, Spock, 1967); and as they grow older, children bring their fathers more into the picture, because their needs are less basic and their demands increase. As was mentioned in the previous chapter, men become more active in caretaking tasks over the year. They do so partly to 'help' their wives, but also because these activities facilitate contact between father and child. Men often perform them in a light-hearted manner, as part of their daily play routines. Thus twenty-three men who did not bath their one-year-olds commented that they would 'play' while their wives bathed them, and most did this on a regular, if not daily, basis.

When I asked fathers to consider their relative involvement in caretaking over the first year, sixty-three said they were more actively involved now (at a year), twenty-seven felt their commitment had not changed, and only ten were less involved now than when the child was very young. A few men's contact with the child changed for practical reasons; for example, their hours altered at work, or their wives returned to employment. However, many became more involved because the early ambiguities in the father–baby relationship were eroded by time and by the child's developing competence. Ten fathers mentioned that they were more involved now because they no longer perceived the baby as 'fragile', and forty-one considered that the child at one year was more responsive and therefore easier to relate to:

> I spend a bit more time with her now than what I did when she was born, 'cos I enjoy the fact that she can walk around and she's a bit stronger. As I've said before, I was a bit frightened when she was a bit weak . . . you know, when her head was flopping about the place. I was a bit worried . . . and I would, er . . . I wouldn't stay away purposefully, but I'd seem to edge away . . . sit in the single chair sooner than sit on the settee with her, you know.
>
> (Transport manager's assistant)

> Now he's a year old, he's more attentive, and he responds more than he did . . . well, obviously, when he was born, but, you know, when he was six months. . . . The older he gets, obviously, the more involved the father gets *because* of this. He plays with him more and he responds more . . . it's sort of psychological, I suppose.
>
> (Factory manager 1)

This 'psychological' change is echoed in men's descriptions of their *perceptions* of their developing children. At first, the father may perceive the child as unrewarding and incapable of engaging in reciprocal activities. However, these perceptions gradually change, and child and father come to regard one another in a more favourable light:

> I've got used to her now. . . . like I say, it's strange at first . . . I suppose it's different for a mother . . . but for a father . . . you come to hospital and you see a baby lying there and somebody says, 'That's yours.' Mother's gone through having her . . . I've warmed to her now . . . I've got more used to it . . . play with her more. She's started to respond a bit more now . . . she's not just a sort of blank.
>
> (Unemployed builder's labourer)

> I think when they're first born and they're lying there and they are having a go at you in their own little way, and then they go through a stage when they're just sitting there and looking around . . . to me, I don't know . . . it's like having a little dog, that you're sat there looking at. . . . There's nothing you can do with it, you know . . . he just sits and laughs at you or ignores you completely and just sits and looks at something in his own little way. But now he's crawling round, he's getting to the stage where any time now he'll be wandering off of his own, his two little feet running off somewhere. But he's at a better stage now. He's at a nice stage now. [Prompt: 'So it's a stage you find much nicer than the . . .'] Oh, I enjoy it much, much more, yeah . . . He's giving you things now, he'll come and put his head on your knee, which I presume is his own way of showing affection.
>
> (Goods representative)

The fact that men involve themselves in play, rather than in more mundane care-giving tasks, had led to the charge that play is a means of escaping the 'dirtier' or demanding chores of parenthood (La Rossa and La Rossa 1981). While this is to a certain extent true, the men in this study suggested that their involvement is far more complicated than this. It is clear that their relationships with their babies are hampered by their diminished initial role. For example, those men whose wives breast-feed often feel at a psychological disadvantage:

> Until she stopped breast-feeding she wasn't really interested in me either. . . . Not that I wasn't interested in her but she wasn't receptive, if you know what I mean. [Prompt: 'Is that because of her age or because she was breast-feeding?'] Well, I think she tended to go to her mother, 'cos she was a human dummy, if you know what I mean [laughs].
>
> (Lift engineer)

It is often considerably later in the first year of the child's life, then, that a special relationship between him or her and her father becomes a reciprocal affair. A mother's closeness to her child is expected to come naturally, while a father's relationship has to be worked at and often starts later. One mother described the sudden crystallization of her husband and son's relationship towards the end of the first year:

> There was one instance when Kim [son] showed his recognition for Tony [husband] and Tony's recognition was shown back. When the evening[s] started to get dark . . . Tony comes home at about quarter past five . . . and I just had Kim in my arms, but watching for the bus . . . and I just stood there and Anthony was walking down the path and for the very first time Kim responded to him and he started to jump up and down in my arms. Tony just stood there and . . . oh, it was fantastic, it really was, because he [had] never shown anything before and there it was, it was real! And I know that Anthony just couldn't get over that. . . . It was terrific!
>
> (Housewife, whose husband is a factory porter)

Fathers and one-year-olds at play

While they placed a high priority upon play, the fathers found it hard to assess the extent to which they engaged their one-year-olds each day. Many commented that their play routines varied greatly; on some days they might not play at all, while on others, particularly at weekends, they might spend long periods attempting to involve the child in activities. As a result, attempts to measure the frequency of father–infant interaction have long been regarded as problematic (Underwood 1949), and any measure of reported involvement must be treated with caution. Table 7.1 shows the responses to specific questions about the typical time spent by men in play on a day-to-day basis. It consists of their 'average' estimate over a complete week, including the weekend. While this measure does not show each father's specific involvement it serves to demonstrate the variations in men's contact with their offspring.

Table 7.1 Average amount of time fathers play with their one-year-olds each day (including weekends)

Time	Frequency
(a) 10 minutes or less per day	4
(b) 11–30 minutes per day	13
(c) 31–60 minutes per day	37
(d) 61–120 minutes per day	30
(e) 121 minutes or more per day	12
(f) Varies according to shift	2
Total:	98

Dividing the fathers into those who reported playing with their children for at least an hour per day and those who did less revealed two factors which seem to be associated with the amount of time fathers devote to it. Firstly, men appear to play for longer if their wives work (62 per cent of those with working wives vs 38 per cent others played for at least one hour per day; χ^2 = 3.99, df = 1, p<0.05). Fathers whose wives work on twilight shifts tend to act as baby-sitters more than caretakers during the time between their wives' departure for work and putting the child to bed. Secondly, more fathers from the middle of the class spectrum (71 per cent of both groups in social class III) claimed to play for an hour per day than the professional and unskilled manual workers (29 per cent of classes III and V; χ^2 10.15, df = 1, p<0.002).

Mother–Child and Father–Child Relationships Compared

Mothers' and fathers' play styles

The observational literature tends to suggest that fathers concentrate upon active physical play (Lamb 1981b). When asked to list the activities which they engaged their one-year-olds in, the fathers gave detailed accounts of their daily routines. Few conformed exactly to the stereotype depicted in the observational literature, by citing only social or physical play. Indeed, mothers and fathers gave similarly lengthy lists of activities usually involving both social and 'educational' games, like fitting shapes into a posting box. At the same time it is clear that fathers specialize in the active games which they demonstrate in front of observers, while mothers' play routines are fundamentally different.

Fathers' play fits into concentrated and regular periods. As a result it often takes on a ritualized quality. While their play may well be varied, they place more emphasis on *activity* during these brief episodes. There are many practical reasons why the father is often boisterous. First of all, the time that is available for a man to play is usually in the evening, when he has not been at home all day, and both he and his child are often a welcome relief for one another. His usual role is to occupy the baby at a time when he or she is almost ready for bed (when many one-year-olds become irritable unless they are kept 'amused') and when his wife may want either to escape from the child or to cook the evening meal. Alison Clarke-Stewart (1978b) found that mothers also withdraw at this time in order to allow the father an opportunity to develop their relationship. Similarly, at weekends fathers play in order to allow mothers time to do other things. When asked if they had any 'special' games with the child that he or she looked forward to, seventy fathers felt that they had such a game. These included many types of play, but a majority specialized in games involving chasing, physical contact and surprise – particularly those activities which took place in the excitement of dad's return from work:

Just mostly chasing her, ain't it, when I . . . if I come home and walk through the door . . . she likes playing hide and seek. [Prompt: 'So she almost expects it as you come through the door?'] Yeah, I walk through the door, and she'll know what I'm going to do to her. I'll take my jacket off, and I'll creep up to her and she'll start giggling and trying to climb up Helen (wife).

(Coal-miner)

Significantly more first-timers mentioned a special game (78 per cent first- vs 57 per cent second-timers; $\chi^2 = 4.96$, df = 1, p < 0.05). These are more likely to be able to play on a one-to-one basis. At the same time special games were more common to father–son pairs (79 per cent vs 62 per cent for father–daughter pairs; $\chi^2 = 3.69$, df = 1, p < 0.06). Close father–son ties have been noted in many observational studies of infancy (Power 1981). However, such patterns are not clear-cut at one year (Lewis 1986) and seem to be much more obvious beyond the child's second birthday (Lewis *et al.* 1982, McGuire 1982).

As Lorna McKee (1982) found, mothers tend to perceive play in very different ways. In keeping with their role as primary care-givers they fit play in when they can, or if the need to stimulate the child arises.

[Interviewer: 'Is there any special time which is her playtime with you?'] Not really, no. . . . It's just that if she is getting fed up we'll start playing.

(Housewife, whose husband is a welder)

I'm usually doing housework and I'm washing. We play mainly as I'm doing the housework – it takes a bit longer but it's a game at the same time.

(Housewife, whose husband is a civil servant 2)

When she is not simply trying to occupy the child while doing housework, the mother often sets aside particular periods during the day to help him or her 'work' at constructive play, involving books or toys deemed to be educational.

Many fathers appeared to be unaware that their brief episodes of play were any different from those of their wives. The mothers are significantly more likely to regard father's playtime as special to the child (61 per cent vs 37 per cent of the fathers in the small sample; $\chi^2 = 4.59$, df = 1, < 0.05), and they were more likely to emphasize the differences between mothers' and fathers' play styles when comparing them (63 per cent vs 37 per cent of the fathers in the small sample; $\chi^2 = 4.27$, df = 1, p < 0.05). Such differences in parents' perceptions may well reflect the basic difference between their play styles. Fathers entertain their children usually with their wives close at hand and within earshot. Mothers' play is much more private. So, while half the fathers claimed that their play styles matched those of their wives, many commented that they each placed particular emphasis on different activities:

I think she plays generally the same way. I think what she does tend to do, um, in the time she's with him, she p'raps tends to read books with him more than I do. As I say, mainly because of the fact that she's with him more, er, the time when I'm with him, er, then it's generally play.

(Police constable 2)

I think Brenda [wife] tries to teach her a bit more than I do. . . . I think with having such a short time . . . I mean, I get more at night and Brenda says, 'I had her on my knee today and we was doing such-and-such', and you know she tries to bring her on speech-wise and things. . . . [Prompt: 'Well, what do you do?'] We just generally fool about [laughs] . . . although when she was trying hard to walk we, obviously, were both trying hard that way.

(Hairdresser)

The following comparisons of a father's and a mother's play come from a husband and his wife answering the same question. The mother stresses the use of play to teach and quieten her child, while the father emphasizes his own physical strength and its influence upon his son's development:

[Interviewer: 'Does Jim [father] play in the same way or differently?'] I think differently. With Jim it's more play. With me it's more educational. I read to him as well. It's one way to encourage this bedtime business. I point things out and his eyes start closing. I hope, when he's older, I'll be able to read a story, take him upstairs with his book and read him a story. I hope that will get him to sleep. He does like books.

(Housewife, whose husband is a mobile grocer)

Well, she don't . . . she can't swing him about and things like that 'cos, as you can see, she's not that big and she might . . . I think she's a bit frightened of dropping him. Anyway he's getting a bit heavy now. [Prompt: 'So she plays differently from you?'] Yeah, well, how she plays, she always tries to educate him with her play, whereas I'm just a bit boisterous with him, you know. . . . I think it's a basic difference of . . . of men like to play with their boys . . . like to feel that they're boys, you know. Where with a girl, it would be different. You wouldn't swing a girl round, or you wouldn't wrestle with a girl.

(Mobile grocer)

The 'Closeness' of Parent–Child Relationships

Much of the parent–infant-interaction research in the 1970s was concerned with comparing the closeness of fathers' and mothers' relationships with their young children (Lewis 1982a). Many studies, for example, have examined the nature of the child's 'attachments', using Mary Ainsworth's 'strange situation' experiment (Ainsworth and Wittig 1969). This consists of a series of episodes, during which the infant, in the presence of a stranger, is exposed to the departure and return of his or her parent – a stress-provoking experience. By and large, children use their mothers and fathers in similar ways – as secure emotional havens (Feldman and Ingham 1975, Kotelchuck 1972, Willemsen *et al.* 1974) – although they may demonstrate different patterns of attachment to each of them (Main and Weston 1981). However, in times of heightened stress, some studies reveal that toddlers seek out their mothers more than their fathers, suggesting that the maternal haven is more secure (Cohen and Campos 1974, Lamb 1976).

The present study examined whether parents' descriptions of their relationship with their infants matched those found in observational studies, and also sought parents' descriptions of their 'attachments'. Their accounts closely match the observational data. Most fathers have developed very close relationships with their one-year-olds. However, while the variety of paternal styles is great, the nature of the relationship is usually qualitatively different from that of mother and child.

Table 7.2 gives a breakdown of fathers' responses to two specific questions about the child's behaviour in particular settings: who would he or she turn to for play, or if frightened, when both parents were available? Half of the fathers suggested that the child would turn to either parent for fun, while the other half felt he or she would turn to one parent rather than the other. In some cases he or she turns to the mother (17 per cent), while in nearly twice as many cases he or she prefers the father (31 per cent). However, in contrast, sixty-four fathers felt that when the child needed comforting he or she would automatically turn to the mother. In these circumstances, only four felt that he or she would turn to him in preference to his wife. Indeed, significantly more wives than husbands in the small sample felt their one-year-olds would turn to the mother when frightened (73 per cent mothers vs 46 per cent fathers in the small sample; $\chi^2 = 4.44$, df = 1, p < 0.05).

Table 7.2   Who does the child turn to (a) for fun and (b) when frightened? (Fathers' reports)

Child turns to	For fun	If frightened
(i) Mother	17	64
(ii) Either parent	52	31
(iii) Father	31	4
Totals	= 100	99
		(1 missing)

Table 7.2 also shows that thirty-five children were reported to turn to their fathers when frightened, either as someone equally as close as the mother, or as the primary 'attachment' figure. While there is a significant difference between parents' assessments, these data still suggest that there is no necessary link between the amounts of parents' practical involvement and their closeness to the child. However, certain conclusions can be drawn from the large number of children who appear to prefer their mothers. While both parents may act as 'playmates', mothers, as primary care-givers, usually have a deeper attachment to the child. This closeness is demonstrated particularly in times of stress. As one mother put it:

> He's happy with John [husband] most of the time. If he's a little bit upset, you know, it's bad, and even if he's really upset it's me he wants because he cuddles up like when I was breast-feeding him . . . and he likes me singing to him, for the comfort. I think it's just the fact that, you know, he associates me with the comfort, you know . . . when he was younger.
>
> (Housewife, whose husband is a legal executive)

The fathers were asked to consider just how important they were to their one-year-old. Table 7.3 outlines their responses to this question.

Table 7.3   How important is a father to a one-year-old?

Fathers' answers	*Frequency*
(a) Is not necessarily important	5
(b) Performs a complementary 'function' to his wife (subtotal = 40)	
(i) providing 'security' to the child	20
(ii) as a provider	5
(iii) as a discipliner	4
(iv) to educate	3
(v) as a playmate	6
(vi) for more than one of these	2
(c) He should be 'involved' (subtotal = 48)	
(i) but less than his wife	38
(ii) in the same way as his wife	10
Total:	98

Five men considered that the father's impact upon the child is negligible:

> You know, anyone could come in and once he'd got to know them he'd be . . . I think he seems to be equally happy with them, or could easily be. [Prompt: 'Is this the same with the mother?'] I don't know . . .

it's a bit different with the mums 'cos of the amount of time spent with her. They spend a lot of time with them. . . . I could be substituted . . . that's what I mean. He recognizes me, things like that, but give him five minutes and he'd be happy with someone else. I suppose I could flit out of his life without him bothering a great deal.

(Panel beater)

In keeping with the recent models of fatherhood suggested by Fein (1978b), (see Chapter 1), the vast majority of men asserted initially that they are important contributors to the child's psychological well-being. Forty adhered to what Fein terms the 'modern' belief that fathers provide either a specific function, like play, or, more typically, general 'security' for both mother and child. These sentiments echo the division made by Parsons and Bales (1955) between the 'instrumental' male, who links the family with the outside world, and the 'expressive' female who maintains the emotional stability of the family. A larger group (forty-eight) appeared to adhere to the ideal of 'emergent' fatherhood, considering that mothers and fathers provide the child with the same type of emotional and practical support. However, further questioning suggested that deep down many fathers do not hold these beliefs. When asked, only ten thought that mothers and fathers are 'interchangeable'. Thirty-five men felt slightly distanced:

The father can never be as close to his child as a mother can . . . I think . . . I believe that there's that maternal bond, that indescribable, undefinable thing that a male can never break into.

(Industrial relations officer)

I think it would come down to the fact that, taking a whole day – any twenty-four-hour period – I think that they soon realize that Mummy can't be with them all the time and there comes a point when they need a substitute for Mummy. It's nothing *against* Father, but he steps in and fills the gap. [Prompt: 'Is there anything special in the child's relationship with the father that makes it possible for him to fill that gap, or could it be anyone, there is something special between the two. . . . . All I know is that the baby can differentiate between mother and father and then father and another . . . that of another person. And why he should feel close to a father, especially where the father is out at work all day . . . it must be instinctive.

(Civil servant 2)

It's a strange role, really, because I'm the one who rattles the key in the lock and comes in. She always seems very pleased to see me. . . . . I'm always the one who's just dashing off. . . . She sees me for about ten minutes in the morning and I dash off. So in a sense it's special in that it's not the same as Joan [wife]. . . . At the moment we're the only people in her life anyway, and if I were taken as the norm, Joan would be special. . . . This afternoon I met Joan walking

home from town, pushing Sarah, and she was very pleased to see me.
[Prompt: 'Would you say the father's less important than the
mother?'] Yes, I think so, in as much as she can get on without me.

(Customs executive officer)

Discipline and control
Most fathers, as this chapter suggested, cast themselves into the role of
'super-pals' to their children:

[Interviewer: 'Can a father and his son be as close as a mother and
her son at this age?'] Yes, but in a different way. . . . With a mother
it's a bond which is obviously . . . all mothers . . . you have with all
mothers. Whereas with a father its a – he's a mate, probably a friend.
[Prompt: 'That's the difference, then?'] Yeah, I think one's a love
thing and one's a friend thing.

(Warehouse labourer)

The distinction between mother as attachment figure and father as playmate
has far-reaching effects. In this final section, I will examine parents' attitudes
towards disciplining and controlling the child. Even at one year, discipline
has become a major issue in many households. The child is able to spend
the day happily tampering with the television or family ornaments, without
necessarily responding to requests to stop. Sixty-six fathers used some sort
of physical punishment. Smacking was a frequent topic of conversation
among couples, and only fourteen differed over the strategy to be used.

However, as a result of their different relationships with the child, there
were clear qualitative differences in parents' approaches to discipline. The
wife was usually the one who decided how the child was to be disciplined.
As one wife said: 'I've got them, so I've got to deal with them.' Four men
claimed that they were important to the child because they were more
disciplinary than their wives – see Table 7.3. These were in a very small
minority, however. Observational research in the United States suggests
that fathers tend to discipline their two-year-olds less than their wives do
when both are at home (Fagot 1974 and 1978). Similar results were apparent
in most of the hundred fathers' accounts. As 'mates' to their babies, most
men appear reluctant to live up to the stereotype which has existed for
generations and which their wives often expect of them.

Many men were aware that the nature of their contact with the child
was so brief that an active disciplinary role might jeopardize the relationship
they were developing. So two-thirds of the smacking fathers and many of
those who avoided using physical punishment felt uneasy about taking a
disciplinary stance – a finding which speaking for both himself and his wife,
echoes the thoughts of many fathers on disciplining the child:

Well, what we normally do . . . give her a smack and immediately
afterwards comfort her. [Prompt: 'So you find that's sort of . . .']

I'm not sure if it's . . . I feel as though, if we smack her we must comfort her. . . . Otherwise she'll go off us.

(Garage proprietor)

Other men gave the impression that they rarely even got cross with their one-year-olds:

[Interviewer: 'What do you usually say to him when you're feeling a little bit cross with him?'] Well, very rarely . . . I don't get cross with him. . . . To me, you know . . . it's hard to explain but he's my son and to me he's the apple of my bloody eye, you know. Probably Jacqueline [wife] being with him more, so during the daytime is, you know . . . he's doing more things annoying to Jacqueline than he is to me. At night time, you know, I play with him for a couple of hours before he goes to sleep and things like this, and he don't normally do things wrong when I'm here. He obviously does when Jacqueline's here because she's told me.

(Despatch controller)

As this father suggests, the issue of controlling the child is perceived differently by each parent. Mothers often perceive the child as difficult to placate, 'naughty' or at least wilful. Fathers tend to depict him or her as easy to placate, less culpable and more 'fragile' then their wives do. So, for example, significantly more fathers in the small sample felt that they could calm the child down once a tantrum had set in (70 per cent vs 29 per cent of the mothers; $\chi^2 = 5.76$, df = 1, p < 0.02).

Similarly, mothers were more likely to agree with a policy of leaving the child to cry – in his or her cot at night, for example. Significantly more fathers in the small sample felt that doing this would do the child harm (83 per cent vs 34 per cent of mothers; $\chi^2 = 5.24$, df = 1, p < 0.05). For mothers, a one-year-old's crying is much more likely to be perceived as part of a battle of wills in a power struggle:

[Interviewer: 'How long would you leave her to cry?'] About twenty minutes, 'cos they find at this age that they get crafty and cry and cry. And as soon as you pick her up she's happy and laughing, and as soon as you put her down she's off again. So we've sort of weighed her up now and we know that . . . you know, we just leave her.

(Part-time typist, whose husband is a central-heating mechanic)

[Interviewer: 'How long would you leave him to cry?'] If my patience would hold out . . . until he stopped. But often it's a matter of, 'oh, I can't stand that noise any more.' [Prompt: 'And how long is this?'] Um . . . *now* I can leave him because if he's crying I know he's just playing up. . . . He can cry for half an hour if he feels like it, but I'll still leave him.

(Housewife, whose husband is a factory porter)

While fathers also mentioned that their reactions often depended upon the type of cry and how long their one-year-olds had been left, it is clear that many have far less tolerance of crying than their wives. Not only do they tend to be less able to stand the noise, they also regard themselves as 'soft'; the father–child relationship is often described as a more indulgent one than that between mother and child:

> [Interviewer: 'Do you think it does a child of this age any harm to be left to cry?'] Lindsay [wife] don't think so. . . . I think you've got to go and pick her up. We do differ on that, but not a lot. . . . Lindsay will now leave her . . . not too long. She'll say, 'You're not going to be picked up all the while.' This is the trouble, you see, I spoil her and Lindsay's got her all day. I'm in the wrong really, 'cos Lindsay's got to do her. [Prompt: 'How long would you leave her if you thought there was nothing wrong with her when she was crying?'] Oh, I'm too soft with her. . . . I'd go over to her in a minute and pick her up.
>
> (Records clerk)

Mothers were often upset by the imbalance between their own and their husbands' roles as discipliners. Sixteen (of the thirty) mothers felt that their husbands were easy-going, and many of these criticized the father's lax approach to discipline:

> [Interviewer: 'How does her daddy feel about that (smacking)?'] He doesn't do it as much as me. He didn't think much of smacking at all when we first had her, but I think he realizes now that it needs to be done sometimes because there's no other way you can get the message across. I . . . you know, we only tap her, we don't sort of go hammer and tongs at her. [Prompt: 'Does one of you seem to be more easy-going than the other?'] Robin [husband] tends to be slightly softer. I think he thinks if he didn't see her very often at this stage he's not got to be too hard in case she didn't like him [laughs].
> (Housewife, whose husband is an assistant contracts officer)

> [Interviewer: 'How does her daddy feel about that (smacking)?'] He never does, and I feel it is going to show when they get older. I'm really quite worried about Donna [older child] as she's so disobedient. I know she gets bored and is ready for school, but if I say, 'I'll tell you dad', she knows he'll do nothing. . . . He says, 'If you want to smack her, you do, but I won't.' . . . And I feel he don't support me. [Returns to this point later.] As I've just said, they're getting out of hand and I think it's all his fault. I get jealous, yes, jealous, of them with him. He just lets them do anything. [Prompt: 'Do you tell him, or have you told him you're jealous?'] Yes, I have and he says, 'Don't be daft.' [Prompt: 'But there's more to it than that, you feel?'] Oh, yes, I think it's a serious problem that should be sorted out.
> (Part-time cleaner, whose husband is a sawyer)

Conclusion

This chapter has attempted to describe the nature of the relationship between fathers and their one-year-olds in contemporary culture. Like their participation in child care, fathers' emotional involvement appears to change over the first year of the child's life. At first the ambiguous nature of fatherhood is accentuated. Men usually become 'engrossed' with their new-born offspring, but at the same time they can feel distant and cut off from the mother–infant 'bond', since their practical role in child care is often limited. As the year unfolds men come to relate to their children more closely, mainly because infants need less practical attention and they develop social skills which facilitate relationships with those other than their primary care-givers.

In many respects the 'playmate' role comes naturally to fathers, and many men adopt it, since they want to build a special link with their children in the limited time they have available, and this role is culturally prescribed. At the same time father–infant play often occurs at a time of day when the child may need to be kept occupied. Fathers call upon a wide variety of activities when playing. However, many appear to specialize in active games, and these are perceived as an important feature of the father–child 'attachment', particularly by their wives.

When mothers' and fathers' descriptions of their children were compared, their views seemed to differ in ways which reflect their daily involvement with and responsibility for them. For example, mothers tend to describe the crying of the one-year-old as wilful and attention-seeking, while men are far less likely to leave a child to cry. Fathers, as their children's 'mates', tend to be more indulgent than their wives, who have to deal with them all day. Similar differences between parents often exist when it comes to disciplining their children. While on the surface they appear to follow the same policy, in many families fathers withdraw from a punishing role so as not to jeopardize their relationship with their one-year-old.

The descriptions of fathers' relationships outlined in this chapter are consistent with their accounts of their experiences in pregnancy and their practical involvement in the care of the child. In the next chapters the focus on men broadens to include an examination of how their role as fathers fits in with other aspects of their lives.

Part Three
Fatherhood in its
Wider Perspective

8   Marriage and Early Parenthood

Marital Satisfaction and Parenthood

When examined collectively, the studies of the 'transition to parenthood', discussed in Chapter 1, suggest that the arrival of a child effects families in a variety of ways and usually brings mixed blessings. The research on marital relationships over this period paints a similar picture (Belsky *et al.* 1983 and in press). Oakley (1979) found that 73 per cent of mothers report a decline in marital satisfaction five months after delivery. Such trends have been seen to worsen during the second half of the child's first year (Miller and Sollie (1980). Early parenthood is reported to be more stressful than other stages in the life-cycle (Campbell *et al.* 1976). However, other research indicates a more complex pattern. Some, for example, found no decline in marital satisfaction (Cowan and Cowan 1981, Entwisle and Doering 1981). Other studies suggest that parenthood has both negative and positive effects on a marital relationship (Feldman 1971, Meyerowitz and Feldman 1966). The nature of change may be influenced by the state of the marriage before the arrival of the child (Dyer 1963), Feldman and Rogoff 1968, Hobbs, 1968).

Recent research has attempted to explain the differences in these findings. Much of this work has tried to attribute marital satisfaction to the division of domestic labour after the delivery. Again the results are equivocal. One study (Fein 1976) suggests that coherent and distinct roles (whether egalitarian or traditional) are an essential ingredient to marital satisfaction, while others provide evidence to support the view that increased father participation is correlated with increased marital satisfaction (Cowan and Cowan 1981, Dickie *et al.* 1981). Yet another suggests that marriages which were 'equal' (or symmetrical) before the arrival of the child fare worse after his or her arrival since the shift to traditional roles is more marked, and the baby encroaches upon the relationship (Feldman 1971). While each of these findings is plausible, the differences between them lead us to question their validity, particularly as other researchers have criticized the appropriateness of the usual tools employed to measure both role division (Oakley 1974) and marital 'satisfaction' (Spanier *et al.* 1978).

Theoretical models of the effects of parenthood upon marriage have thus become more dynamic, indicating that a relationship is more subject to change than previous authors suggest (Hoffman and Manis 1978, La Rossa 1977, Rollins and Galligan 1978). Hoffman and Manis, for example, detail a number of potential advantages and disadvantages which parenthood might bring to a marriage simultaneously. The results of the present study support this position.

When asked to discuss the changes in their relationship many parents admitted that their new status brought both joys and hardship. Two questions asked directly whether parenthood 'brings a couple closer together' or 'pushes them apart'. Most fathers (seventy) felt closer in some way to their wives, while a similar number (sixty-eight) admitted to feeling that parenthood drove couples at least slightly apart. Thirty-five men felt both closer to and distanced from their wives. In short, mothers and fathers suggest that marital satisfaction over the first year of parenthood ebbs and flows.

Indeed, rather than portraying early parenthood simply as a time of either marital stress or satisfaction, it seems more salient to examine the *nature* of the relationship over this period in both its positive and negative changes. The patterns of emotional dependency described with reference to pregnancy in Chapter 3 continue after delivery. On one level couples adhere to the symmetrical ideal, describing parenthood as a shared experience. However, as the last three chapters suggest, mothers' and fathers' roles are so clearly differentiated that they can divide a husband and wife. We have to understand these contrasting perceptions simultaneously.

The experience shared

The arrival of a child, whether first- or second-born, brings to most parents changes in their life-styles, their finances, the time they can allocate to various activities and, partly in consequence, their marriage. While the term 'crisis' might exaggerate their psychological states and also deny and positive experiences during the transition, it is clear that some disruption in the routine and the emotional atmosphere of the family almost inevitably takes place (Rossi 1968). At times this has a deleterious effect upon a marriage. Couples commonly stress their relative isolation or loss of freedom. In keeping with previous authors (e.g. Oakley 1979) I shall argue later that this can have a harmful effect upon a couple's relationship. Neverthelesss, a repeated theme in the interviews suggested that couples regard this disruption as being in some way of *benefit* to the relationship.

Milestones in the child's life serve as rites of passage in the establishment of a joint parental identity. The delivery, for example, takes on the meaning described by the 'progressive' obstetricians in Chapter 3, and is seen as a turning-point in the relationship:

> [Interview: 'Would you say that having a baby brings a husband and wife closer together in any way?'] I think that the actual birth experience brought us closer together without any doubt. [Prompt: 'And does this have long-lasting effects?'] Well, just the whole sort of overwhelmingness of it . . . er, the trauma, the traumaticness of it, er, and sort of coming through the other side with a beautiful baby, sort of thing. . . in that we're both pleased and delightful with him and we're able to sort of talk about him and say how wonderful he is to each other. . . . Then I think it's . . . again, I suppose . . . definitely a plus in our relationship.
>
> (Engineering lecturer)

A key feature in our understanding of parents' perceptions during this period is that they feel somewhat restricted by their new roles. Many first-timers and even some second-timers recall that they did not know how much the new arrival would alter their lives, however much they anticipated change.

> It's amazing . . . I never thought how much it would disturb your normal pattern of life. You get this preconceived idea of . . . the baby will fit into you life. You don't realize how much they take over, whatever pattern you had before, whatever routine or anything. . . . It's a period of adjustment, that is, you know . . . I don't think that people can settle into parenthood.
>
> (Industrial relations officer)

A considerable proportion of the seventy couples who felt closer mentioned that their joint involvement in the baby was an important cause of this. The child continues to be a 'major talking-point, as the journalist put it. He or she 'bonds' parents together and may even give meaning to a relationship:

> You've created them, after all, so it's bound to be a big bond between you, and of course most of your conversation is made up of what you've been doing.
>
> (Housewife, whose husband is a general studies lecturer)

> I was working, and Beryl was here, like . . . and we weren't seeing much of each other, like, really. I used to come home and we never used to speak, you know, it was just a matter of coming in, saying 'hello' to be polite and that was it. So when Elaine came along it was something to do together then.
>
> (Refuse collector)

Younger parents were more likely to stress not only the struggles of early parenthood but also the closeness that this brings to a marriage. Trends in the data show that more men under twenty-six experience negative feelings towards the child (57 per cent vs 37 per cent men twenty-six and over; $\chi^2 = 3.49$, df = 1, p < 0.07); and they were less likely to mention the positive aspects of parenthood when describing the changes in their lives (20 per cent vs 43 per cent of older men; $\chi^2 = 3.297$, df = 1, p < 0.10). Younger fathers (those whose wives were under twenty-six years old) more often agreed that they had 'given up a lot' for the child than their older counterparts (87 per cent vs 44 per cent for older middle-class fathers; $\chi^2 = 8.41$, df = 1, p < 0.005). At the same time, significantly more younger men reported that parenthood had made their marriage closer (72 per cent vs 46 per cent of fathers twenty-six and over; $\chi^2 = 6.41$, df = 1, p < 0.01). These claimed that they had 'matured' as a result of their new shared duties as parents:

> [Interviewer: 'Would you say that having a baby brings a couple of closer together?'] I think the fact that he's sort of the number one, if you like . . . so you're both working towards his end initially, trying to bring him up . . . so you're thinking about him more. I mean you've got to try and show your affections and share your attentions to some extent . . . but he's the king-pin I s'pose. So I think like that side . . . so you're working together.
>
> (Brick company representative, aged twenty-five)

A different experience

(1) Time, fatigue and early parenthood

The adjustments made during early parenthood serve to unite the parental 'team' in many respects. At the same time, many studies suggest that the arrival of a child increases the potential for conflict. While each partner may respect the other's endurance in 'adversity' and their part in the procreation, it is clear that in some important ways a marital relationship can change drastically. Studies which find no change in marital satisfaction often describe other stresses. For example, Cowan and Cowan (1981) found that six months after delivery thirty-seven of the forty parents studied reported an increase in the number of disagreements with their spouses, but no overall change in satisfaction. Entwisle and Doering's (1981) data indicate that couples often channel their conflict through the child. In the haze of sleepless nights, a concern for the baby reduces the amount of time and energy which parents can devote to each other. So, for example, 70 per cent of Entwisle and Doering's respondents reported a reduction in the wife's sexuality during early parenthood. Without being asked directly about their sexual relationship these parents mentioned similar themes:

To a certain extent, actually, you become a little more detached. In fact, *we* did, didn't we [to wife]? We sort of drifted apart . . . not intentionally, we probably . . . [Wife: 'We were very wrapped up in him.'] Yeah, we were so wrapped up with him that you forget a little bit about your relationship. . . . It's only now that we're starting to get back whatever we had lost.

(Sales representative and wife, a part-time shop assistant)

[Interviewer: 'Would you say that having a baby brings a couple closer together in any way?'] Well, it does in one sense, but the fact is that since Mandy [older child] was born we've never been able to sort of sit with our arms round each other. [Interviewer: 'So would you say in that sense it pushes them apart?'] Well . . . in a sense . . . mentally it's brought us together but sexually it's pushed us apart . . . you know. . . . As I say, the only time we put us hands together is just before we go to sleep . . . and put us arms round each other and say, 'Oh yeah?' . . . and then . . . [snores, then laughs].

(Factory labourer)

You feel tired. You feel so drained at the end of the day that you haven't got any time for each other. You can speak with your eyes, sort of [closes eyes] . . . 'I can't speak to you, I'm too tired'! We'd both do the same thing . . . before we'd sit and chat. . . . As soon, as he settles we just want to go to bed and go to sleep.

(Housewife, whose husband is civil servant 2)

(2) 'Restricted' mothers and 'sturdy oak' fathers

The pressure of domestic work and the presence of a third or fourth member of the household in some way alters and detracts from a marriage. Further important influences upon the relationship stem from the division of parental roles into primary care-giver (i.e. mother) and secondary care-giver (i.e. father). Early parenthood is qualitatively such a different experience for men and women that it may also divide them. Oakley (1979: 234) suggests three reasons why such divisions may arise: the man becomes jealous of the baby; the woman resents her husband's role as playmate; and a 'communication gap' arises, mainly from the man's 'trained incapacity to share'. Similar themes were common in this study. Many fathers did appear to distance themselves from their wives. However, this is caused as much by the pattern of marital dependency between them as by any inbuilt trait in the man.

As in pregnancy, the father plays a psychologically supportive role during much of the child's early development. Adjusting to parenthood makes women experience a 'crisis' which is far deeper than that of their husbands. Russell (1974), for example, found that mothers showed a heightened concern for their appearance, their figure and their state of fatigue. Such feelings correlated with their expressed marital satisfaction.

Epidemiological research has long shown that many mothers, particularly blue-collar workers, suffer from depression in various forms. One study of 166 working-class women before and after delivery found that one-quarter had symptoms of clinical depression at four months post-partum (Zajicek and Wolkind 1978). There is much debate on the causes of the many types of depression in this period, but recent research emphasizes the importance of sociological and psychological factors (Clulow 1982, Oakley 1980). Given the weight of evidence concerning depression in mothers, I did not seek directly to quantify the number of women or men in this sample who experienced depression over the first year. However, fathers and mothers frequently mentioned the subject. For example, in a discussion about each parent's emotions over the year, forty-six men mentioned without prompting that their wives had experienced mood swings or depression during the early weeks and sometimes beyond.

Recent evidence on the nature of post-partum depression supports the view (Feiring 1976) that the secondary care-giver father plays an important role in alleviating or exacerbating his wife's adjustment to her new role. Studies of both normal populations (Ryder 1973) and women experiencing post-partum psychiatric disturbance (Kaplan and Blackman 1969) indicate that mothers often show deep concern that their husbands are not supporting them. A close examination of two accounts of this period shows the influence of the fathers:

> I found myself resenting everything after about four months. I didn't like anything then . . . I got very depressed. Oh, I must have been a horrible person to live with [laughs]. [Prompt: 'Did you do anything about it? Did you go to the doctor?'] No, I didn't go to the doctor's because I didn't want to associate it with depression. I thought, 'Oh rubbish', you know, and I just thought I was becoming resentful. It might well've only been that, but I would never want to go through that again because I made life miserable for me and made life miserable for Anthony [husband]. And he wasn't giving me the attention I wanted, so he was resentful towards me and it just became a vicious circle. . . . And I just had to pull myself out of it. . . . It made me a very nasty person. [Prompt: 'Did Anthony tell you that . . . or?'] Well, Anthony is . . . as I said, you can't tell what he's thinking. And I used to tell him how I felt and he'd say, 'Well, don't be daft' . . . and that's not any help, so he didn't help very much at all. . . . So I just had it all by myself. It might have been all me anyhow. You can just never tell.
>
> (Housewife, whose husband is a factory porter)

> [Interviewer: 'Have there been any bad moments for either of you since he's born, when you've felt a bit desperate?'] Oh, yeah, I mean . . . again, it's not bin him [child] causing us trouble . . . what . . . where that's arisen from post-natal depression. Anne's [wife]

suffered from that very badly for, er, several, er . . . life really was sheer hell. It wasn't the youngster. I was coming in for the brunt of that, wasn't I [to wife]? I mean, there really was . . . it was a matter of 'I hate you', you know, 'I wish you'd get out', or you know, that sort of thing. [Wife: 'Two choices and he knew whichever one he took was going to be the wrong one anyway' (laughs).] I, I . . . [her] short temper would be going off . . . and no matter what I did or what I said was going to be wrong. I mean, I knew . . . I knew this . . . I spoke to the health visitor about it and I knew the only thing I could do was to try . . . try and let it wash off . . . try to keep my temper. I mean, the big time I lost my temper she told me, 'Ooh, shut up', you know, I mean, it does get on top of you. . . . You've just got to sort of just . . . just keep going. [Prompt: 'You managed to?'] We got through it. [Wife: 'It's been a lot better this last couple of months.'] It's . . . it's one hell of a time to go through.

(Police constable 2 and his wife, a housewife)

These two descriptions are extreme accounts of the tensions which can build up in marriages in the first months of parenthood, since most women do not remain depressed after the early days. Yet they reflect a typical pattern in marital relationships, and explain why nearly seventy fathers felt that couples drifted apart in certain respects during this period. It was clear from their general accounts of psychological change over the transition that men and women usually experience early parenthood in different ways. For many couples the wife's physical 'sickness' in pregnancy (see Chapter 3) and during the early days post-partum continues. Rather than being seen as 'ill', the wife often comes to be described as 'restricted' or 'tied down'. Despite a change in terminology, these descriptions bear a strong resemblance to one another.

Table 8.1 gives a breakdown of fathers' responses to two general questions about the effect of the child's arrival on each parent's life.

Table 8.1   Father's account of changes in his own and his wife's lives since the birth

| | Frequency of change in: | |
Response category	*Father*	*Mother*
(a) Life is restricting	(subtotal = 23)	(subtotal = 43)
(i) only restriction mentioned	5	15
(ii) restricting and yet positive	18	28
(b) I have more responsibilities	23	7
(c) Little/no change	14	13
(d) Positive change	(subtotal = 40)	(subtotal = 37)
(i) more mature	21	17
(ii) happier/fulfilled	19	20

Obviously it is hard to summarize just how oneself and one's spouse have changed over a year in an answer to two interview questions, or to represent the complexity of paternal responses in a table such as this. However, it enables us to compare fathers' general impressions. It shows that about 40 per cent of men felt that they and/or their wives had 'matured' or become fulfilled since the child's arrival.* While some men (twenty-three) say that they themselves have become restricted by the child (and the majority of these also perceive positive change in their lives), almost twice as many feel that their wives have been influenced in this way by parenthood. Men may use the term 'responsibility' to summarize change in their own lives, but they often describe the change to the wives' lives as 'restricting'.

This semantic distinction is shown more clearly in the details of fathers' accounts of change during the period. In keeping with the comments of the factory porter's wife and the policeman quoted above, many men paint a fairly bleak picture of their wives' new life:

> [Interviewer: 'How much difference has it made to Mandy's (wife) life that you have a baby?'] Ooh, a hell of a lot, . . . Well, she's depressed . . . she's got no life in her . . . well, that's what she says. She thinks that all her life's gone into Wendy [child] . . . with her being full of joy and that she never wants to go to sleep. She thinks all her's [wife] drained into her [child], you know. . . . She's still the same but she doesn't . . . she thinks she's depressed and everything . . . gets headaches. . . . Sometimes she regrets that . . . you know, she don't mean it, it's just one of those things. . . . She's still the same, I suppose, you know . . . a bit nasty. [Prompt: 'Is that because . . . ?'] She's lost her freedom, really, hasn't she? I know we was married, but . . . when you've got a kiddie, that's it. You're tied down and you haven't got the choice of what you used to have.
>
> (Scaffolder's labourer)

In contrast, this man felt about himself that, while parenthood had 'hit me hard as well', the effect was less than that upon his wife: 'Oh, the fella's got it ever so easy . . . they aren't so tied down . . . they don't have to be at all.'

The impression that motherhood is more 'restricting' than fatherhood is suggested further by a comparison of the mothers' and fathers' accounts in the small sample. An equal proportion of parents (just under half) describe the mother's routine as restricted. However, significantly fewer women than men described the father's role in terms of added responsibility, or

---

* Such responses are culturally prescribed particularly in interviews, so I will not discuss these here. A similar proportion of fatters focused on the less positive aspects of parenthood.

restriction (8 per cent women vs 42 per cent men in the small sample; $\chi^2 = 8.39$, df = 1, p<0.005). Given that parents were not asked directly whether or not their lives had been restricted (and yet so many volunteered this description), it seems fair to suggest that this is a key feature of many perceptions of motherhood. This role requires the father to play support to his wife in times of crisis. As Kathryn Backett (1982) found in her study of parents with a three-year-old, couples devise 'coping mechanisms' for dealing with the restrictions placed upon the wife. The father is particularly required to show sympathy for his wife's current and 'temporary' loss of freedom.

Middle-class fathers were more likely to emphasize the differentiation of parental roles and the wedge this drives between couples. They were more inclined to describe their wives as being more tied down than themselves (60 per cent vs 40 per cent of the working-class fathers; $\chi^2 = 4$, df = 1, p<0.05). As Table 8.2 shows, they also more often admitted that parenthood make a marriage drift apart.

Table 8.2 Does parenthood drive a couple apart?

Social class	Yes	No
I/II	22	3
III (w.c.)	18	7
III (m.)	14	11
V	14	11

$\chi^2 = 8.09$, df = 3, p<0.05.

While-collar workers usually pointed out that their wives' new life-styles contrasted dramatically with their old ones, and this was likely to influence the marital relationship:

> I think she feels quite restricted. . . . I think it's not being able to do what she wants to. Because she's got the baby she can't go out to where she wants to . . . go to work . . . meet people. [Prompt: 'Does it just have it's restrictions?'] Oh, it has its advantages. [Prompt: 'So what are they?'] Um, it's somebody to be proud of. . . . She's met people in a different sphere – mother-and-todler group and that sort of thing. [Prompt: 'So it's broadened her outlook in some respects?'] In some respects, yeah. [Prompt to wife, who had tried to interject earlier: 'Would you agree with that – restricting in some respects, broadening in others?' Wife. '*Yes* I, I . . . er, at one point, um, I went through a phase where I felt very vegetablized, because Ted's (husband) not a very communicative person. He doesn't talk very much, so I'd be at home with her (daughter), who obviously

doesn't talk very much . . . not in an adult way, anyway. And Ted would come home and *he* didn't talk very much and I felt that I was vegetating mentally . . . and I wanted to get a job purely to go out and meet people. . . . It's difficult to understand, because he's at work all day . . . it's not the same restriction as me at home with a baby. Although one would think that I would be freer, being at home and being my own agent, but it's not that way at all. And it's difficult when you've worked and you've been amongst people. So this is why I . . . do go out an awful lot. I have a car and I, I take her shopping, anything . . . just to get out, yeah . . . because I couldn't bear to, I mean I'd die if I didn't, hadn't got the car. I think I'd slowly crumble if I didn't have the car. We're a little bit isolated up, here, really. . . . Fortunately there are . . . it's quite a baby-minded estate, this is . . . and having lived here for almost a year, we've got to know people and got a little circle of friends now, and it's getting better . . . and I think in five or ten years' time, we'll be quite sort of established . . . and you know it'll be quite nice then.']

(Police constable 1 and his wife, a housewife)

(3) Motherhood as 'fulfilment' and the distancing of husbands

This negative image of the primary caretaker's role is balanced by a more positive ascription. Not only does motherhood appear to tie women down, it is also depicted as the fulfilment of the woman's biological function. She is deemed to be naturally closer to her child. A man has to work at his paternal relationship and even then, as suggested in Chapter 7, this tends to be less close than that of mother and child. Hoffman, and Manis (1978) found that mothers are more likely than their husbands to describe parenthood as 'fulfilment'. This emerges clearly in parents' accounts:

How have I changed? I feel, um . . . a sense of satisfaction with my life . . . more than I felt before. Obviously I was very satisfied with the work I did but I feel so much a complete woman now, having a baby . . . having the experience . . . definitely more satisfaction, more calm than I tended to be before. . . . Things tended to worry me more before Simon [son] was born . . . I've definitely calmed down more. (School teacher, whose husband is a finance company representative)

I think it's been a very important thing to her. . . . I think if we'd have no children for any reason, that, you know, she would have felt that a major part of her life was missing and she, um, was missing a great deal. She would have failed if she hadn't've been able to produce children . . . it's been important to her as a woman. I think, you know, she feels that this is her role . . . part of her role, and . . . they've added a lot to our lives that we just didn't anticipate before. . . . You know, the *amount* of pleasure that, um, you get from watching them grow up, you know, from the things they did. [Prompt: 'Have there been any other changes in her?'] Yeah, well, I . . . . I think it's helped her with identity, if you like, as a person. She now feels that she has a relationship with other women that she knows, her mother, her grandmother.

(Primary schoolteacher 2)

I shall argue in the next chapter that the experience of fatherhood is usually intense. However, men as secondary care-givers recognize that their wives' involvement is even closer as a result of their primary role. This 'deference' to the mother is important since it may both influence the distribution of 'power' within the marital relationship and distance the father psychologically from his wife.

As Oakley (1979) suggests, their different statuses as child rearers can make parents complete for the baby's attentions. Women often feel let down by their husbands' aloofness. At the same time, fathers may often feel their contribution is not recognized, or even that they are in some ways being excluded by their wives. Many men stated at the start of the interview that it was about time someone recognized their contribution. There was also a distinct feeling among some that the baby had divided the marital relationship, by stealing the father's 'limelight':

> There's a saying that once your wife's had a baby, you might as well pack your bags and leave for the first two years. [Prompt: 'Would you agree with that?'] I should think so, yes . . . in some ways, yeah. I think the father gets ignored a little bit when the new baby comes along. The wife's more to the new baby for probably the first year or so.
>
> (Unemployed builder's labourer)

> You see, you get married and all of a sudden you're in the limelight, so to speak . . . from your wife, from your in-laws, from your mother. Then all of a sudden you have this baby and he's pinched all this limelight. I suppose really in that way I could see how it pushes a couple apart.
>
> (Product development officer).

Leisure and Early Parenthood: Reflections on the Marital Relationship

I have argued that the arrival of a baby experts contrasting pushes and pulls on a marital relationship. The strengths of these relative forces are hard to discern, but are hinted at in couples' accounts of the changes in their lives. One such change is the way in which spouses spend time away from the child in leisure activities – going out, or keeping up a hobby or sport. Two patterns emerge from a consideration of these activities, which shall be considered in turn below. Firstly, parenthood greatly restricts and alters mothers' and fathers' time outside the home, particularly that spent together. Secondly, husbands and wives appear to perceive leisure time in different ways. Fathers often seem more concerned about their loss of freedom, despite the fact they are more likely to spend time in a leisure activity. Just how parents divide up their spare time reveals a great deal about individual and general patterns of marital cohesion.

Changing leisure activities

Parenthood alters most couples' leisure activities by forcing them to stay at home. They go out less, and their circle of friends often changes considerably. Table 8.3 gives a breakdown of the couples' reported joint evenings out both before the pregnancy and when the baby was one year of age.

While this table shows a shift in couples' joint leisure activities over the period as a whole, it by no means describes the complexity of changing influences upon parents at this time. The most important of these is the difference between first-and second-timers. Most first-timers went out once, if not more, each week before the pregnancy (67 per cent vs 28 per cent second-timers; χ^2 = 14.7, df = 1, p<0.001), and they experienced far greater change over the transition to parenthood. Indeed, second-timers often had a 'fling' during the pregnancy, going out more than before.

Few couples venture out together in the early months. In almost half (42 per cent) the families, neither parent went out at all in the first three months. By the child's first birthday variations between couples were apparent, but the overall picture depicts a home-centred family, with few outside links. Table 8.3 shows that by the child's first birthday twenty-seven were going out together at least weekly. However, at the same time, forty-three couples had had less than twelve evenings out in the year, and a majority of these (twenty-seven) had less than six. These figures are roughly similar to those obtained by the Newsons (1963: 141) more than twenty years ago.

Table 8.3   How often did the couple go out before the pregnancy and when the child was one year old?

	Before pregnancy	*When child was one year old*
Never	3	8
Less than monthly	12	35
1–3 times per month	19	30
Once a week	15	19
2–3 times per week	42	8
At least four times per week	9	0

Fathers suggested three reasons why their social lives altered as they did. Firstly, some, like many parents in the Newsons' study, had firm ideas about finding a suitable baby-sitter for the child. First-timers were less likely to employ a baby-sitter (26 per cent vs 48 per cent second-timers; $\chi^2 = 4.45$, df = 1, p < 0.05), and many of these appeared to be more protective towards the child:

> I know people like to have a break, have a night out. We often do now but only when Jacqueline's [wife] brother and girl-friend come up and look after Ian [son]. . . . But they know him. We discussed this . . . we don't agree with having any baby-sitter. You know, we want somebody who Ian knows.
>
> (Despatch controller)

Secondly, fathers often commented that financial constraints prevented them from going out as much as they used to. These mentioned factors like the expense of the baby and, in the case of first-timers, the loss of half the couple's earnings:

> I would like to [go out] but finances have been a big restraint . . . 'cos we moved here . . . the mortgage rate went up. I do not have to tell you we've been crippled in a lot of ways financially. If you go to the pictures with bus fares and everything it costs you four quid. [Prompt: 'So that's ruled out most of the time?'] I'm afraid so, yeah.
>
> (Civil servant 1)

A third, more basic change seems to occur in addition to the problems of money and finding suitable care for the child. A consistent theme in fathers' descriptions of their leisure activities over the transition to parenthood – which echo mothers' accounts of two decades ago (Newson and Newson 1963) – is that parenthood makes couples more family-centred and less interested in activities outside the home. As was mentioned in Chapter 3, for many couples these changes start to occur during the first pregnancy, or even after their marriage. Not only do 'nest building' and 'maintenance' continue to be part of many fathers' spare-time activities, but also their social lives often alter.

Many men reported changing their leisure pursuits. They have to fit these into the few spare hours they have available and also within the family budget. Many men change their spare-time activities to include their families. For example, three fathers took up caravaning so that the family could enjoy weekends together. More typically, men found home-based activities to suit their newly acquired family- or child-centredness:

> Well, when she was pregnant we didn't go out as much . . . but when she was pregnant . . . we've started now to visit friends or they come here. We make an evening of it here. [Prompt: 'But you didn't go out as much. . . . Was that for any particular reason?'] Money, I think, especially going out for meals, anyway. [Prompt: 'So you just

went to friends?'] We went to friends . . . yes, and then after Alan
was born, you know, it carried on from there. We tended to go to
friends more than, say, going to . . . we haven't been to the pictures
for ages, or to the theatre . . . because those things have become very
secondary in your life, you tend to talk more about babies, and things
like that. We have the occasional meal but not as often as we used to.

(Factory manager 1)

The existing evidence suggests that great changes occur in parents'
friendship patterns during early parenthood. It shows that kin become an
important part of married couples' social networks (Ukoza 1979),
particularly in the early years of parenthood (Hoffman and Manis 1978).
Secondly, the general literature on friendship shows that the onset of
marriage and parenthood usually marks a decline in the numbers of friends
people tend to have (Schulman 1975) – a process which continues over the
life-span (Dickens and Perlman 1981). Thirdly, in keeping with the patterns
reported above, the research demonstrates that married men spend most
of their leisure time at home, and fathers across the social spectrum tend
to include their families in their leisure pursuits (Young and Willmott 1973).

The extent to which fathers become family-centred is shown in the
responses to a question asked about how often they discussed the child with
their friends outside work. It became apparent that some fathers have no
or few friends, while others change their social circle when they become
fathers. Twenty-three men discussed their children only with their family,
and sixteen others claimed not to talk about them with anyone. When
probed, many of these thirty-nine men made comments like: 'Oh, I haven't
got any friends outside as such, you know, I'm an unsociable swine' (factory
labourer). Most of these fathers gave the impression that as they took on
the responsibilities of parenthood they slowly lost touch with their friends.

A similar group of twenty-three men made it clear that they discussed
children only with other parents. A shared involvement in parenthood or
prospective parenthood appears to keep the link between them:

Um . . . don't see them very often now. I see friends that I used to
have very rarely now, you know. . . . There's probably one guy that I see
fairly often that, you know, I knew for a long while. Now he's married
but he hasn't got no children. . . . He's thinking about . . . they're
thinking about having a family so he's been asking me how we went
on when they were young and things like that. . . . So I tell him.

(Computer clerk)

There's a lot of . . . there's one or two couples with babies, same age,
so it's a case of swapping notes, you know. I suppose when you get
a small child, you tend to develop your friends in a similar position.
[Prompt: 'So you keep up your contacts with the ones with similar-
aged kids?'] Yeah, I should say far more than with friends without.
[Prompt: 'Is there any particular reason for that?'] I think you both

tend to appreciate that you're tied down to a greater extent, whereas when you haven't got a baby you want the freedom more, and I suppose if somebody wanders along with a baby you are restricted to an extent.

(Building-society trainee)

This father echoes a finding of Susan Bram's (1974) study of childless couples. She found that many felt uncomfortable with, and even consciously avoided, old friends with children, since parents appear to be so obsessed with their babies. Certainly many fathers were aware that they had been taken over by the child and that discussing him or her a great deal in company was, as the journalist put it, 'a little bit inevitable'.

Husbands and wives compared

While husbands and wives may make equal 'sacrifices' of their leisure pursuits, there often remains a significant difference between them in the activities they follow individually. In the early days, for example, there seems to be less pressure on men to stay at home to care for the baby. The vast majority of mothers never go out without their husbands during this period. However, more than half of the fathers (58 per cent) took the opportunity to go out alone during the first three months. Just how often men go out is unclear. In the small sample, the mothers were far more likely to say that their husbands went out once a week in the early days (53 per cent vs 20 per cent of fathers; $\chi^2 = 7.18$, df = 1, $p < 0.01$). Such a discrepancy appears to arise from parents' different interpretations of the term 'going out'. Husbands' descriptions of a quick drink at the pub compare with wives' accounts of a night out. As the first year of the child's life unfolds, fathers maintain this advantage.

A year after delivery, forty-seven men went out by themselves, usually for a night out with the 'lads'. This group contained more working-class fathers (58 per cent vs 36 per cent middle-class; $\chi^2 = 5.33$, df = 1, $p < 0.05$). However, we cannot infer from this finding that middle-class men are more home-centred, since they were more likely to find other, perhaps more legitimate reasons for leaving the home in the evening. They performed more hobbies and sports (60 per cent middle-class men performed at least two regularly vs 38 per cent working-class men; $\chi^2 = 4.84$, df = 1, $p < 0.05$), and had more 'commitments' to social activities at work, which included entertaining clients and office nights out (63 per cent vs 17 per cent working-class; $\chi^2 = 18.89$, df = 1, $p < 0.0001$).

Whether they simply 'go out' or pursue an organized activity, fathers are more involved than mothers outside the home. Even before the first child is expected the husband is far more likely to have these 'commitments' than his wife. For example, forty women were reported not to pursue any hobby or sport (and the mothers' data supports this) before they had a child. This contrasts with only eighteen of the men ($\chi^2 = 11.75$, df = 1,

$p < 0.001$). Men's activities seem to be so much better organized and expected:

> Well, always I've gone out a lot more than Christine, you know, 'cos I have me night out with the boys. I also go to the football match. [Prompt: 'That might be an evening one?'] Yeah . . . yeah, an evening one. Say, they played an evening one on a Wednesday, then I'd go to the match on Wednesday and have me Friday night out with the boys and praps take Christine out on a Saturday, see. [Prompt: 'What about Christine's sports and hobbies, what sort of thing did she get up to before the pregnancy?'] Ooh, hobbies . . . well, I think, you know, with going out to work and then coming home and having to do her household chores I don't think she had a lot of time, you know. [Prompt: 'So she didn't really have any regular ones?'] Um . . . not that I can think of, no.
>
> (Stock auditor)

In absolute terms fathers give up more leisure pursuits than their wives. Mothers tend to forgo their one activity, while only thirty-one fathers gave up all theirs. Most of them kept up their one or two favourite pastimes. Mothers and fathers appear to place different emphasis on the value of activities outside the home. Despite the fact that more men become involved in these, a clear trend in the data from the small sample suggests that it is they, rather than their wives, who express dissatisfaction about not being able to go out more (50 per cent vs 27 per cent of the wives; $\chi^2 = 3.45$, df = 1, $p < 0.07$).

Fathers' accounts of their outside leisure pursuits throw light upon their marriages and their commitments to the ideal of marital symmetry. For example, when asked about whether their wives minded them going out alone, the fathers divided into three groups. Firstly, fifteen men appeared to maintain their 'right' as bread-winners to go out, in defiance of their wives' preference:

> [Interviewer: 'Does Carol (wife) mind you going out alone?'] Yes [laughs]. [Prompt: 'Well, how do things work out, then?'] Er . . . she sometimes falls out with me. . . . I'm, as I say, I work hard and if I can't have a bit of leisure time, it isn't worth me . . . [Prompt: '. . . working so hard?'] . . . working so hard. That's the way I look at it. [Prompt: 'Does she usually agree with that?'] No, she doesn't agree with that. [Prompt: 'A fairly permanent disagreement?'] Yeah, we agree to disagree.
>
> (Plasterer's labourer)

A second group, of thirty-two men, went out regularly without reporting any matrimonial conflict. Their wives were more likely to go out to work or to have their own social activities. A sawyer, for example, traded his two nights out a week for his wife's outing on a Friday, the 'best night'.

The third and largest group of fifty-two fathers did not go out regularly without their wives. These either stressed a belief that husbands and wives should do things together, or claimed that their wives were reluctant for them to go out alone or together:

> When we were first married we decided that, you know, if we went out, we'd go together. . . . You know, we don't believe in going out separately because we believe it causes a rift . . . yeah . . . then such like as we'd say, 'Right, we'll go out perhaps on a Saturday night.' [Prompt: 'So you go out every week?'] That was very early on . . . but not now as we've got the babies and that, it's hardly ever.
>
> (Barreller)

> *Interviewer*: Does Sandra [wife] mind you going out alone?
> *Father*: No, I take her along as well.
> *Interviewer*: But you don't . . .
> *Father*: We decided that before, you see.
> *Wife*: I'd feel . . . I'd feel . . . if he said he was going out, I'd feel jealous 'cos I weren't going out.
> *Interviewer* (to wife): Then would you let him go out?
> *Wife*: Yeah, then we'd really have a row, you know.
> *Interviewer* (to wife): Yeah, but you said he hadn't done it that much?
> *Wife*: No.
>
> (Grade-room worker and wife, a housewife)

> [Interviewer: 'What about your outside interests?'] Yeah, well, you don't have the time or the money, now that she's packed up work so you've only got one wage and things have come up more . . . so . . . it all has to stop now, you see, from going out seven nights a week. We *did* realize that we would have to stop it. [Prompt: 'So you were living it up a bit, were you?'] Yeah, this was it, you see . . . see, we said that, when we spoke about having her, we said, 'All this has got to stop', you know. [Prompt: 'So you were ready for it, anyway?'] Yeah, but I'd just like her to go out at least once a week . . . but she won't leave her [baby]. [Prompt: 'Not even with you?'] No, well, I'd like to go out together, you know. [Prompt: 'Does Lindsay (wife) manage to get out by herself?'] She won't do it. . . . I'd said she was free to but she won't.
>
> (Records clerk)

> Well, we've always been together. It was only courting, I used to have one night off a week and I used to go up-town with me mate just for a drink. [Prompt: 'What about since you were married?'] Oh no, we've always been together. It's only this week that she's said I can go out on a Thursday night if I like. [Prompt: 'So it's going to be a regular thing?'] Well, it *might* be. It's only for a game of pool or snooker, like. . . . She don't mind, *I* leave it up to her, see. I say, well you know, 'Can I go out?' and if she says, 'All right', then I go.

It's up to her. *I* don't want to upset her. [Prompt: 'Have you ever asked her before and she's said no?'] She'll always say yes. If I say I want to go she'll always say yes.

(Plant operator)

Conclusion: Do mothers resent their husbands' less restricted role?

Parent's accounts of the changes in their marriage since the arrival of the child are too complex to measure along a singular dimension, like 'marital satisfaction'. Relationships undergo varying amounts of positive and negative change. A baby may give an unrewarding marriage some meaning, but may also detract from a relationship. Given that parents perform such different roles, their marriage almost necessarily will alter.

Not only do husbands undertake less child care; they also have more leisure pursuits than their wives. Mothers tend to be perceived as being 'tied down' or 'restricted'. We might, therefore, expect these women to resent their husbands' less restricted role. Yet close examination of the thirty mothers' interviews suggests that this is not usually the case. Not only do mothers expect to be more tied to the home, but they also appear to be pleasantly surprised by their husbands' contributions to family life. Men often give the impression that they are detached from any emotional involvement in relationships, and this has two effects upon their wives' perceptions of fathering.

Firstly, large numbers of women either have little to compare their husband's involvement with, or simply assume that their spouses are uniquely participant. Table 8.4 gives a breakdown of mothers' responses to a question concerning the differences between their husband and 'other fathers'. It shows that one woman felt her spouse was particularly non-participant, and five could see no difference between their own and other husbands. However, a majority of the women stated adamantly that their spouses were different, in that they were 'superior' or more involved than other men.

Table 8.4   Mother's impressions of her husband's involvement compared with other fathers (small sample)

Response category	*Frequency*
(a) Father is less involved than other fathers	1
(b) Father is involved as much as other men	5
(c) All fathers are different/Don't know	4
(d) Father is more involved than other men	16
	(Uncoded: 4)

The conviction with which mothers answered this question suggests that they were not simply trying to defend their husbands' self-esteem or their own reasons for marrying them. These mothers seemed genuinely surprised that their husbands 'helped' them so much and were convinced that they had a deeper relationship with their children than other men. This indicates either that I selected a uniquely involved sample of fathers, which seems highly unlikely, or that fathers will display their repressiveness and involvement only within a narrow social circle, which usually is confined to family members.

This latter alternative seems to be supported by the second feature apparent in the maternal interviews; irrespective of how participant the fathers actually were, seventeen (of the thirty) women expressed surprise that their husbands had become so involved with the child (and three others felt that they had been more involved in the early days than they expected). Occasionally chinks in the father's armour appear. His involvement and expressiveness are often a revelation to his wife:

> If I see him and he's reading a story and I'll be in here tidying up . . .
> and Thomas [older child] will be sat half on his knee and Jenny
> [one-year-old] will be on his knee . . . that looks lovely. I could never
> have pictured Dave [husband], before we had children, doing that.
> . . . He looks as though he loves them and its lovely.
> (Housewife, whose husband is a welder)

Despite the rhetoric about the symmetrical family, companionate marriage and emergent fatherhood, the mothers suggested that their husbands' emotional involvement is simply not expected of them. It is seen as a bonus by many. Such an expectation allows men the latitude to spend more time outside the home in leisure activities, as long as they perform the little that is demanded of them. It also means that when they display their emotional commitment to their children, such intimacy surprises their wives. As I shall suggest in the next chapter they also surprise themselves in the depth of feeling which they experience.

9   *The Experience of Fatherhood*

Discussion about the relationship between paternal involvement and the man's identity is rare, perhaps because we all too often cast men into the role of 'provider' – a figure who is detached from family intimacy. At the end of the last chapter it was suggested that the commitment of many fathers comes as quite a shock to a large proportion of their wives. Their expressive involvement contrasts with both the stereotypical picture of men and the part which many play in marriage.

Even to themselves, men's perceptions of fatherhood contain contradictions. They admit that they are less involved than their wives with the baby; and, as many of the excerpts from the interviews show, fathers often describe their roles in the prescribed 'detached' manner. Yet the interviews also repeatedly revealed a deep commitment to fathering, suggesting that many conceal their expressive feelings even from themselves.

Becoming a father usually involves experiencing hitherto unknown feelings. The three sections of this chapter attempt to characterize different aspects of the psychological change that are frequently mentioned by fathers. On one level the intensity of emotions generated by parenthood makes men find the experience continually surprising. Their involvement with the baby, however brief, repeatedly exposes the intimate side of the man's character; the child is a mirror, repeatedly bringing the man face to face with his emotions. Secondly, fatherhood fits into a man's pre-existing roles and relationships – hence its varied and complex nature. Fulfilling the roles of worker and father can cause psychological strain, but also initiates many into a new code of practices. Having more responsibilities commonly makes men perceive the world in different ways. On a third level, fathers have a great deal of themselves invested in their children. A baby both allows a father to be altruistic or expressive and also enables him to look to the future and measure his 'success' as an adult.

The First Year of Fatherhood: a Surprising Experience?

A number of the questions I asked the fathers attempted to go beyond the traditional stereotype of sturdy masculinity. These discussed the extent of the man's emotional involvement in fatherhood. To the question 'Have there been any surprises in what it is like to be parents?' more than half of the fathers (fifty-five) felt that parenthood was at least partly 'surprising' (some answered 'no' as they had expected their lives and feelings to be disrupted). More middle- than working-class men were in this group (66 per cent vs 44 per cent; $\chi^2 = 4.89$, df = 1, p<0.05). However, this class difference is probably far less important than the great variations in individual experience. The reasons given by men for such feelings of 'surprise' ranged from the depth of their involvement (15 per cent) to the anger and worry they had felt since the child's arrival (11 per cent). These fathers shared the belief that paternal involvement jolts a man into feelings of intensity, although many of these appeared to be unable to express such emotions:

> Some of the things Robert [older child] or Louise [one-year-old] does . . . I mean, it just gets you . . . I mean, there's no expressing it! [Prompt: 'What sort of things?'] Well . . . the first time he spoke . . . I mean, same as Louise the other night . . . I was having a milk the other night and she took her first step. . . . You know, I mean . . . you can't really put it into words . . . it's just a feeling of joy you get.
>
> (Disabled labourer)

> Well, if you've never had one you can't [describe what it's like to be a father]. . . . I don't think you can, really . . . like people have said to me, 'Oh, it's great to have a youngster and that.' But you can't feel the emotions until you've had one yourself. It's a really great experience, I mean I'd never swap her for the world now. [Prompt: 'so what sort of emotions do you feel that you'd never experienced before?'] Well, um . . . it's stumping me, this one, really. You know, when you walk into this room and you see her there . . . as soon as she sees you and her eyes light up, you know . . . bloody hell . . . and the next minute she's there, she's crawling, all over you, and you sit there and think 'Bloody hell, I never thought', you know, 'she's mine'.
>
> (Records clerk)

Fortunately, a few men were less tongue-tied and could summarize what made them feel so moved by the experience. Usually this meant linking a number of contrasting feelings:

> A sense of fulfilment . . . a sense of worry and a sense of wonder . . . being a father's so mixed up that you can't put your finger on any one thing. . . . It's all the emotions you've ever felt and probably will ever feel . . . so mixed up that you never know when they're going to come.
>
> (Primary schoolteacher 1)

It is these feelings – worry and wonder – which strike men almost out of the blue. As 'sturdy oaks' they often find that they cannot understand the feelings of intense love for, and sometimes hostility towards, the child. These surge up inside them, despite the role which many adopt as a support to other family members. Indeed, men themselves often dismiss their own feelings of involvement even though they may, for example, admit to missing their children while at work or if they arrive home to find them asleep.

A sense of wonder

In order to gain an impression of the depth of fathers' involvements with their children, I designed certain questions to breach convention and ask men directly about their feelings. For example, I invited them to comment upon whether anything about the child gave them a 'thrill'. Only five men complied with the traditional stereotype and said that there was nothing about the child which did so. The rest took the question very seriously, and their responses show that when asked they are able and willing to discuss their feelings in depth:

> I never thought I could . . . care, you know. . . . When other people talk about their children, you know, they feel . . . it just doesn't seem to register with yer. But now I understand the bond. . . . You know, it's made me more . . . I never thought I could have that sort of feeling for another person, outside of love for your wife, you know. It's another kind of love in fact, it's not a physical love . . . it's love.
>
> (Warehouse labourer)

> He's much more a great source of delight than I ever imagined possible . . . because, I'd say . . . to tell you the truth, I've never been very much, er, sent on babies. . . . As you've probably heard, I've never known much about babies. I've never had any real contact with them before Richard so, er, yes, he's been very much more a source of delight and pleasure for me than I would ever thought possible. [Prompt: 'What exactly about him makes him so . . . ?'] What exactly about him? I don't know, really . . . the fact that he does things . . . um, the fact that he sort of responds to . . . to one talking to him and so on, and this . . . talking about what he does now, really . . . but even in the earlier stages, the fact that he was there and attractive and I suppose I thought he was a beautiful baby and still do . . . you know he was a continual pleasure . . . well, not continual pleasure, no, not at three o'clock in the morning . . . but a great deal of fun to be had out of. [Prompt: 'And which sort of things had you thought weren't going to be as pleasant as that?'] No . . . I hadn't really . . . I hadn't really thought about that side of it in any detail. I suppose we had . . . I sort of wanted children because *people* wanted children, not because I knew much about them [laughs] . . . because we put it off long enough, sort of thing. . . . I never really thought about just what it would involve for me, what [the] pleasures

would be. I thought of the disadvantages and they're at least as bad as I imagined, but the advantages weren't clear to me in advance.

(Engineering lecturer)

In contrast to the belief that fathers make efforts to avoid becoming involved in child care, seventy-five men mentioned that their daily involvement in care-giving had struck them as being a rewarding and enjoyable experience. A few raised unexpected topics:

[Interviewer: 'Most fathers find that there are some things about looking after a baby which are much nicer than they expected. Has there been anything like that for you?'] Oh, yeah – er, minding the baby and changing the baby's nappy, which I thought I would hate, you know. . . . But it was like . . . one of the things I used to do was when the baby was sick, smelling the sick to make sure it wasn't . . . hadn't got acidic . . . that it was normal . . . that she'd just had enough and didn't want any more . . . the fact that the milk hadn't curdled in her stomach . . . so smelling sick and examining stools and what-have-you. [Prompt: So you enjoyed all that?'] Oh yeah, fabulous.

(Industrial relations officer)

More typically fathers mentioned routine aspects of care-giving, like putting the child to bed, or as was discussed with reference to the early days of the child's life, checking him or her at night:

We always look at Mark before we get into bed ourselves and I'm usually last in bed. Almost every night I go in to make sure he's all right and I just say to him, 'Night-night, sweetheart', or summat like that. I feel something . . . what? Love . . . and he's laid there so peacefully, you know. . . . He's such a good lad, it's great having him . . . he's bags of fun.

(Spring maker)

Fear and loathing: a sense of worry
As the engineering lecturer quoted above suggested, fatherhood is obviously not just a bed of roses. There are aspects of the experience which do not give men a thrill. After a year of fathering, they usually suggest that the positive feelings outweigh the negative ones in their intensity, but many admitted that they still experienced a mixture of extreme emotions. For example, twenty-eight men had been surprised by the anger or despair they had felt. These fathers were struck by the intensity of their hostility towards their children, particularly at times when they disrupt their parents' sleep or are grizzly:

We've been surprised as to how angry we can become with a defenceless thing like a baby and we can understand more how people do hit them. 'Cos the pressures are unbelievable when they're screaming for hours on end . . . and how much they provoke you really . . . I think that's the biggest shock of anything.

(Lift engineer)

Since these twenty-eight men recalled having experienced extreme emotions in the early days without being asked direct questions about such feelings, it may well be that more fathers experience them, particularly in the early days of parenthood. At this time parents have to adapt quickly to the baby's needs and also to their own emotional reactions. As the lift engineer implies, some may feel intense anger after a succession of sleepless nights, while others, like the spring maker quoted above, are often taken aback by the responsibility for their dependent children. Indeed, some of the men who reported only 'positive' emotions found their feelings hard to cope with. For example, eighteen men described their emotions as being 'protective' and many of these also reported feeling over-anxious or even disturbed in their attempt to protect the child.

In a recent study Kerr and Mckee (1981) concluded that while women experience acute worries about the child's well-being and health their husbands adopt the 'sturdy oak' role and perceive worrying as pointless. They found that half their sample of women admitted to these fears, but only two out of a sub-sample of thirteen of their husbands did so. The results of this larger investigation suggest that the proportions of fathers and mothers who report having acute worries are similar and (like the mothers in Kerr and Mckee's study) just under 50 per cent report having experienced these anxieties. These fathers mentioned a variety of fears, which included the future of the world, the rate of the child's development and most frequently the fears that arise when the child is ill or hurt.

[Interviewer: 'What's the worst thing for you?'] Not being able to help when they're ill or anything and they can't tell you what's the matter with them, you know, and you keep giving them different things and it doesn't seem to be helping them. I think that's the hardest thing to cope with.

(Refuse collector)

The Social Institution of Fatherhood

In order to understand the experience of fatherhood we must secondly consider the relationship between the man's two 'lives': his home and his work. Sociologists (Allen and Barker 1976) and psychologists (Pleck 1977) have pointed out that researchers have failed to link these two spheres. The small amount of existing research suggests that men suffer conflicts in trying to fulfil obligations to one or both parts of their lives (O'Brien 1982). The following two sections will argue that work necessarily reduces a father's involvement in parenting, but at the same time he may confirm his status as father in his daily interactions with his work-mates.

Home–work conflicts

I asked the fathers directly whether their work prevented them from leading a 'full life' at home. The unemployed men were asked either to recall a time when they were not in work or to consider the circumstances of men with children. Fathers responded in two ways. Thirty-nine men accepted their role as provider for the family and saw no conflict between home and work because their domestic role was limited.

> [Interviewer: '(What about) your life in the home?'] In the home . . . sort of family? . . . As full as the social 'norm' for England at the present time [laughs] . . . in that it is expected that the father goes out to work and so on . . . and sees the children mostly in the evenings the weekends. . . . Then, yes, I think they we comply with that 'norm' reasonably well. . . . I think one can . . . you've got to strike some sort of balance between work and home and we're reasonably happy with the balance we've got.
>
> (Engineering lecturer)

Sixty-one fathers felt that their work lives impinged upon their roles as fathers. Given the length of some men's work schedules, this response is not surprising. However, the father's employment status did not seem to influence his views on the matter. All but a few of these men seemed to accept that their domestic role was necessarily limited:

> Well, I find, you know, when I do come 'ome . . . 'cos I do a lot of overtime . . . so when I come 'ome I am tired, you know. . . . I can't . . . I don't play with her more than two hours. . . . If I'm tired, you know, I don't feel like going up, I don't feel like helping to wash the dishes or anything.
>
> (Power-station labourer)

> I'd like to spend more time with him . . . obviously . . . you can't that's it. . . . You've . . . you've got to pay for the house and all this sort of thing . . . it's just the system, ain't it.
>
> (Road construction worker)

> I'd like to spend more time at home when he's awake. At the moment I seem to get in when he's just going to sleep or leaving when he's waking up. [Prompt: 'So what do you think you miss out on?'] Well, things like . . . you know, you asked me earlier what he has for his meals . . . I don't know every detail. Sort of thing, I haven't thought to ask when I get home. It's only when you come along and ask me questions that you realize that you're missing out.
>
> (Bank clerk)

Status changes

The relationship between a man's work and home lives cannot fully be understood in terms of the conflict between them. As was mentioned in Chapter 8, many feel more 'mature' or 'responsible' as a result of becoming fathers. These often experience such feelings through investing more of their efforts and commitment at work:

> Well, it's obviously altered socially. . . . Er, you feel you're more dependent upon work. You know, you've got to make more effort to get there and stay there . . . not inclined to have a week off. [Prompt: 'Anything else?'] Not really, apart from, you know, I look forward to seeing him when I can.
>
> (Panel beater)

> The responsibility is a big one with me. You know, I've got to think three instead of two . . . a sort of progression, you know. You sort of think one, then you get married . . . you think two and then you think three. . . . I've got to think about the way things are at work . . . work's it going to be like in ten years' time? I've got to supply for three now and soon four.
>
> (Product development officer)

Work may be drudgery, but it can also give men certain rewards. Apart from earning the main family income and being able to 'escape' from home during the day, employment is usually socially stimulating for fathers. The onset of parenthood seems to increase some men's social status at work. Firstly, it may enhance a man's perceptions of his standing amongst his colleagues:

> I feel more sort of experienced about life. Having been through it and having a daughter, I feel more responsible. Um, at work I find that . . . with sort of being the youngest on the management grade at work, I think that being married and having a child . . . I think other women especially've got more respect for you because you've got the child . . . obviously you've got more responsibility. . . . I think they see that as a sign of being a bit more mature than somebody at that age who was single and not having a child.
>
> (Assistant contracts officer)

Secondly, new parents often become part of a social network. They may join in discussion about children, learning from others, or relaying messages about child care to their wives. This man talked regularly to a colleague with older children:

> I tell him what she's been up to and he'll sort of compare it with what his kids was like when they was little. [Prompt: 'Does he give you advice or is it just a question of comparing notes?'] Um . . .

yes . . . comparing notes. I went and told him we was having trouble with her teeth and he went back and told his wife and she sent a message back, 'We used to use this', you see.

(Central-heating mechanic)

They also relish giving advice to 'pregnant' colleagues and those with younger children. The fathers were significantly more likely to discuss their child at work than with friends (76 per cent vs 61 per cent? $\chi^2 = 4.82$, df = 1, p<0.05). Fifty-five men engaged in regular, if not daily, conversations.

As with their friends, men appeared to discuss children with other parents, not just anyone. Two further factors seemed to be associated with the amount men discussed their children at work. Firstly, those who worked long hours were significantly less likely to do this (50 per cent vs 74 per cent of fathers who did not work long hours; $\chi^2 = 5.29$, df = 1, p<0.05). Secondly, and not independently, more fathers from the middle of the class spectrum, and significantly more non-professional white-collar workers, became involved (86 per cent of social class III (w.c.) vs 54 per cent of other classes; $\chi^2 = 7.13$, df = 1, p<0.01). These differences arise for a number of reasons. To begin with, clerical workers say they find the time to chat during work hours more than their professional or blue-collar counterparts. They also appeared to have more invested in their roles as parents; for example, some exchanged photographs with their colleagues.

'Being' a Father

Variations between fathers

It has been argued above that the transition to fatherhood must be understood in terms of both the disruptions to a man's life and the social changes which occur as a result of the onset of parenthood. I will turn now to examine briefly the impact of these changes upon the father's perceptions of himself. There is great variation within the social institution of fatherhood, and men can experience their new status in many seemingly contrasting ways. Let us, for example, examine the accounts of two men who were asked to summarize the experience of fatherhood. The first channels his emotions through his work, while the second describes the joy of his daily interactions with his children:

> I am quite incapable of describing it. I'm inarticulate. . . . It's so tied up with an emotional state, I mean . . . you describe it? It's certainly brings out in me a protective instinct which I feel is quite natural . . . and I suppose probably shows itself. . . . I react to that instinct by working harder than I might otherwise, so that ultimately somebody can collect the insurance when I pop off . . . which is a slightly peculiar way of looking at it. . . . I have set that as one of my targets in

life . . . to provide them with an adequate education, which I think they can thereafter do what they please. . . . I know that was the way my father looked on it with me.

(Managing director)

To explain to someone what it's like being a parent is practically impossible. . . . Um . . . what I get out of it is to get up in the morning and . . . well, the best part about being a parent is at night before you go to bed, is to go into Roy's [older child] bedroom, look at . . . fast asleep and even now you check whether he is breathing . . . kiss him good night . . . out the room into Adelle's [one-year-old] room . . . make sure she's all right. And to me that is being a parent – to be able to do that. And for him to come up to you . . . the first thing I remember with him, really remember, is the first time he came up and said, 'Dad, can I have . . .' and I thought that was brilliant. I went out and bought it. He's never stopped it since [laughs]. [Prompt: 'So what is it about checking them to make sure they're OK that sort of sums it up?'] You know, you're checking them to make sure they're OK and everything, but you look down and you think, 'That's ours', you know. [Prompt: 'So . . . anything else about being a dad?'] Yeah, you also like this bit where they're dependent on you. It's nice to have a family and . . . when people turn round and say, 'Oh, kids are awful', and . . . when you hear people saying, 'I'm not going to have any kids when I get married', and 'I'm not going to get married . . . not going to have any kids', you know you could really sit down sometimes and tell them what you think of them. [Prompt: 'What would you say to them?'] What would I say to them? I'd . . . you know, I'd ask them to come round to our house on a typical Sunday. . . . O.K. . . . sometimes we get up and have a moan at each other and a moan at the kids, but you know, throughout the day . . . if you only have ten minutes' joy a day playing with them, you know, it's brilliant, it's . . . something everyone should experience, at least. When people turn round and say, 'Oh, it's a nice baby – who's is it?' It's . . . great. It brings people together, it brings families together. To care for somebody, that must be the best part.

(Transport manager's assistant)

However, fathers involve themselves in the business of caring for or protecting the child – by working harder or simply enjoying their company, for example – we cannot assume that one type of man 'experiences' the role in a qualitatively 'better' way. Such judgements can only be subjective. Throughout this study I have stressed the commonalities between and variations in men's approaches to parenthood. By and large there appear to be few differences between the members of the four social class groups that were examined. However, it seems fair to suggest that some fathering styles are more common to men with certain occupations. For example, the managing director quoted above is typical of many professional workers who invest a great deal of commitment in their jobs. These often describe such efforts as being of benefit both to themselves and to their children.

The one occupational group which stands out as being more directly involved in the role of father is the non-professional white-collar workers – social class III (w.c.). As has been said in earlier chapters, these men were more likely to participate in child care and family-centred activities at key times during the period of study. For example, they tended to take longer periods of leave around the time of the child's delivery, they scored consistently highly on individual measures of child care and, since they often work flexi-hours, were significantly more likely to assist in the care of the child in the mornings. In addition, as a group they were more likely to express a belief in becoming directly and openly involved with their children. So, for example, more members of this group would engage their colleagues at work in discussion about their one-year-olds' antics. Their accounts of parenthood, like that of the transport manager's assistant quoted above, show this emphasis. For these workers more than any other group parenthood is often depicted as a central feature of life:

> What does it mean to me personally? . . . It means fulfilment . . . my life, actually, as far as *I* see it. . . . There are two things . . . well, three things, I wanted. The third, which I put as happiness, is sort of coupled with the other two; I wanted to get married and have children. I've got my child and as far as I'm concerned my dreams are fulfilled. It doesn't matter what financial reward I get from anything, it will never compensate for the happiness I'm getting from the family. [Prompt: 'Does that sum it up completely?'] No, well, just to add to what . . . it's made me a responsible person rather than a person with responsibilities. It's settled me down, anyway. Yeah, outlook *does* change . . . it changes quite dramatically, but it changes for the better. It doesn't matter *what* age you are when you become a father. . . . It's at that point that you grow up.
>
> (Civil servant 2)

Fathering and identity: shared experiences
Fatherhood, defined by men of all ages as the 'point that you grow up', can effect an alteration in the ways in which men see themselves. The change in life-style and added responsibility usually give rise to shifts in the father's perceptions of his past, present and future. My colleague, Rex Stainton Rogers (personal communication) coined the term 'life-phase identity', to describe the man's identification with a position in the life-span.

(1) First- and second-timers compared
Implicit within most studies of the transition to parenthood (discussed in Chapter 1) is the belief that the arrival of the first child marks a shift in

the parent's progression through the life-cycle: from youth to adult, for example. Similar sentiments are apparent in parents' accounts, perhaps because they reflect a cultural prescription about how one will change. However, the notion that first parenthood marks a single transition is too simple. Firstly, the arrival of a child initiates a feeling of change, but one which does not necessarily suggest 'growth' through the life-cycle. For example, two men in their forties were convinced that paternity had rejuvenated them. I therefore use the term 'phase' rather than 'stage', because it does not imply that 'development' is a single, one-way process. Secondly, first- and second-timers usually describe parallel life-phase changes in their perceptions. While there are differences between them, which I shall discuss first, there are also obvious similarities.

First-time parents almost always experience greater change in their lives, simply because they have few experiences to compare it with and also as their life-styles usually change in more dramatic ways. They may, for example, move out of their parents' home during this period. Their psychological adjustment at key times in early parenthood was reported to be more intense. As was suggested in earlier chapters, their emotions around the time of delivery are heightened. They tend to describe the early months of parenthood as being more restricting, even though they usually have more time to devote to their child on a one-to-one basis.

However, second-time fathers experience similar a sort of shift in their perceptions. They appear to feel that the new baby disrupts their life-styles in other ways. Chapter 3, for example, showed that second-timers were more likely to be cast into the role of 'sturdy oak', protecting their wives, who become 'ratty' during pregnancy. After the child's arrival there was no indication that second-timers settled into their new roles more easily. For example, I asked men whether they had ever found having a baby around difficult, expecting first-timers to be far more likely to give an affirmative response. In fact, significantly more second-timers described their adjustment to the baby as being problematic, although, as Table 9.1 shows, this result was accounted for by a difference between first- and second-timers in the middle-class groups. Working-class men and middle-class second-timers were more likely to state that having a baby around was difficult. Blue-collar workers mention the financial strains caused by parenthood. For second-timers the main reason given was the demand imposed by having two children to care for, as well as having an extra mouth to feed.

Despite some differences in the nature of their experiences, first- and second-timers describe changes in their lives and perceptions that are very similar. Consider the following accounts. The first quotation comes from a young father who was twenty at the time of his son's delivery. He recalls how he became an adult and a parent at the same time. The arrival of his child enabled him to leave his parents' household, set up his own home

Table 9.1   Fathers' adjustment to parenthood ('Have you found it difficult having a baby around or has everything come quite easily?')

	Some difficulties	None
Middle-class men		
First-timers	11	19
Second-timers	14	5

$\chi^2 = 6.38$, df $= 1$, p < 0.02.

Working-class men		
First-timers	22	8
Second-timers	16	4

$\chi^2 = 0.29$, df $= 1$, NS.

and adopt a different way of life. Like many other fathers he gave up being 'cheeky' or fighting and has become 'respectable'. He attributes the cause of this change in attitude to his son. The second quotation comes from a father of two children. He experiences similar feelings of psychological movement through the life-cycle.

> I tell you, it's given me a lot . . . it's put me in, like, a new world, I tell you. I got me own responsibilities, I've got no orders from me dad . . . me parents or nobody. I've got me own responsibilities. I can do what I want. I've got me own home. Got a wife, kid . . . and she does what she wants, you know. We talk about things ourself, you know. Mum can't say, 'Get out.' You know, I do what I want. I got what I want. [Prompt: 'And this is the result of having a kid, do you think?'] Yeah, I think . . . all to do . . . I think it's Thomas [one-year-old] who's brought me and Judith [wife] up to what we are now. He's brought us up . . . he's respectable . . . we're not cheeky, you know. I used to get involved with a lot of things, fighting especially, but now when you're married you don't want to. . . . He's made me grown up, that's all I can say. . . . I've been like a kid.
>
> (Scrap-yard labourer)

> Er, it's a full life. . . . I'd say, don't have one . . . [have] at least two . . . because your life alters with one, from just being a couple. . . . Your life completely alters with one, but when the second one comes along it completely alters again. [Prompt: 'How does it alter again?'] Well, your whole attitude alters again. . . . Instead of just having one child to look after you've all of a sudden got another one, and you think to yourself. . . . Where people had told me before I had children

life would alter as much as it did I'd have said, 'No way.' It's completely altered. [Prompt: 'How has the second one altered it?'] Well, the first one you still have that feeling of, er, independence. . . . With two you've got to give yourself entirely . . . you can't say, 'I'm going to do such and such' . . . [Prompt: 'For any particular reasons?'] No . . . you couldn't say, 'I want to go to the motor racing this weekend', because basically it's not a family 'do'. . . . If you're going to be a family person, you say, 'Right, we'll go . . . take a picnic to the park, where you can have swings, or take a ball and play', whereas. . . . You've got to give your life to your family.

(Newsagent 2)

(2) Thre life-phase identity changes: achievement, sacrifice, investment
All the fathers admitted that they had been changed in some way, when asked to reflect on how fatherhood had influenced them. The descriptions of both first- and second-time fathers contained three themes, which I shall outline here. Firstly, they describe their current role as 'fulfilment' or an 'achievement'. Having a dependant marks a shift from one status to another irrespective of whether the child is the first or second:

It's an achievement, really, great . . . great achievement . . . watching him grow up and that, like . . . seeing if you can make him a bit better than yourself, like.

(General labourer)

Well, for me, it's been just a big . . . terrific experience. I've really enjoyed it. I think it's like nothing else you could experience. Oh, it's really fulfilling in a way, but how you could explain it I don't know. [Prompt: 'Well, I'm asking you to . . .'] Well, you're . . . I mean, a child is somebody who's completely dependent on you – you know, they're completely dependent on you, and you also know that everything you do in life with them is going to affect them – how they grow up, and . . . I'm a real believer in the nature and nurture thing. I believe you can change a child, how they grow up, by what you do with them. So in a way it's a great responsibility; if you make a mess of it it's your fault. And I think you've got to give as much experiences as possible. I think that's what's enjoyable about it. It's really rewarding seeing how they grow up and depend on you. [Prompt: 'Do you think that dependency could be an upset to the father, because of the pressures put on you?'] It could upset some people. It doesn't upset me, 'cos I think if you feel you're doing your best for them, you can't do any more, can you? I mean, I wouldn't think, 'Oh, should've done this', or . . . if we don't take the kids swimming for a few weeks 'cos we can't be bothered, I feel bad, you know – or if I think I'm too lazy to take them out for the weekend, I feel a bit guilty, I suppose.

(Primary-school deputy head)

Like mothers, fathers will commonly compare their offspring with other children. A man's children become a measure of his success as a parent and therefore as an adult. Other children tend to be seen as less bright or unattractive. These feelings were repeated many times during the interviews. Whatever the reasons for fathers' claims, it is clear that their frequent comparisons of their own children with others influence their attitudes towards their new status as parents:

> He's even handsome. Well, I mean, it's obvious [laughs]. [Wife: 'Yes, he takes after his mum'.] What was his name, that little lad . . . ugly . . . 'My God, he looks like a monkey.' . . . That was his father talking. He was dead right. The ugliest baby you've seen in your life, looked better from the back. This one's quite a reasonable specimen, really.
>
> (Financial controller)

Secondly, fatherhood changes a man's outlook, since it forces him to make 'sacrifices' for the child. The father gives up his freedom or 'youth' in order to nurture the child. His sacrifice is a measure of his new 'middle-aged' outlook:

> I've matured a lot since, since he's been here. I realize I've got more than meself to care about – got to be a bit more careful, you know – work to keep this house, work to keep us together and work to keep us comfortable. [Prompt: 'Is your life different in any way?'] It makes you, yeah, it puts a burden on you, it does, er, I think it does because you know that you've got a child and, you know, that you want your best for him. It's just the actual getting the best for him that's the problem. You know what you want, it's just a question of gerr'in it and how about it. How about gerr'in it. [Prompt: 'So that puts quite a strain on you?'] It does sometimes, yeah. I do feel as though I'm working a lot harder – but I will get the benefits when I see him perhaps, you know, such as yourself at university or something like that, he'll be gerr'in something I've never had.
>
> (Mobile grocer)

> He's added to it dramatically. He's made me drift into the . . . what Elizabeth, both Elizabeth and myself felt was middle-aged . . . boring . . . I don't know, middle age, middle class. It's what we epitomize as the family life which we now absolutely fill to a tee. And I suppose the only reason I'm prepared to accept that . . . the alternatives that we would enjoy are the socializing, pub-going, restaurant-going, cinema-going . . . and as I say, the only reason we are prepared to accept this dramatic change is because of his, the benefits he brings. Of course we would have been prepared to accept it whatever he was like, and he happens to be a pretty ace child.
>
> (Doctor)

Thirdly, as the fathers quoted above suggest, the child is an investment for the future. The work that fathers invest in nurturing the child may pay off in two ways. The child will fulfil ambitions not achieved by the father himself, or will become a friend later in life. In both cases the man casts his mind to the future:

> Well, I think a lot of it is seeing them grow, the development . . . um. They develop far more quickly, whereas with your wife I s'pose you don't tend to notice the development 'cos you're both growing old at the same rate, whereas the child – one minute he's not walking, then he's running about and no teeth and then teeth. . . . Um, I s'pose you could put – I s'pose you can try and help and hope that they can achieve some of your unfulfilled ambitions. [Prompt: Do you think that that's a general feeling that dads have?'] I should think so, yeah.
>
> (Building-society trainee)

> It's nice. I can't imagine going through life being married without kids. . . . I don't know why. OK, you get married, but why do you get married, then? OK, it's only a roll of paper and people have kids without getting married, but . . . I don't know why . . . I like the set-up, the way it's run, and you get married and you bring up a family in time. And you enjoy it. You can look back on it and think you've achieved something while you've been alive. And, er . . . it's great. . . . I want to grow up with them. . . . I don't want to be the dad or the old man, sort of thing . . . I want to be alive with them and I want to enjoy things. I want to be a friend. [Prompt: 'Is it going to be easy, do you think . . . that sort of relationship?'] Oh, no . . . I'll have to work at it, yeah, but now's the time. I never had that, you see . . . and I think, 'Well, it's great.' My biggest pal is my step-father . . . and he still is. And that's only the relationship from when I was about nine, and that's kept with me. . . . I didn't have a father up till then. Then we started to play cricket, football . . . I did all the things I didn't do with my real father. And I want to do that with Luke . . . not necessarily with Heather 'cos she's a girl . . . but definitely with Luke anyway.
>
> (Carpet salesman)

Conclusion

Whatever a man's previous parental status, parenthood will most likely make him experience a feeling of disequilibrium. Just as fatherhood usually heightens a man's emotions and influences the way he perceives his social status and relationships, it also has the potential to change or reinforce many of his basic ideals. Some express a firm belief in the importance of parenthood to men. They may do so in order to reduce the dissonance caused by the disruption to their lives. Alternatively, they may genuinely feel that life is better with children. Whatever their reasons, many used the interview to preach the virtues of fathering, or to state emphatically that life before they became parents was 'boring' or unfulfilling:

> Well . . . I feel that when it all boils down to it, that's what we're basically on earth to do – procreate the species – that it would be perversion, no, not a perversion, a diversion from natural route to consciously avoid having children. And I thought this before having Sophie, and having had Sophie I'm even more convinced that it's the case. And I'd say to anyone . . . 'It's great and go ahead.'
>
> (Customs executive officer)

> In a way it's like being part of . . . part of one whole person. Er, the four – in our case the four – of us . . . if it was just the three of us even . . . tend to be like me. You seem to share moments that you wouldn't if you was on your own, if you see what I mean . . . certain things amongst you . . . it's just a matter of sharing – something shared always seems to be more enjoyable. . . . Plus the supportive bit where you're helping between you to bring the child up. [Prompt: 'So you're equally supportive?'] Rather than a dominant one, yeah. I'd say we're equals . . . hopefully a helping hand along the way as they grow up, you know, there to be able to admire and to share moments with them. And help them with whatever they're interested in.
>
> (Lift engineer)

The vast majority of fathers claim that their child has a major influence upon their identity. For example, the transport manager's assistant quoted above said that he liked the fact that his children were dependent upon him. Earlier in the interview he had remarked that this dependence was reciprocal; he relies upon them as much as they do on him:

> It's . . . it's great, you know – to notice them doing things and to . . . you know. But in fact they seem to help you rather than you helping them all the time. [Prompt: 'In what ways?'] They bring you a bit closer together as regards . . . um . . . they depend upon you. . . . You tend to depend on them, you know – they mean a lot.
>
> (Transport manager's assistant)

Similar sentiments were expressed in other interviews. So strong are parents 'bonds' with their one-year-olds that the following statement reflects many fathers' perspective upon their relationships:

> I suppose I've been surprised at my emotions sometimes, but . . . yeah, to me, without the kids, you know, I don't know what I'd do. . . . And things like this . . . and if anything ever happened to them I'd crack up . . . I think I would crack up, actually . . . you know, that sort of emotion and . . . you're probably just as dependent on them as they are on you . . . that sort of emotion, really.
>
> (Engineer's clerk)

10 All Change? The Historical Context of Fatherhood

Introduction

This chapter will discuss some of the wider issues which were raised in the introduction to this study. The stage of fatherhood which I have examined forms but a short part of a 'career' that can last almost a lifetime and changes considerably as father and child progress through the life-span. This discussion will consider fathers' perceptions of their past and future, and will compare the accounts they give with some evidence concerning the changing patterns of fatherhood, both generally through the life-cycle and during the lifetime of the present generation of new parents.

The chapter divides into three main sections. Firstly, I will examine the fathers' comparisons of themselves with their own parents. In keeping with the 'emergent' image of fatherhood, many men describe themselves as being more involved with their children than their parents were. In the second part I will consider this view from other angles. These suggest that the optimism of contemporary parents may indeed be partly caused by a shift in parenting roles, which has been influenced greatly by technological changes. However, the optimism of new parents also reflects their stage in the life-cycle. Longitudinal data and these fathers' perceptions of the future suggest that their future roles as fathers may not always be as bright. In the third section I will return to the issue of social change, by focusing particularly upon the employment patterns and prospects of the parents in this study. The apparent dramatic changes in maternal employment will be contrasted with the parents' attitudes towards the divisions of labour between the sexes at home and at work; the stereotypes of man as bread-winner and woman as mother seem to be as strong as ever.

Then and Now: Men's Reflections on Changing Fathering Roles

I asked the men and women to compare specifically their own parenting styles with those of their parents. Both mothers and fathers suggested that

166

parenthood today is different from what it was twenty years ago and before. While the nature of the discussion varied considerably it is fair to suggest that, in keeping with the new emergent ideal, a majority of parents feel that dramatic material change and increases in parental involvement with their children have taken place during their own lifetimes. This feeling of change was apparent in three areas of discussion, which I will turn to now: (1) child-care patterns in recent times; (2) attitudinal differences between the respondents and their own parents; (3) fathers' reflections on their own fathers' involvement in parenting.

General changes since the parents' own childhood
Table 10.1 gives a breakdown of responses to the general question, 'Do you think that it's much the same bringing up children now as it was for your parents, or do you feel there are big differences?'

Four men considered that parenthood is more difficult now than it was for their parents. These were all young, working-class fathers who found it hard financially to afford to care for a young baby. While some young fathers, particularly in times of increasing unemployment, may perceive their role as hard for financial reasons, a majority (including all the fathers in this sample who *were* out of work) felt that times are far easier now than they used to be. Both working- and middle-class men often mentioned the support given to parents from professioinals and commented even more frequently upon on the dramatic increase in household aids:

> It's different now . . . a lot easier now. You've got more things to buy now from what you used to buy. . . . Well, a few years ago there wasn't any nappy-pads, no sterilizing equipment. You didn't have a choice of babies' clothes in those days 'cos we wasn't so well off as we are now. Nowadays you can buy what you want. Well, I can . . . a lot of people can't. If she wants something now she gets it.
>
> (Warp knitter)

Table 10.1   Fathers' comparisons of the similarities and differences for themselves and their parents as parents

Response category	*Frequency*
(a) It is easier for us	62
(b) There are no differences	11
(c) The differences are mixed	19
(d) Parenthood is harder these days	4
	(Uncoded: 4)
Total:	100

It's a lot easier for . . . I would have said . . . women nowadays to bring up children now with all the amenities such as automatic washing-machines and . . . and stuff like that, than it was then . . . um. . . . I would've said so . . . I mean, when I was a child it was a mangle and . . . um, a brush rather than a Hoover. [Prompt: 'So apart from the equipment are there any other differences?'] Um, that, er, again depends very much on the parents . . . I suppose, on how good they could or how bad they could cope. Beside that I wouldn't have said there was a tremendous amount of difference in that.

(Unemployed sales representative)

Certainly material advances such as these have taken place. These are often cited by fathers as a cause of increased paternal involvement. However, as was argued in Chapter 1, such changes in domestic technology make it difficult to compare one generation with the next.

Attitudinal differences between parents and their own parents

Table 10.2 shows fathers' responses to a question asking them to compare their attitudes about child care with those of their parents. One-third (thirty-six) felt that their ideas were roughly similar. This group contained significantly more skilled manual workers (52 per cent of class III (m.) vs 32 per cent of men from the other social class groups; $\chi^2 = df = 1$, $p < 0.05$). While this finding is not explained by the data or accounts, I got the impression that the skilled workers were closer to their parents, since they generally lived nearer to them than white-collar workers and expressed a closeness that was not often described by unskilled workers.

While some saw few differences in outlook, a majority of fathers felt that they differed from their parents, as Table 10.2 indicates. These men espoused the belief that today's fathers are more involved with their children. Some mentioned that they are less strict, while others stressed that they,

Table 10.2 'What about your ideas and attitudes compared to your parents – do you think your ideas on bringing up children are different from theirs?'

Response category	*Frequency*
(a) Our ideas are similar	36
(b) A few 'minor' differences mentioned	8
(c) I am more child-centred (e.g. more involved psychologically = 22; less strict = 24)	54
(d) I am more strict	1
Total:	99

unlike their parents, had more to offer in terms of help. Companionship or affection.

> I know it sounds awful, but I try to base the way I bring my children up the opposite to the way I [was] brought up. I don't think I [was] brought up very well. . . . I don't think they had much thought for either myself or my brother. I don't think they had much consideration, nor much . . . what shall I say? . . . affection. The course of actions during their lives . . . didn't have a very good effect on me. I didn't have a very happy home life. It had its good moments, but it had a lot of bad moments. I don't think, from a discipline point of view, I hardly had any discipline. I could have turned out to be the typical 'bad-home' juvenile delinquent or what you want to call it, but I didn't take advantage of the situation. . . . Well, they never . . . from a schooling point of view, there was no interest. With my kids I'm not going to say I'm going to shove schooling down their throats but I shall give them encouragement, let's put it that way.
>
> (Sales engineer)

> Very, very different . . . [Prompt: 'In which respect?'] Um, I think that their idea of a good upbringing was to provide a warm place to sleep, adequate clothes and plenty to eat and that, um . . . if you'd managed to do all three things while your child was growing up, then you'd succeeded. That was what parenthood was about, that, um, generally. . . . The concept of what parents can do for their children nowadays has expanded greatly beyond that . . . um, partly because it's now easier to provide the physical comforts and partly because of the realization of what parents can do with their children. [Prompt: 'So is it just the realization or is it something more than that . . . that's caused this shift?'] Well, I think that work has been done to show parents what they can do for their children, you know . . . at all levels, really, um . . . that you know . . . I think that you will find very few people who don't realize that a parent can influence the . . . you know, their young children and that, er . . . how well they do and how happy they are, and how well they get on at school. . . . A lot of them, you know, haven't got any idea of what they should do in order to do it but, um, they realize it should be done.
>
> (Primary schoolteacher 2)

The wives in the small sample were significantly more likely to stress the similarities between themselves and their parents (54 per cent vs 24 per cent of the husbands in the small sample; $\chi^2 = 3.98$, df = 1, $p < 0.05$). This may suggest that men, more than women, feel that they are breaking new ground in developing a family-centred role.

Fathers' recollections of their own fathers

When asked specifically about their own fathers' involvment with them as children the men seemed to give clear support for the emergent view

Table 10.3 Fathers' own fathers' involvement with them as children

Response category	Frequency
(a) No father (died, or separated from mother)	8
(b) No involvement	12
(c) Involved less than weekly (i.e. on special occasions	23
(d) Regular involvement (i.e. played more than weekly)	42
(e) Regular involvement and some care-giving (i.e. put to bed weekly)	8
(f) Regular involvement and (daily) care-giving	6
Total:	99

of fatherhood. Table 10.3 gives a breakdown of their recollections. It must be set in context by the fact that 73 per cent of the fathers claimed to be involved in one child-care activity on a daily basis. Only one of these admitted that he undertook no child care from one week to the next. In contrast, as the table shows, only fourteen men remembered their fathers doing *any* care-giving at any age in their development or even felt that it was likely that they became involved.

The largest group of fathers (forty-two) remembered their own fathers as playmates, and thirty-five felt that they showed absolutely no interest or became involved only on special occasions, like family outings. Typical comparisons are:

> My father? . . . My father virtually had nothing to do with my brothers and sisters at all. . . . This was because he was an old-type miner. . . . You know, he went out to work, he did a good day's work for a bad day's pay and he came home and he went to the nearest pub. [Prompt: 'What about in the home, did he help at all?'] Very, very seldom. [Prompt: 'So what sort of things did he do with you?'] What did he do with us? . . . Er, I can't remember, going back . . . I can't actually remember my father ever playing a game with us as children, apart from when we started going on holidays . . . when I would be about nine, ten years old.
>
> (Finance company representative)

> Well, I think there's differences certainly. I think I take more part in the bringing up of my children than my dad ever took up in bringing me up, you know . . . but that's possibly a matter of opinion. I mean, I was always very close to my mother at home and if ever I wanted

to talk over anything I always felt more comfortable talking to me mum than me dad. That's possibly . . . I don't know . . . maybe in those early days it was mainly me mum that was lumbered with me, as it were.

(Computer clerk)

A Tide of Change? Fathers' Attitudes in Perspective

So a large proportion of the fathers adhered to the emergent view of fathering, claiming that we are in the midst of a shift in the domestic role of men. Not only do fathers feel that they are more involved with their children than their parents were, but as we saw in Chapter 9 they have, at the child's first birthday, a great deal invested in his or her future. However, it is always possible that men regard the past through tinted spectacles. As the Newsons suggest, 'it is all too easy to be misled by one's own personal memories of childhood (Newson and Newson 1963: 219). We have to distinguish between real social change and shifts in the ways we talk about parental roles.

In the two parts of this section, I will consider this optimism of contemporary fathers from different perspectives. Let us first reflect upon the reliability of the fathers' accounts reported in the previous section, by comparing such accounts of paternal roles in the 1980s with the Newsons' data collected from mothers in 1960 about their own parents as parents. This exercise will suggest that, while changes have taken place over the past twenty or so years, the increase in fathers' involvement has been relatively small. Recent discussion about participant fatherhood has been exagerrated. The second part of this section considers the optimism of fathers of one-year-olds with the perspective of men whose families have progressed further through the life-span. The optimism of men with babies may well reflect feelings that are characteristic of parents at a particular stage in the life-cycle. The men themselves realize that their involvement in fatherhood may not be as intense beyond the child's early years.

Evidence for a change in paternal involvement

(1) Parental attitudes
In their study, Newson and Newson (1963) asked almost identical questions about the parenting styles of respondents' own parents. Two decades later the striking aspect of the mothers' comments in the Newsons' study is their similarity to those made by today's fathers. Like the parents in this study, mothers in the 1963 study mentioned three basic changes with regard to child-rearing that had occurred within their own lifetime. Firstly, they acknowledged the great material advances that had been made in people's

standards of living, particularly in light of the Depression and the Second World War. Indeed, it seems likely that fathers' comments of today reflect upon a continuation of this trend.

The other two changes mentioned by the mothers in the Newsons' study were the decline in general authority or discipline between their parents' and their own generation and, partly in consequence, the child-centredness of the contemporary generation of parents – themes frequently raised by the fathers in this study. The similarity between parents in both studies is striking. Parents in 1960 and 1980 tended to share the belief that their own parents were restricting, partly because of their restrained material circumstances. Parents in both generations saw themselves as members of new, more egalitarian families. As the Newsons commented, in the forefront of mothers' minds was 'A better chance: for many, this was the criterion of social progress and it was a point that recurred again and again' (1963: 222):

> 'Well you try to do a bit more for them, don't you? I always think you try to do a bit more than you think was done for yourself.'
>
> (Miner's wife,
> quoted in Newson and Newson 1963: 222)

As was suggested above, it is perfectly feasible that material advances have continued to improve the standard of living for young parents. Yet the Newsons' respondents and these parents were commenting upon more than the effects of post-war economic growth. Among both generations were many who were convinced, with regard to their own peers, that past values had been rejected and that now 'there's a much closer relationship between parent and child' (driver's wife, quoted in Newson and Newson 1963: 227):

> 'I never had what you'd call – any love – from my mother. Now with ours I think that's the main thing, because even with our Patricia (five) – I'll put her on my knee and nurse her, and she comes to me and asks for it; well I never remember having any of that. I could never hold a conversation with my mother, well even now I can't. Seems as though we're distant somehow, funny isn't it.'
>
> (Machine operator's wife,
> quoted in Newson and Newson 1963: 223)

Such optimism and confidence may well be characteristic of parents with young children, since most fathers' memories do not extend as far back as their early years. As was mentioned in Chapter 1, the belief that fathers are becoming more involved has been around for many years, if not generations. Twenty years before the Newsons' study, Gardner (1943) reported findings similar to these. I will turn now, therefore, to examine whether we can really be sure that changes in paternal involvement have taken place, by comparing data on child care from the present study with those of the Newsons' research.

(2) Evidence for a change in father involvement

Like the fathers in this study, the new fatherhood literature discussed in Chapter 1 has tended to suggest that men are coming increasingly into the picture (Beail and McGuire 1982a, Lamb, in press). But are men becoming more participant in the daily domestic routine? In attempting to answer this question it is immediately striking that hard comparative data is lacking (Hoffman 1977). There are two main ways of examining changes in practices over time. Firstly, some rely upon parents' recollections of previous generations' involvement. These tend to suggest a major increase in paternal involvement in recent years (e.g. White *et al.* 1982), but as I have argued in previous discussion this evidence is far from convincing.

Secondly, we can compare parents' accounts collected in previous generations with those gathered today. Again this procedure has its shortcomings. Methods change over the years; past assessments of paternal involvement lacked specificity and tended to be collected from maternal reports. Recent research has attempted to obtain more precise data. More important are probable ideological sifts over time; fatherhood is a vogue issue these days, and men may be under more pressure to appear to be involved.

With such cautions in mind, we can compare the evidence collected in this study on fathers' involvement with parallel data from the Newsons' research on mothers. As was explained in Chapter 2, both studies share the same location, methodology and sampling techniques. In 1960 the Newsons asked mothers questions about specific aspects of child care, some of which we compared directly with those of fathers today. This comparison suggests that some aspects of the man's involvement have changed. I mentioned in Chapter 4, for example, that birth attendance figures have risen from below 10 per cent to above 60 per cent.

Table 10.4 shows two directly comparisons betwen the fathers in this study and a sub-sample taken from the Newsons' study that matches the current sample for birth order, sex and social class. The figures show that on both measures fathers appear to be more participant in the recent study. Half the fathers in families with one or two children in 1960 never got up to attend to the baby at night whereas, by 1980, 87 per cent of a comparable sample did so. As was mentioned in Chapter 5, many more men now become involved at home in the period following delivery (77 per cent in 1980 vs 30 per cent in 1960).

That all these comparisons reveal consistent differences in the same direction over time shows that real change has occurred. However, we must interpret such measures of involvement in terms of the social context in which the activities take place. It was suggested in Chapter 5 that more

Table 10.4 Participation measures for first- and second-time fathers of one-year-olds in 1960 and 1980 (matched for sex of child and social class)

	1960 (N = 100)		1980 (N = 100)	
	No	Yes	No	Yes
Husband gets up to baby at night $\chi^2 = 33.18$, df = 1, p < 0.0001.	51	49	13	87
Husband helps in the period after the birth	70	30	23	77

$\chi^2 = 44.48$, df = 1, p < 0.0001.

husbands help in the period after delivery because they are the only available adults to care for mother and child. In addition, figures like those concerning getting up to the child at night might indicate greater change than has actually taken place. In only thirty-three of the eighty-seven families in 1980 where the father got up to the child did he do this as often as, or more than, his wife.

Comparative data on more routine child-care tasks in the two studies, shown in Table 10.5, suggest that change in paternal involvement is less apparent. In keeping with research practices of twenty-five years ago, the Newsons simply divided fathers into those who 'never' performed an activity, those who occasionally 'helped' their wives, and men who 'often' participated.

Table 10.5 presents the closest match between the Newsons' data and mine. Their category 'Never' included men who had not carried out a task and those who had done so only a few times, so the 1980 data are subdivided into those who had never done a chore and those who had carried it out a maximum of twelve times in the child's first year. When the two categories of minimal involvement in 1980 are compared with the 1960 data on men who never perform, the figures are roughly the same. So, for example, at both times roughly 40 per cent of men changed less than thirteen of the two thousand or so nappies that each child had worn over the first year!

Table 10.5 shows that more fathers in 1980 involved themselves regularly in these activities. However, the differences between the two generations are not great. Only one statistical comparison between the two groups approaches statistical significance. In 1980 more men put their child to bed regularly (35 per cent in 1960 vs 48 per cent in 1980; $\chi^2 = 3.75$, df = 1, p < 0.06). A shift in men's basic working week in the last twenty years may well have facilitated this change.

Table 10.5 Level of fathers' involvement with their one-year-olds in caretaking tasks: 1960 and 1980 compared (birth order and social class composition of 1960 sample matched to 1980 sample)

| | *Activity* | | | | | |
| | *Putting to bed/ getting to sleep* | | *Bathing* | | *Nappy changing* | |
Involvement	*1960* %	*1980* %	*1960* %	*1980* %	*1960* %	*1980* %
Never	29	(7	54	(30	37	(11
Rare/little (<13 times in year)		(19		(32		(29
Occasional	35	24	26	9	43	32
Often	35	48	20	29	20	28

Between 9 and 11 per cent of responses in the 1960 data were incomplete, being marked 'yes'. I have therefore divided these responses equally within the 'occasional' and 'often' categories.
Note: The data presented here have been modified since they were presented in Lewis *et al.* (1982). A more robust interpretation of the 1980 figures was used.

While there has been a slight increase during twenty years in their practical involvement, the figures show no evidence of any increase in men's ideological commitment to the daily care of their children. The obvious feature of Table 10.5 is the great variation between fathers. At both times some men appeared to be hardly involved in the care of the child, while others were highly participant. There is no evidence to suggest that father–infant relationships are closer today than they were. We might expect to see differences in the small amount of comparative data that exists, but in effect the figures which Schaffer and Emerson (1964) produced twenty years ago are broadly similar to those presented in Chapter 7.

Fathering over the life-span
When examined in context the optimism expressed by parents of one-year-olds seems valid and deeply felt. The child's first birthday, as many fathers commented, is a time for reflection. A year after delivery parents look forward to a relationship which, as we saw in Chapter 7, was usually developing in a fruitful way. However, it would be foolish to assume that the nature and closeness of a parent–child relationship remains constant over time. I will briefly outline here some evidence from the Newsons'

longitudinal data and the accounts of fathers in this study to suggest that parent–child relationships change as they both progress through the life-cycle.

(1) Longitudinal data

Elsewhere, the Newsons and I (Lewis *et al.* 1982) have examined fathers over sixteen years of parenthood. Throughout their longitudinal study (Newson and Newson 1963, 1968 and 1976) the Newsons paid close attention to the father's role, even though their main respondents were mothers. Our comparison of fathering over this period illustrated the obvious point that, as the child develops, the nature of his or her relationships with parents and others changes. As was mentioned in Chapter 6, fathers might be expected to change a one-year-old's nappy or play with him or her in a particular way, but these skills soon become redundant. The art of parenting requires different talents, which become less practical and more 'social' as the child develops.

The Newsons examined the father–child relationship over the life-cycle by asking questions appropriate to various age groups and developing a measure of father participation at each stage. The overall scales of father involvement intercorrelated with one another at the five ages over the first sixteen years (at one, four, seven, eleven and sixteen), so it seemed meaningful to describe this involvement as a consistent phenomenon (Lewis *et al.* 1982). Not only did these measures intercorrelate, but father participation seemed to be clearly demarcated at each age. We showed that participation in the middle years of childhood related to the child's sex, and their social class and family size. Fathers were reported to be more involved with their sons than with their daughters, in middle-class more than working-class families and in small families rather than large ones. These findings were consistent at three stages in the study — a factor which provided some assurance that they are reliable.

Our analysis suggested that there are clear cultural and subcultural 'rules' of appropriate fathering in different circumstances through the life-cycle. While a man's activities relate to his social class membership and the other factors listed above, the impression gained from this study was that throughout the child's life they perform a role which complements and adds to the 'necessary' mothering role of the wife. Indeed, fathering at each stage was perceived as 'a bit of a luxury', as one mother put it (Lewis *et al.* 1982: 188).

In Chapter 7 it was suggested that the father has to work at maintaining a relationship with his one-year-old, while the mother, as primary care-giver, is assumed to be naturally close to the child. This impression is consistently gained from the transcripts taken from the interviews at each stage of the Newsons' study. In middle childhood, for example, mothers would still report a special closeness to the child. Fathers generally made contact with their offspring in leisure activities, particularly sport. However, in contrast to the evidence which finds little to distinguish between the 'attachments' of mothers and fathers to their one-year-olds, their research suggested that, as the child grows beyond infancy, men usually assume a role which is far less close than that of their wives. We concluded:

> There is obviously a certain amount of negotiation in individual families, but it always takes place against a background of assumptions about what 'normal' fathering consists of. Occasionally there is overt disagreement between husbands and wives but more typically fathers settle for fairly narrowly defined roles. Some are cast as benign adults whose main function is to amuse and play with their children as 'super pals', but this can be a role which lacks emotional depth. In other families, particularly those with older children, fathers are not even this much involved.
>
> (Lewis *et al.* 1982: 187–8)

So throughout the middle years of childhood a mother would often excuse the secondary role of her husband by saying of her child, for example: 'I have time to be with him and perhaps Ted [husband] thinks he isn't needed.' (Lewis *et al.* 1982: 188). Such an account of fatherhood over the life-span is consistent with other data. For example, I reported in Chapter 6 Pressman's finding that father participation is greater in men with children under two years of age. A cross-sectional study of 1,569 families in the United States by Hoffman and Manis (1978) found that the birth of the first child marks a decline in the husband's involvement in the home – a process which continues as the family progresses through the life-span.

(2) Fathers' attitudes towards the future

A feeling that the father is an added bonus, rather than an essential member of the family, was also communicated by many men when they attempted to compare their present role with their anticipated experience as fathers. They looked to the years ahead in contrasting ways. As was suggested in Chapter 9, a majority of men depicted the child's future in glowing terms. Both middle- and working-class men placed great stress upon the child's education and had high hopes for his or her career prospects. Only two fathers envisaged their children in a manual job. These were not simply vacuous high hopes; many men were already making concrete efforts to help them move 'a bit further up the scale in a job', as the machine-setter put it. One father described his practical involvement in furthering his older son's educational career, at the age of two years and ten months:

> He's had these ABC books, you know, and we've read these words to 'im for him to pick it up. We took it in turns . . . Jan [wife] and me, like . . . doing that. And now and again he'll bring his books to us and ask us to read or whatever. . . . I want to teach my son,

'cos with me being bad at spelling I suppose . . . English, 'owt like that, I want him to be better. I want them both to do well.

(Barreller)

Unemployment, though only one-third as high as it is today, was rising at the time of the interviews. About half the fathers placed great emphasis upon persuading their one-year-olds to obtain as many qualifications as they could. While there was no class difference in men's aspirations, a feeling of pessimism was present in many working-class fathers' ideas about their children's future.

Fathers were generally optimistic for their one-year-olds in times to come. However, their feelings about their relationship in the coming years showed a marked contrast to this generally positive view. When casting their minds into the future, sixteen men gave what I classified as a 'naïve optimistic' response. They claimed that they would take each stage and enjoy it as it comes. Of the rest, the vast majority (sixty-six) selected a period within the first ten years of the child's life as the 'most enjoyable for fathers', and most of these (forty) focused specifically upon the pre-school years. The general impression given by men was that the child increasingly grows away from his or her father, either because of contact with peers or hours at school, or because the nature of the relationship between men and their older offspring is more distanced:

[Interviewer: 'Looking ahead, what stage of childhood do you think you're going to enjoy the most?'] Well, before he was born, I would have said about ten or eleven. But now, having grown up with him since he was born . . . I would think a lot earlier than that. I would think when he's about three, even two-and-a-half upward. You know, when he can converse . . . you know, quite reasonably. I would think about three upwards, or something. [Prompt: 'Till when?'] Six . . . so he can go to school and get his own friends and own ideas and be influenced by everybody else . . . and come back and tell me what a right idiot I am.

(Factory manager 1)

Enjoy him now . . . I think that as he starts to communicate and, er, takes an interest, then that is going to be stimulating, in that one is going to be able to teach him things. [Prompt: 'Which sort of age range would you think that would be?'] I . . . I must admit I like the sort of . . . probably in the nought-to-five bracket. I think then they're nice at that age. . . . I'm not saying he's not nice at any other age but, you know, at the stage when you can get hold of them and cuddle them if you like, you know.

(Factory manager 2)

In the same vein eighty-one men felt that the later years of childhood, especially the teens, would be the most difficult or worrying time for them as parents. This period is envisaged as a nightmare by many, as it can be a time when children break away and demonstrate the success or failure of their parents. Mothers and fathers often commented that other parents had warned them about the problems faced by adolescents 'dropping out' or becoming 'tearaways'. Underneath this feeling that they will be judged by the success or failure of their children during this period is the fear that they will continue to lose the love of their children. Many men hoped that they would become 'best mates' with their children when they had grown up. Others reflected back upon their relationship with their parents during their own adolescence, and considered that this would be a difficult period for them to let their offspring leave the nest:

> Well, I know that my parents worried about me, so I would say about the teens . . . [Prompt: 'For any particular reason?'] Well, no . . . only one, I should imagine, and that's because they're growing up, and they'll have a life of their own then, sort of thing. [Prompt: 'And how does that effect parents, do you think?'] Oh . . . I . . . well, I mean it must affect them a lot when they've brought them up for sixteen years, and then they just sort of up and off and so . . . I should imagine it affects them a lot. [Prompt: 'So do you think it might be a fairly depressing time?'] Yeah . . . yes.
>
> (Machine setter)

Work and Family Life: a Shift in Parental Roles?

Throughout this chapter I have attempted to show that changes in paternal involvement have been smaller and more complex than contemporary authors have suggested. It is necessary here to consider a very real social change: the increase in the employment of mothers outside the home. This has been central to the 'emergent' view of fatherhood, both in recent literature (Beail and McGuire 1982, Fein 1978a) and in theoretical statements early in the century (Cutter 1916). Young and Willmott's (1973) account of the symmetrical family, for example, depicted a 'revolving door', through which wives were entering the labour force, while their husbands were becoming more involved in family life.

Certainly great changes have taken place. For example, 10.4 per cent of the mothers in Newson and Newson's (1963) sample were in some sort of paid employment. Twenty years later 30 per cent of these mothers were working. Similar trends are apparent throughout the industrialized world (Ratner 1980). Other demographic changes have occurred in tandem. Families are becoming smaller (OPCS 1979) and the age spacing between children has been 'compressed' (Moss 1980), allowing mothers to return to work much sooner than in previous generations.

Yet closer examination of these trends indicates that changes in the couple's division of labour in employment have not been as great as the figures might imply. Nor can we assume that any increase in maternal employment makes fathers adopt radically different parenting roles. As was reported in Chapter 6, men with employed wives do score highly on measures of child-care – particularly when it comes to looking after the child single-handedly. However, these men were not so different from those fathers whose wives were full-time mothers. The three parts of this section will explore just why current figures of change in the numbers of mothers working do not indicate an emergence of participant fatherhood. Firstly, the nature of maternal employment is such that it remains an activity which is secondary to the maternal role. Secondly, parents' attitudes towards change in their roles in the home and the labour force reveal a basic conservativism; women are perceived as being better equipped to cope with caring for a baby. Thirdly, moves towards increasing paternal involvement have not been successful.

The nature of maternal employment

While the large number of mothers in paid employment suggests that substantial change has taken place, their patterns of work reveal that for most participation in the wider economy is marginal. Women with young children tend to drift into part-time jobs for brief periods of time. If we examine the amounts the thirty women in this sample worked, we find that twenty-five of the thirty employed mothers worked part-time and fifteen of these worked fewer than fifteen hours per week. As Ratner (1980) states, mothers such as these are a 'reserve army' in the labour force. Firstly, their work plans are often very flexible. For example, eight of those working were making plans to cease doing so in the near future, while thirty non-workers were hoping to find jobs in the next year.

A second reason why mothers form part of a reserve army lies in the nature of their employment. Research shows that not only do mothers' jobs tend to be part-time. They also predominantly offer low pay and no opportunity for promotion, training or even sickness benefit (Moss 1980, Ratner 1980). The reasons for working given by the workers in this study are consistent with those given by other employed mothers (Moss 1980). Firstly, many parents mentioned that the wife's part-time job enabled her to have a 'chin-wag' or to get away from the child for a few hours for a 'break':

> In a sense what it is, is it's a way of getting away from the kid for half an hour. She has them all day, sort of thing, and then . . . even though she's working, it's still a break from the kids.
>
> (Factory labourer)

Secondly, the wage earned in the mother's job was cited by many as a boost to their income:

Well, I don't *want* her to work but these days it's a necessity, I'm afraid. If you want to have the good things in life, you've *got* to.

(Disabled clerk)

The idea of maternal employment is not appealing to about two-thirds of fathers. Yet many working-class men stated, like the father quoted above, that their wife's earnings were a financial necessity; it is not by chance that significantly more unskilled labourers (social class V) approved of the principle (48 per cent vs 23 per cent of fathers from social classes I/II, III (w.c.) and III (m.); $\chi^2 = 4.2$, df = 1, p < 0.05). It is to parents' attitudes towards work and child care that we now turn.

Attitudes towards work and parenthood

Mothers are increasingly likely to find part-time work, but there is little indication that they are ideologically committed to the principles of equal employment and shared parenthood. Attitudinal studies reveal many ambiguities in their attitudes towards work, home and parenthood (e.g. *Employment Gazette* 1981, Mason and Bumpass 1975, Moss 1980, Paloma and Garland 1972, Weingarten 1978). Mason and Bumpass, for example, found that most women in a large sample supported the principle of women's employment and equal pay, but at the same time 76 per cent agree with the basic differentiation between women's domestic duties and men's role as providers. Similar views were apparent in the accounts of the parents in this sample. Discusssion about their ideal work arrangements and the possibility that they might exchange roles with their partners revealed deeply conservative views about paternal roles outside the home and maternal attachments to their children.

Few parents appeared to be keen on the idea of the wife working full-time. Fathers reported that only five of them and nine of their wives would prefer the wife to work in an ideal world. There was a high concordance between partners in the small sample on this issue; we can accept the reports of the fathers as an approximation of their wives' views. On part-time work, parents divided into two groups. For about one-third of the men (32 per cent) this was an acceptable option, although a majority of these stipulated that they favoured only the sort of work which fits in with the wife's running of the home:

Well, she'd like to go back part-time, we've both discussed this and we don't think it's right for a wife to look after the kids and work full-time. I mean, when the children are at school, er . . . probably Jacqueline [wife] would like an afternoon job back in the printing type of trade where she was before . . . where she can work about three or four hours in the afternoon . . . occupy herself . . . get a bit of money in for the family and also look after the home as well. To me, [a] housewife with children and a husband shouldn't be to work full-time because I think house gets neglected, children gets neglected,

you know. And we discussed this. I mean, [when] the children get
school dinners, she can stay at one o'clock . . . until they come home
at night.

(Despatch controller)

I'd like her to go back to work – 'cos I think it's best for my wife, 'cos
it would give her a bit more sense, not sense of progress, more of a
break. Part-time . . . really, that would be the best of both worlds.

(Civil servant 1)

Almost two-thirds of the fathers (63 per cent), and half of the wives in
the small sample, were more conservative. This group, which included
fifteen of the men with employed wives, expressed an antipathy to the idea
of mothers working:

I wouldn't let her. She only gets . . . I mean, I wouldn't let her go
to work, really. She don't have to go to work, but it's . . . say . . . 'cos
it gives her a couple of hours to herself, like . . . just to get out the house.

(Sawyer)

Implicit in most fathers' accounts was the belief that employment outside
the home was likely to upset the family routine. On a practical level, some
mentioned the problems of organizing a dual-worker family, where the
husband works long hours or shifts. Other men felt they could earn more
doing overtime than their wives could in a part-time job. In addition, a
majority stressed the woman's primary function: her role as mother. To
be a 'proper' mother a woman has to be available to care for the child
and family:

Well, I would put it to her that the kids come first – before work, I
mean; financially we've got to get by on my salary. This 'equal rights'
thing is a bit twisted – it's not quite right. They seem to forget one
or two major roles of women in life, I think. [Prompt: 'Does that mean
you don't want her to go back till the kids are at school, or . . . ?']
well, no, I think if they were at school I should think it's up to Barbara
[wife] – but I shouldn't think she'd want to, actually.

(Financial controller)

No, I don't . . . I don't think so. [Prompt: 'You wouldn't like her
to go back?'] I don't think it's right for any mother to go to work
when they've got children. I might be a bit old fashioned in that respect.
[Prompt: 'Until the children are what age?'] Well, at least until
they're in their teens. I think possibly by then they may be a bit bored
at home, if they didn't have their children, um, but I don't think it'll
arise in our case, because we've both got so many interests, that when
the children . . . even if any of them leave home for instance, we've
got so many things that we can do, I don't think it'll ever arise.
We're both in the same mind that with all this unemployment about,

er, it's stupid for any woman who is married and got a family to be
at work.

(Company director)

When asked about the principle of role reversal, twenty-seven men agreed
with it. Just how many of these would take up such an offer is impossible
to estimate. The remaining fathers were opposed to the idea, and fifty
expressly stated that men and women are equipped with different skills.
Some (21 per cent) rejected the idea immediately, since they felt that no
man is endowed with the ability to care for a baby:

> Well I mean . . . you don't mean during the day? [Prompt: 'Yes'.]
> No, I think that's wrong. . . . [Prompt: 'Can you say exactly why?']
> Well, I think essentially to bring up a baby is a female occupation. . . .
> [Prompt: 'Which parts particularly are?'] Um . . . everything, you
> know, early childhood. [Prompt: 'Can you put your finger on exactly
> what is wrong?'] Well, I don't know. Child and mother go together,
> you know, like bacon and eggs. I don't think the child and the father
> are sort of compatible, you know. I think that mothers tend to be
> more closer.

(Factory porter)

A similar proportion of wives agreed with this view. This woman, for
example, had been a staff manager at a large chain-store and had been
reluctant to give up her job before the birth of her child. A year later she
had changed her mind considerably:

> I'm not one of these who believe that this age . . . it's important that
> as a mother I am at home. I don't believe in having a baby and going
> straight back to work. I think it's wrong. [Prompt: 'Some people say
> there's no reason why the father shouldn't look after the baby while
> the mother goes out to work. How do you feel about that?'] Yes,
> Simon's [husband] often joked about that. I think *he* would quite enjoy
> that sort of role, actually. [Prompt: 'And how do you feel abot that?']
> Er, um . . . I dunno . . . I wouldn't want to, I shouldn't think. I
> think a mother's important at this early stage.
>
> (Housewife, whose husband is factory manager 1)

A second group of parents opposed to the idea of role reversal mistrusted
the father's capabilities. Twenty-one fathers felt that they personally could
not cope:

> I couldn't do it . . . well, I don't really know how Denise [wife] felt
> deep down when the baby came along and she had to be here to look
> after the baby . . . but no doubt she got used to it. . . . But I think
> I'd find it one hell of a strain . . . having to care for, run round after
> and play . . . and be with the child all day. I think I'd find it very
> hard . . . endlessly . . . that's what it seems to me.

(Spring maker)

One father had tried to look after the baby while his wife went out to work in the evenings but had found it too hard to cope:

> Well, you know, she went out at first, like, you know, but . . . it was a couple of hours at night and I told her to pack it up. [Prompt: 'Why was that? It was too much for her, was it?'] Well, it wasn't too much for her but she was going out at five and back at seven, like, you know, and the baby was ready for feeding and changing like. . . . So I says, 'You'd better stop at home', you know. . . . I didn't really know how to look after the baby . . . how to keep her quiet, you know, and what could be wrong there.
>
> (Plant operator)

Again similar sentiments were expressed by some of the mothers. This woman had been critical of her husband's lack of involvement in the family:

> Well, it's all right in principle, I suppose, but it does depend on what the father is like with them . . . how he could cope, and if he could earn more money, it wouldn't be practical . . . it wouldn't be . . . I don't think *men* who stay at home all day actually can care for the children. You've got to be exceptionally fatherly . . . not *any* man.
>
> (Housewife, whose husband is a carpet salesman)

In addition to feeling that mothers are more capable of caring for children than fathers, many women echoed the respondents in Oakley's (1979) study, who felt dependent upon their baby, having spent so many months caring for him or her:

> I would *like* to go back to work, but I don't . . . I mean, when I was first pregnant, I wanted to go back to work. But now I wouldn't want to leave Kim [son]. I think I'd miss him too much.
>
> (Housewife, whose husband is a factory porter)

So, without any prompting apart from two general questions about their ideal work arrangements and the idea of role reversal, a large majority of parents indicated that parental roles are or should be divided. Mothers are imbued with the skills of child care – either naturally or as a result of constant contact with their baby. Fathers either collectively or individually are thought to be less capable. While the reasons for these beliefs have been discussed frequently, the extent of the divisions between male and female worlds have yet to be fully explored. As I have argued in Chapter 6, it is the case not only that men exploit their wives by 'dodging' their responsibilities in the home. Both mothers and fathers actively strive to perpetuate the differences between parental sex roles.

When considering the possibility of role reversal, mothers reject the idea for reasons other than a belief in their own abilities. On pragmatic grounds they see men's pay and career opportunities far outstretching their own. At the same time many realize that, while the world of work is essentially a man's one, as parents their social world revolves upon the institution of motherhood: a network of ties which includes organized functions like mother-and-toddler groups, and less formal arrangements. The isolation experienced by lone fathers reveals the sex appropriateness of these links between mothers (Hipgrave 1982).

Fathers work not only to gain power from earning the main family income or to avoid the mundaneness of child care. Many fathers felt that outside employment was the harder option of the two traditional parental roles. These men felt that role reversal would exploit women, or that their own jobs were too demanding physically for a woman to cope with:

> I think it's the man's job to go to work, really. [Prompt: 'For what reason?'] Well, not for the reason [of] a woman stopping and doing the housework . . . but, er . . . You know, a woman shouldn't *have* to go out to work . . . I don't think so, anyway. Well, if a man can put in overtime and that to keep his wife at home, like, [Prompt: 'What about the situation where a man stays in all the time . . . doesn't work at all . . . the *wife* goes to work and does overtime?'] That's daft . . . well, it's just idleness, I put it down to, really. You can't let the missus go out and do all the work and, er . . . [Prompt: 'Well, what happens if she hated it at home and . . . ?'] Oh, if that's the case then it's all right, like, I suppose. . . . Can't see many women volunteering, though.
>
> (Dyer's labourer)

> Me and Eileen's [wife] joked about it. You know, I've said, ''ere, get off to work and I'll stay home all the time.' You know, to me women's housework . . . and how they carry on about it . . . You come home at night and they say, 'I've had a grueller today.' . . . The odd afternoon, I've come home for a cup of tea and they've been dossed out on the settee fast asleep . . . and I've said, 'Cor . . .' Yeah, I wouldn't mind it. I mean, I work hard for my money. . . . If Eileen could earn as much money as I'm earning, I'd let her do it. You know, I'd be quite willing to stay at home.
>
> (Lorry driver)

Moves towards participant fatherhood

Parents' attitudes towards work reveal in many cases an underlying belief in a basic differentiation between mothering and fathering roles. In concluding this discussion, I shall briefly examine some case examples of the men in the sample who appeared to be carving a new and more participant role for fathers. In Chapter 6 I discussed the overall participation of the fathers in this study and found that their involvement in child care depended to a large extent upon their own and their wives' working hours. Two groups of men were significantly more involved than the other fathers: those who were unemployed or disabled and four men whose wives worked while they took responsibility for the child during the day. That these fathers participated more in the home might suggest that these families are taking the lead in a trend towards a more androgynous parenting role. However, further examination of the transcripts suggests that with one exception these fathers are far from pioneers of a new way of life.

Unemployment forces men into the home in such a way that might enable great change to take place in the domestic division of labour. While they were more participant, the unemployed men were involved in child care and housework for only a small part of their available time at home. These fathers often commented that their daily presence at home caused considerable friction between themselves and their wives, and three made special arrangements to cut themselves off from their families. One man had his 'room' at home which he reserved for himself to sit in during the day, away from his family. The other two went out all day (one went fishing and the other claimed to be looking for work) to 'escape' a life of domesticity. Indeed, when asked about role reversal, a majority of these men argued strongly in favour of the traditional division of parenting roles:

> Um, well, we've thought about it. I mean, I've never objected to Joy not working anyway. I, um, I prefer her to be at home because if I'm working all day I like to come in, say, and have a meal. I don't mean particularly *ready* for me on a plate or anything like that but I like a meal to be cooked for me and that sort of thing. I don't think it's fair on a woman anyway if she's married and has a child. If you wanna bring a child, um, or children in a proper family atmosphere and bring 'em up well, I think it's necessary, er, that one of the parents should stay at home and look after the children properly. [Prompt: 'So you've thought about it. Is that as far as you've got or are you going to make vague plans about that?'] Um, well, we've talked about it before we got married, um, and Joy agreed that she'd rather be a proper mother than go out to work and have the child in, er, um, I don't know, play centre whatever or have somebody coming in and have her look after the child during the day. We didn't think that was right anyway, or the right way to bring up our child or children so. [Prompt; 'So you've thought about it but never put it into practice?'] Er, well, what we said was that, um, Joy would prefer not to go to work. I would prefer her not to go to work. [Prompt: 'And so it suits both of you.'] And so it suits both of us. At the same time, I'd have no objection later in life for her to go back to work if she wanted.
>
> (Unemployed sales representative)

Fathers with employed wives undertake more child care than the average, but as was stated above these men were not necessarily committed to a more participant role. It may be that only in families where the wife works full-time does the man's role compensate for her absence from the home. Of the five women in such jobs, two working-class families placed the child with a child minder, so the fathers were not involved much more than their peers. In the three middle-class families where the wife worked full-time and in another where she worked part-time, the fathers were involved far more than the average. As was mentioned in Chapter 6, these men took care of the baby for at least part of the day. Perhaps, then, they are breaking new roles for fathers?

Two of these couples highlight the transient nature of involved fatherhood. One ('newsagent 1') had taken his child each day to his shop during her first year, since his wife worked as a community nurse. However, two days before the interview they had employed an au pair to take responsibility for the child, since she was beginning to take up too much of his time at work. The second father (the 'house-husband') had given up his work in order to care for the baby full-time, enabling his wife to continue to earn her larger salary. Yet at the time of the interview he was building up a career as a photo-journalist so that his wife could be 'allowed' to become a housewife. His response to the question about role reversal suggested that his aspirations were far from androgynous:

> [Interviewer: 'Some people say that there's no reason why the father shouldn't look after the baby while the mother goes out to work. How do you feel about that?'] I suppose there's no reason really [why not] . . . but I suspect there's something built into the male of the species that wants to go out and earn the bread, because . . . Although I've now finished up doing what *I* wanted to do, occupation-wise . . . albeit rather part-time at the moment . . . in as much as I'm not doing a forty-hour week yet. . . . Admittedly I don't *like* domestic chores. I find them trivial and irritating . . . I can't say I'm wildly happy about the present arrangement. I'm tolerating it, you know, rather than enjoying it. [Prompt: 'Is it just the domestic chores or is it looking after Laura (daughter) as well?'] Oh, I thoroughly enjoy any aspect of dealing with Laura, yeah, that's great fun. . . . I don't like things like washing and vacuuming and this and that. . . . I mean, I just can't be bothered. I'd rather work eighty hours a week literally. [Prompt: 'So do you think that there's something inhibiting about staying at home and looking after the baby?'] Well, I suspect that it's not quite the natural state of affairs, but you know, I can't put a finger on it. *I* wouldn't be 100 per cent happy with that. *I'd* rather be the bloke that goes out and brings in the gold, you know [laughs].
>
> (House-husband and part-time photo-journalist)

It is foolish to generalize from just two case examples, but these are in keeping with the feelings of studies on role-reversed couples. The small amount of literature on these families indicates that their problems are great. For example, Russell (1982 and 1983) found that the mothers in these families tended both to feel guilty about leaving their children, and to 'take over' when they arrived home from work. Indeed, two years after his fieldwork a follow-up study revealed that half of the families with this role pattern had reverted to a 'traditional' family type.

Among the fathers only one, a finance company representative, who arranged his working hours so that he could look after the child while his wife taught at a primary school, considered that he would continue to take care of his child in the foreseeable future. His was a special case, however, since he had been left with his older children by his first wife and had spent eight years as a single-parent father before remarrying. Being so experienced with children, older than his wife and in a job where he could arrange his hours of work made him especially well qualified for the joint caretaking role which he and his wife assumed. Not many fathers share his experience, however.

> [Interviewer: 'What do you feel about Tina (wife) working?'] I suppose Tina could finish work tomorrow and it wouldn't affect us financially in any way, shape or form. [Prompt: 'Would you prefer her to (stop)?'] No, because, I . . . I think, er, Tina working actually keeps her young and it keeps her occupied. I don't think . . . my personal opinion is, I don't think there's enough work at home to keep a woman occupied, you know, if she's dusting and polishing all day long. I think . . . my opinion is that we're following this way because I ran a house and a family for eight years on my own and I suppose my life sort of changed a little bit by, er, me doing all these three things together. [Prompt: 'You realize the house is not . . .'] The house is not sufficient to keep a person occupied . . . unless she's a mothers' union fanatic and this type of thing.
>
> (Finance company representative)

Such is the pressure upon parents to adopt traditional roles that they also appear to resist many attempts to change their attitudes and behaviour. In recent years concerted efforts have been made in 'preparing' men for parenthood before the child arrives and initiating 'paternity leave' in the early weeks of the child's life. As was suggested in Chapter 3, attempts to increase paternal participation in domestic life, by including them in the 'official procedures' of prospective parenthood, both at school and during pregnancy, have been unsuccessful. Indeed, the fathers' attitudes towards both becoming publicly involved in the events of pregnancy (see Chapter 3) and changing the nature of men's and women's contributions to the labour force (see above) suggest a very basic opposition to change. While institutional attempts to effect change have gained momentum in recent years, even the most concerted efforts have been unsuccessful (Clulow 1982). The twentieth century has in fact witnessed many such attempts to effect change. For example, Gardner (1943) cites examples of parentcraft courses for men in the 1930s. Schlossman (1976) details the unsuccessful attempts to effect social change through 'parent education' at the turn of the century.

The main impetus to effect lasting changes in the nature of fathering roles comes in the move to make 'paternity leave', during the period after delivery, statutory, in the same way that maternity leave is available in most industrial nations. Again, as was mentioned in Chapter 3, there is no state provision in Britain for fathers to take time off work after the arrival of their children, despite recent recommendations to effect such a policy (Bell *et al.* 1983). However, in other countries such provision has been made, and the most notable example is Sweden. The Swedish government has initiated a system of leave for parents, and fathers have been granted time off work around the time of their children's birth since 1974 (Lamb and Levine 1983). Couples may now share between them 270 days off after the delivery at an index-linked rate of pay which is close to their normal salaries. In addition, they are entitled to other periods of leave up until the child's eighth birthday.

However, the result of such a wealth of provision for parents is that few men take the leave that is available to them. As recently as 1980 only 10 per cent of eligible fathers took any such leave, and these usually took far less time off than was available to them: an average of forty-two days (Jalmert, personal communication). Moss and Fonda (1980) suggest that the low number of fathers who take up paternity leave in Sweden may reflect the novelty of the policy and that its effectiveness should not be judged immediately. While the paternal role in Sweden has undergone some change (Sandqvist, in preparation), the evidence suggests a general reluctance of the Swedes to change their care-giving patterns as a result of government policy. As Lamb and Levine (1983) comment, the failure of the scheme to be taken up by large numbers of new fathers appears to reflect a basic conservatism not only among parents but also among their employers and the society at large.

Conclusion

Throughout the book I have attempted to explore the ambiguities inherent within contemporary fathering roles. During pregnancy the expectant father is likely to display an air of detachment, while privately either sharing in the psychological change which his wife goes through, or bottling up his emotions by adopting a 'sturdy oak' role. Early in the child's life he spends more time at home than usual, performing a key role in the family. Yet this rarely involves caring for the baby; this is the mother's prerogative. As the baby develops, his or her father may pay lip-service to the idea of equality in parenthood (that spouses should share responsibility for the child), but work and a traditional emphasis on the differentiation of parental roles prevent him from taking an active part in family life. The father may spend only minutes of the child's waking day with him or her. Yet he usually develops a close attachment and commitment to his one-year-old. Finally, as has been said in the present chapter, the man is likely to regard himself as more involved in fatherhood than his own father was. The evidence suggests that this may not be wholly true; father and child may perceive their relationship in different ways as time progresses and from different points of view.

In industrial cultures fathering continues to be a 'bit of a luxury', which in the vast majority of circumstances is an added bonus to the 'necessary' function of mothering. The fathers studied here were at a stage in the life-cycle when men appear to be most involved in family life (Hoffman and Manis 1978) and they were in stable marriages. We can presume much less contact between father and child in most cases where the man is not living with the mother.

As the literature on fathers grows, proponents of the differentiation perspective increasingly argue that truly participant fatherhood will not become the norm until great changes are made outside the family – in child-care arrangements and in the sexual division of labour in the workplace. As New and David (1985: 210) put it:

> There are increasing numbers of men who are not afraid of being 'like women', of fathers who want to participate in *all* aspects of looking after children. The story of modern fatherhood is one of a movement from controlling to sharing, even though, without further institutional change, this process cannot get very far.

Certainly true symmetry between spouses cannot occur without major societal reorganization. Yet two major institutions which are resistant to such change are motherhood and fatherhood themselves. Each clings on to its responsibility for child care and the world of work respectively. While a belief in social change is a strong motivating force behind research and theory on the family, the mothers and fathers cited here give this a low priority, if they consider it at all.

Appendix: the Interview Schedule

**University of Nottingham Child Development Research Unit:
Guided Interview Schedule (for Fathers of First and
Second Children Aged 1:0)**

Orientation data
Child's full name ....DOB .... B/G
Siblings name ....DOB .... B/G

Mother
Name .... Age ....
1   Is X working at all?   FT/PT/Not working
                                                             FT ed/PT ed
2   Before having N/the children what job did she have?
      (If any)   Was this part-time or full-time?
3   (If in work or education now) Who looks after the baby while she's at . . .
4   How far did she get with her education?
      (If stopped in last 2 years) Was the baby an interruption to her education
      or would she have stopped anyway?

Father
Age .... Work: FT/PT/Disabled/Ed/Unemp.
5   How far did you get with your education?
      (If stopped in last 2 years) Did you stop partly because the baby was coming
      or did you intend to stop anyway?
6   What job do you do?
      How long have you done this?
      Have you had any other jobs? (specify)
7   What hours do you work each day?
      Is that five days per week?
      Does this vary?
      (specify shifts)
8   Do you have to be away from home at all, except during the day?
      Home: every night/up to 2 nights away/2–5 nights away/normally away
      other . . .

9   (If unemployed) How long have you been out of work?
      What jobs did you have before you became unemployed?
      Did you receive any training or apprenticeship for a job?

Birth
First of all I'd like to ask you some questions about N's birth.
10   Where was he/she born?
11   Was he/she premature or late at all?
12   Do you remember how much he/she weighed?
13   Were you there for the birth?
      All the way through?
         all/last stage/earlier stage/no
14   (If not present) Would you have liked to have been there?
      (What prevented you?)
15   (If present) Did you ask to be there, or did someone persuade you?
      (who persuaded you?)
16   (ALL) Did X (wife) want you there?
      (If older child) Were you there for N's birth?
17   What was the hospital's (midwife's) attitude?
         + ve/ – ve/neutral/dk
      Did there seem to be any difference of opinion between the hospital staff
      on this?
18   How did X get on – did she have a good time?
      (if negative) Was there anything special/else that made it an unhappy or
      unpleasant experience for her?
      (if positive) Was there anything special/else that made it a good experience
      for her?
19   (if present) And what was it like for you?
      Was there a particular moment in N's birth that you think you will
      remember all you life?
      (if negative) And were there any good moments – that gave a thrill or made
      you feel good?
      (if positive) And were there any really bad moments – when you felt scared
      or horrified or just disgusted?
20   (ALL)
      How do you feel now about (husbands being with their wives)
                                (fathers being there   )
      through childbirth?
      (if positive) Do you think it's good for fathers to be there or is it just helpful
      to the mother?
21   What does X think about it now?
22   How soon did you first hold the baby?
      immediately/within the first hour/first day/later
23   Some fathers say that they feel very odd when they hold their baby for
      the first time – was that true for you?
24   Did you feel immediately that N was really yours or did it take some time
      to realize this?
      (if older child) Was this the same with O?

What thoughts went through your head?

26   When did you see him/her again after that?

27   How long was X in hospital?

28   How often were you able to visit?

29   Did you take any time off work after N's birth? (how long)

30   (if older child) Who looked after O?

Were there any problems about that?

31   Can you remember what sort of things you did when you weren't with X and N?

(prompt) Did you spend much time getting the house ready for them?

32   Did X come straight home, or did she stay with someone else?

33   How soon was she up for the whole day?

34   Did she have any help in the house after the baby was born?

Father home all day/relative/ . . . . neighbour/other friend/other

(if neighbour or relative) Did you pay her for her help or was it just for love?

35   (if unclear) What sort of things did you do for N or around the house while things were getting back to normal?

(prompt) Is (that) something that you would usually do anyway, or just at a time like that?

Preparation

Can we go right back in time?

36   How many brothers and sisters did you have?

Father . . . . Mother . . . .

Position . . . . Position . . . .

(if younger sibs.) How much younger is your younger/est sister/brother?

37   Did you ever look after any babies or young children when you were a child?

Before you were married did you bottle-feed a baby?

(if yes) How often?

Had you fed a baby with a spoon

What about nappies, how often had you ever changed any?

(if yes) Whose?   How often?

Or soothed a baby to sleep on your lap?

(if yes to any of the above) Did you do this (these things) because your help was needed or because you wanted to? – perhaps your parents encouraged you?

38   How about school, were there any classes dealing with what it's like to be a parent?

(if yes) What sort of things did you discuss?

(if no) Would you have been interested in this sort of thing?

39   So before you met X did you have any ideas about how many children you wanted to have?

(if yes) How many did you want?

Had you definitely made up your mind about that, or were you going to wait and see?

Can you say what made you decide?

(if no) Did you think that some time in the future you'd have children or were you just not interested in them?

40   How long have you known X?

41   Before having N (the children) did you both discuss the possibility of having children very much?
(if no) Was it the sort of subject you never discussed?
(if yes) Who usually brought the subject up?

42   Did you agree on the number of children you were hoping for?
How many?
(if not) Was that something you both knew was a disagreement or was it just a feeling that there were differences in what you wanted?
How did you think it would sort itself out? Do you still think that?
Would X agree?

Pregnancy

43   How did your wife feel when she first found that she was expecting N?

44   What about yourself – how did you feel about it?

45   Did your feelings change in any way or did you go on feeling like that right through to the birth?

46   How about X – did her feelings change during her pregnancy?

47   Was there anyone in your families whose attitude affected you?

48   Was X well in her pregnancy or did she have problems?

49   Had she had any previous problems – miscarriages or anything like that?

50   What about the antenatal clinics – did you go to any? Y/N
(if yes) What did you do at them?
            Where you made welcome by the staff?
(if no) Were you encouraged to go?
            Would you have liked to go to them?
(if no) Was there any mention of going?
(if yes) What do you think you would have got out of them?

51   Did she go to antenatal classes with this pregnancy?
(if yes) Did you become involved in them at all?
(if no) Could you have gone?
            What put you off?
(ALL) Did you help her practise her exercises?

52   When X was expecting N, did you read any books or magazines about babies?
(can you give me any examples?)
(if older child) Did you read any when she was expecting O?
What about since?

53   Apart from the obvious physical changes, do you think that women change during pregnancy?
(in what way?)

54   (if yes) Do you feel that (......./any change in X) had any effect on you?

55   (ALL) Do you feel that X's being pregnant had any effect on you?
            Do you think that you changed in any way?

56   Is it a time when couples get closer together, or do you think that it tends to make them go their own ways a bit more?

57   Do you feel now that X was as well prepared for childbirth as she could have been, or do you feel that it could have been done better?
(How?)   (Could you have helped?)

58   And what about the first few weeks, coping with the baby yourselves, do you feel that you were properly prepared for that?
(if no) In what way?

59   Most fathers find that there are some things about looking after a baby which are much nicer than they expected – has there been anything like that for you?

60   And most find that there are also one or two things that are much worse than they thought they would be – what's been the worst thing for you?

Feeding
     When N was a small baby did X breast-feed him/her at all?
     How long? (check) Was this when he/she finished with the breast completely?
     When did he/she start having bottles?
     And when did he/she start having solid foods?
          1 2 3 4 5 6 7 8 9 10 11 12 (months)
     Breast
     Bottle
     Solids

62   (if breast-feeding 2 weeks or less)
     Did she have any special reason for not breast-feeding?
     (if physical reasons) Would she have gone on or do you think that she would have stopped anyway?

63   (if breast-fed for more than 2 weeks)
     Did she look forward to feeding N or was she persuaded?

64   (ALL) How did they feel about breast-feeding in the hospital? the midwife feel about breast-feeding?

65   And did you have any views about it?
     Did you influence her in her decision?

66   Had you ever seen a baby being breast-fed?

67   (if any breast-feeding)
     How did you feel when you saw your own baby being breast-fed?

68   (ALL) If YOU could decide which way your next baby was to be fed which way would you choose?

Bottle
69   Did N have any difficulties over bottle-feeding? (even at the beginning?)

70   Was he/she a baby who posseted and vomited a lot or did he/she mostly keep his/her food down?

71   Have you ever bottle-fed him/her?

72   (if yes) How old was he/she when you first fed him/her
     (if no) Is there any particular reason why you haven't?

73   (if bottle-fed) Have you done this on a regular basis, or just occasionally?
     (if regular) Right from when he/she was . . .
     (if occasionally) Has there been a time when you yourself fed him/her on a regular basis, if for only a few weeks?

74   Were you keen to give him/her the bottle yourself or did you do it just to help out?

75   (ALL) I suppose he/she's still on the bottle a bit, is he/she?
      How many does he/she have a day roughly?
76   (if F. has fed) Do you ever give him/her the bottle these days?
      (how often)
77   When he/she was very young/had just started on the bottle/did you use
      to get the bottle ready for a feed?
      (how regularly?)
      (do you ever do it now?)

Schedule

78   Before N started on solids, can you tell me how his/her feeding times were
      managed – was he/she fed at certain times or just when he/she seemed to
      want it?
      (prompts) If he/she cried before his/her usual time, would you feed him/her?
      If he/she was asleep at the usual time, did you wake him/her for his/her
      feed?
      Rigid to clock/Flexibly rigid/Flexible/Demand
79   Did either of you have any special reason for deciding to stick pretty closely
      to the clock/let him/her choose his/her own times?
      (if father) How did you come to want N to be fed in this way?
      (if mother or unclear) Did you influence X's decision – or did you leave
      it up to her?

Solids

80   I'd like to ask you now about the things he/she eats and drinks nowadays.
      Can you tell me everything he/she has to eat and drink on a typical day?
      From the moment he/she wakes to the next morning?
81   Do you give him/her any of this food?
      (if yes) Would you say you did this every day or just occasionally?
      (specify)
      (if no) Do you ever feed N?
82   What about at weekends?
      Do you feed him/her (more) then?
83   Do you ever prepare food for him?
84   Do you ever sit and chat to him/her while he/she is eating?
      (prompt how often, if necessary)
85   (if feeds) What do you do if you're feeding him/her something and he/she
      won't eat?
      (if alternative prepared) Suppose he/she still doesn't want it?
86   Do you find sometimes you or X have to spend the whole mealtime playing
      little games just to get the food down him/her?
87   Do the two of you agree about what you should do if he/she won't eat?
      What would X do?
      What would you do?
      Does one of you tend to get upset about it and the other do the calming
      down, or do you both feel the same?

Sleep

About his/her sleep . . .

88   What time was he/she put to sleep last night?

89   How soon after did he/she go to sleep, or was he/she already asleep when you put him/her down?

90   Did he/she awaken at all during the night?
       At what times?
       How long did he/she stay awake (each time)?
       Did you hear him/her or did you sleep through?

91   What time did he/she wake up this morning?

92   And what time did he/she actually get up?
       (if awake for more than 15 minutes) What did he/she do between waking and getting up?

93   Are these sleeping times fairly normal for N? (state abnormality and why)

94   Is he/she always put down at the same time?

95   Where does he/she sleep?

96   Do you or X do anything to get him/her to sleep at bedtime?

97   Who usually gets him/her to sleep/puts him/her to bed?
       (if X) Do you ever deal with that?

98   What happens if he/she won't sleep, or cries after he/she's left?
       And if he/she goes on crying?

99   (if unclear) Does he/she easily wake in the night nowadays?
       How many nights per week does he/she wake?
          4 + /2–3/1/occ/never

100   Who usually goes to him/her in the night?
       (if X) Would you ever go yourself?
       (ALL) Why is that (X goes rather than you?)
                    (you go rather than X?)

101   (if older child) Who goes to him/her, if he/she needs anyone?

102   What about when N was younger, did he/she ever keep either of you awake at night?
       (if yes) Did you go to him/her more/at all then?
       What did you do?

103   Do you think it does a child of this age any harm to be left to cry?

104   How long would you leave him/her to cry if you thought that there was nothing wrong with him/her?

105   What about your routine in the morning, who gets up first?
       Who usually gets N up?
       Does she/do you dress him/her?
       Is there anything you do with N before he/she gets dressed?

106   (if older child) Does anyone help O get up?
       Who?
       (if X) Do YOU ever help?

Bathing and changing

107   Are you usually at home when N has his/her bath?
       (how often/how many times per week?)

What about weekends?
108   Have you ever bathed him/her?
       (if no) Is there any particular reason why you haven't?
       (if yes) How old was he/she when you first bathed him/her?
       Was this with help or alone?
       Do you bath him/her regularly or have you done so just a few times?
       Is bathing N something that you and X do together or do you do it to
       give X a rest?
109   Do you ever sit and play with him/her while X baths him/her?
110   How about changing him/her – do you ever change N's nappies?
       How often?
       (if yes) Even soiled ones and very wet ones?
       (if no) Have you ever changed them?
            How often?
111   (if ever) Are you as skilled at bathing and changing as X is?
       (if no) Do you think that you could become so?

General caretaking
112   Do you ever take care of N on your own?
       (if no) Not even when X pops out to the shops?
       (if yes) Is this something that you do fairly regularly? (specify)
       What sort of things have you done for him/her when you've taken care
       of him/her?
113   Do you ever take him/her out alone?
       (how often?)
114   Are there any other jobs that you do for N?
115   About other household chores, how often do you help with: (specify)
            Shopping
            Washing the dishes
            Cooking
            Cleaning the house
            Clothes washing/launderette
            Ironing

(Questions 116–18: for fathers with older children only)
116   How much do you have to do with O?
       Do you play with him/her a lot?
       Do you bath him/her?
       Read or tell him/her stories?
       Take him/her out without X?
       Look after him/her when X goes out?
117   Is there anything else you do for O?
       Or anything that you do regularly with him/her?
       (for example? . . .)
       Since N's arrival have you had more to do with O or has there been less
       time to spend with him/her?
118   Looking back to when O was a baby – do you think that you were more

involved with looking after him/her than N?
What sort of things were different?

Communication and play

119 Can I ask you now about what N does during the daytime when he/she's wide awake? What does he/she do – how does he/she occupy him/her self?
120 Is he/she walking at all yet?
121 Does he/she spend a lot of time on the floor, or is he/she mainly in his/her pushchair or high chair?
122 Some people say that you can't really sit down and play with a baby of this age. What do you think about that?
123 Can you describe to me what you do when you play with him/her?
124 Are there any special games that you have between you – that he/she looks forward to?
   Or any little sayings or songs that he/she likes?
125 Is there any special time that is his/her playtime with you?
126 How much time do you spend playing with N on an average day?
127 Does his/her mum play in the same way as you or differently?
   (if different) Do you think that's the usual difference between a mother and a father playing or do you think it's more a matter of personality?
   (if same) Do you think that most mothers and fathers would play the same way as each other or do you think that mothers play differently from fathers on the whole?
128 Do N and his/her mum have any special games or times for play?
129 Is there anyone else who will set down and play with N?
   What sort of things does he/she do with him/her?
130 Does N seem to enjoy one kind of play more than others? (specify) (or any particular toys?)
131 Is there anything else that you wouldn't exactly call play, but that N seems to get a lot of fun out of?
   (prompt) Something he/she does on his/her own?
             Something he/she does with someone else?
132 If you wanted to give N a little treat what would you do?
   If you wanted to make him/her happy and excited how would you do that?
133 I suppose he/she can't say any words yet, can he/she? (list)
134 Has he/she got any other ways of making you understand things?
   What can he/she tell you?
   Can you think of an example when he/she's made you understand he/she wants something?
135 How much does he/she understand of what you say to him/her?
   (prompt) Can you give me an example of something you say that he/she understands?
   (check for context dependence) For instance, if you said, 'Where's Mummy?'
   If Mummy didn't come would he/she go looking for her?
   Can he/she understand, 'Wait a minute'?
136 If you point when he/she's out in the pram would he/she look where you're pointing?

137　In general would you say that N is going to be a chatterbox, or is he/she more likely to be the quiet type?

Temperament
138　I'd like to ask you something about N's personality now. How would you describe him/her to someone who didn't know him/her at all?

139　Is he/she quite content for you to do things for him/her or does he/she like to be independent?

140　Does he/she seem to be a very happy child, or is he/she one of those children who tends to take life a bit hard?
(if happy) Would you describe him/her as placid?

141　Is he/she a cuddly baby?
Has he/she always been like that?

142　Does he/she seem a bit miserable?
Do you know what makes him/her feel like that?
How do you cope with it?

143　Does he/she suck his/her thumb or fingers?
What about other habits, does he/she have any?
Does he/she rock himself, or bang his/her head on the pillow?
Does he/she play with his/her private parts at all?

144　How do you feel about him/her (doing whatever he/she does?)
Does it bother you at all?
Do you try and stop him/her in any way?
How?
Does X try and stop him/her?
Does he/she object to/her stopping him/her?

Conflict
145　Does he/she ever have temper tantrums? (Daily/Most days/1–3 wk/Less/Never)
How does he/she act when he/she's in a tantrum?
What seems to start them off?
What do you do?
Is he/she one of those children who once he/she has a temper tantrum you can't do much about it, or can you distract him/her or comfort him/her usually?

146　How do you punish him/her when he/she's been naughty?
What sort of naughtiness would that be for?

147　Is there anything that you can say to him/her that makes him/her understand that he/she's (been naughty?)
(done something that you didn't want him/her to do?)

148　What do you usually say to him/her:
　　When you feel a little bit cross with him/her?
　　What else do you say to him/her?

149　How do you feel about smacking children of this age?
(if doesn't smack) At what age would you expect to start smacking him/her sometimes?

150　How does his/her mum feel about that?

151   Does N seem to take more notice of one of you than the other?
       Who does he/she behave best for?
       Why do you think that is?

Paternal interest and involvement
152   Do you find that most evenings you and X have a chat about what he/she's
       been doing that day?
153   How do you come to decide to start something new in N's routine?
       For instance: How would you decide when he/she should sit on a potty?
           (prompt) Would one of you decide to try or would you talk about it first?
           Who would bring the subject up?
           Who would decide whether or not to take N to have his/her vaccinations?
           How often do you yourself decide when N is going to do more
           day-to-day things like what he/she's going to eat, or what he/she's
           going to do?
154   Do you and X ever have different ideas about how N should be brought up?
       Do you EVER protest at the things she does with N?
       Does she ever protest at the things you do with him/her?
       (if any) What sort of things do you disagree about?
       How do you usually come to an agreement – or do you just agree to differ?
       Do you think your disagreements are likely to get worse or better?
       (if none) Do you think you're likely to disagree when he/she's older?
155   Do you ever talk with people at work about bringing up young children?
       (who with?)
       (if yes) What sort of things do you discuss?
       What about with your friends outside work?

Perspectives on role sharing
156   Do you think that it's possible to lead a full life at home as well as at work?
       (if no) What do you find that you have to do less of?
       (if yes or don't know) Do you ever find that after a hard day's work you
       would rather collapse in a chair than play with N?
157   Looking back to before X was expecting N, how often did you go out in
       the evenings?
       Did either of you have any regular hobbies or sports?
       How often did you do.............? How often did X do.............?
       (if unclear) Did you always go out/do things together?
158   How did X's being pregnant affect the way you both spent your spare time?
       Did you tend to go out more than before?
159   Did N's arrival affect the amount of time you yourself were at home? How?
       (if unclear) So about how many evenings a week did you spend away from
       home in the early weeks?
160   What about keeping up your outside interests?
       Has that been a problem?
161   Do the two of you ever manage to leave the baby so you can both go out?
       How often?
162   Does someone come in to look after N or does someone just listen for
       him/her or what?

163   Would you like to get out more often than you do or are you happy the way things are?

164   Does X mind you going out on your own?

165   Do you spend any extra time at work, doing overtime or at social activities connected with your job? (specify)
(if any) Has this changed at all since N's arrival?
(if none) Did you before N's arrival?

166   How good are your prospects at work?

167   What about X, has she any plans about (jobs/going back to work?)
How would you like her to organize job possibilities and children if you could choose?
How would she like to do it?

168   Some people say that there's no reason why the father shouldn't look after the baby while the mother goes out to work – how do you feel about that?

169   What does X feel about your helping with N?
Would she like you to do less or more?
Does she see you as someone to call on when she needs some help occasionally or does she expect you to share looking after N when you're at home?
(if shared) Is that an equal share (when you're at home?)

170   Are there any jobs that X does with N that she regards as her own?
(if yes) Is that because she enjoys them/it or does she feel that she can do them better?

171   Are there any jobs which she tries to get you to do more with N?
What about around the home?
Is there anything with N which you'd like to do but she doesn't really want you to do?

172   Looking back over the year, do you think that you have more or less to do with N than when he/she was born?
(prompt) What sort of thing has changed?
(if necessary) Can you say why?

173   Do you think that a father and his son/daughter can be as close as a mother and her son/daughter?   (if no) In what way not?

174   Does N seem to prefer to play with you or X?
Who does he/she seem to have more fun with?

175   What about when he/she is upset or frightened, which one of you does he/she turn to?   Can you say why?

176   Can you say in what way a father is important to a child of N's age?

Values

177   How much difference has it made to X's life that you have a baby/children?

178   What about your life?

179   Have you found it difficult having a baby around or has everything come quite easily?

180   Have there been any surprises for you in what it's like to be parents?

181   Some parents say they are surprised by some of the emotions they feel. Have you found that?

(prompt) Some say that their emotions are much more mixed than they expected – is that so for you?

What about X?

182 Have there been any really bad moments for either of you since the baby's been born – when you've felt a bit desperate?

183 Would you say that having a baby brings husband and wife/a couple closer together in any way?

Are there any ways in which it pushes them apart?

It might be difficult to say this, but how do you think that it affects their relationship?

184 Do you feel that you've had to give up a lot for the baby's interests? (or that you should have given up more things?)

185 Do you think that it's much the same bringing up children now as it was for your parents, or do you feel that there are big differences?

Did your father take much interest in helping to bring you up or in helping in the home?

What sort of things did he do? (specify – child care/play/other) (how often?)

What about your ideas and attitudes compared with your parents – do you think that your ideas on bringing up children are different from theirs? (in what way?)

186 How far would you like N (the children) to go in their education – have you any ideas about that?

187 I know it's very early to talk about it, but how do you see N growing up – would you like to cast your mind forward twenty years and describe to me what he/she'll be like then?

What kind of job do you see him/her in?

188 Looking at N is there anything special that gives you a big thrill about him/her?

Is there anything now that really worries or upsets you?

189 Looking ahead, what stage of childhood do you think you're going to enjoy most?

190 What stage do you think you'll find difficult or worrying as a father?

191 Looking around at other fathers – is there anything that makes you think, I'd never do that with my children?

192 Lastly, what does being a father mean to you personally – how would you sum it up for someone who had never experienced it?

References

Ainsworth, M. D. S. and Wittig, B. A. (1969) 'Attachment and Exploratory Behaviour in One-Year Olds'. In B. M. Foss (ed.), *Determinants of Infant Behaviour*. London, Methuen.

Allen, S. and Barker, S. A. (1976) 'Introduction: The Interdependence of Work and Marriage'. In D. L. Barker and S. Allen (eds.), *Dependence and Exploitation in Work and Marriage*. London, Longman.

Alter, J. L. S. (1978) 'The Relationship Between Self-Esteem and the Male Parental Sex Role'. Unpublished Ph.D. Catholic University of America (University Microfilms no. 78–16858).

Arnstein, H. (1972) 'The Crisis of Becoming a Father'. *Sexual Behaviour*, 2: 42–8.

Atkinson, A. K. (1979) 'Postpartum Depression in Premiparous Parents: Caretaking Demands and Prepartum Expectations'. Unpublished Ph.D. Wayne State University. Original reference not used. See *Dissertation Abstracts International* (1980), 40: 5326B.

Backett, K. C. L. (1982) *Mothers and Fathers: A Study of the Development and Negotiation of Parental Behaviour*. London, Macmillan.

Balding, J. W. (1977) 'Health Topic Questionnaire: Introduction to a Study of its Application'. Unpublished m.s. Exeter, St Luke's College.

Balswick, J. and Peck, C. W. (1971) 'The Inexpressive Male: A Tragedy of American Society'. *Family Co-ordinator*, 20: 363–8.

Beail, N. (1980) 'Transition to Fatherhood'. Paper presented to the British Psychological Society, Division of Clinical Psychology Conference: *The Psychology of Human Reproduction*. Leicester, 27 September.

  (1982) 'The Role of the Father in Child Care'. Paper presented to the British Psychological Society, Social Psychology Section. Edinburgh, September.

Beail, N. and McGuire, J. (1982a) *Fathers: Psychological Perspectives*. London, Junction Books.

  (1982b) 'Fathers, the Family and Society: A Tide of Change'. In Beail and McGuire (1982a).

Bell, C., McKee, L. and Priestley, K. (1983) *Fathers, Childbirth and Work: A Report of a Study*. Manchester, Equal Opportunities Commission.

Belsky, J., Spanier, G. and Rovine, M. (1983) 'Stability and Change in Marriage across the Transition to Parenthood'. *Journal of Marriage and the Family*, 45: 533–6.

Belsky, J., Lang, M. and Rovine, M. (in press) 'Stability and Change in Marriage across the Transition to Parenthood: A Second Study'. *Journal of Marriage and the Family*.

Benson, L. (1968) *Fatherhood: A Sociological Perspective*. New York, Random House.

Berk, R. A. and Berk, S. F. (1979) *Labour and Leisure at Home*. Beverly Hills, Sage.

Bernstein, R. and Cyr, F. (1957) 'A Study of Interviews with Husbands in a Prenatal and Child Health Programme'. *Social Casework*, 38: 473–80.

Bettleheim, B. (1955) *Symbolic Wounds*. Chicago, Free Press.

Bibring, G. L. (1959) 'Some Considerations of the Psychological Processes in Pregnancy'. *Psychoanalytic Study of the Child*, 14: 113–21.

Bird, C. (1968) *Born Female: The High Cost of Keeping Women Down*. New York, David Mackay.

Bitman, S. and Zalk, S. R. (1978) *Expectant Fathers*. New York, Hawthorn Books.

Blendis, J. (1982) 'Men's Experiences of their own Fathers'. In Beail and McGuire (1982a).

Blood, R. and Wolfe, D. (1960) *Husbands and Wives*. New York, Free Press.

Bloom-Feshbach, J. (1981) 'Historical Perspectives on the Father's Role'. In Lamb (1981a).

Bobak, I. (1977) 'Fathers'. In M. Jensen, R. Benson and I. Bobak (eds.), *Maternity Care: The Nurse and the Family*. St Louis, C. V. Mosby.

Bott, E. (1957/71) *Family and Social Network*. London, Tavistock.

Bowlby, J. (1954) *Child Care and the Growth of Love*. Harmondsworth, Penguin.
     (1969) *Attachment and Loss Volume 1: Attachment*. Harmondsworth, Penguin.

Bradley, R. (1962) 'Fathers' Presence in the Delivery Room'. *Psychosomatics*, 3, November: 474–9.
     (1965) *Husband-Coached Childbirth*. New York, Harper & Row.

Bram, S. (1974) 'To Have or Have Not: A Comparison of Parents, Parents to be and Childless Couples. Unpublished Ph.D. Ann Arbor, University of Michigan.

Breen, D. (1975) *The Birth of a First Child*. London, Tavistock.

British Medical Association (1958) 'Round Table Conference of the British Medical Association'. *British Medical Journal*, 2: 321.

Brown, A. (1982) 'Fathers in the Labour Ward: Medical and Lay Accounts'. In McKee and O'Brien (1982a).

Burne, B. H. (1961) Letter to the *British Medical Journal*, 1: 594.

Busfield, J. (1974) 'Ideologies and Reproduction'. In M. P. M. Richards (ed.) *The Integration of a Child into a Social World*. London, Cambridge University Press.

Campbell, A., Converse, P. and Rogers, W. (1976) *The Quality of American Life*. Beverly Hills: Sage.

Cartwright, A. (1976) *How Many Children?*. London, Routledge & Kegan Paul.

Chodorow, N. (1978) *The Reproduction of Mothering*. Berkeley, University of California Press.

Clark, E. (1981) 'Missing Relationships'. *The Times Educational Supplement*, 23 October.

Clarke-Stewart, K. A. (1978a) 'Popular Primers for Parents'. *American Psychologist*, 33: 359–69.
     (1978b) 'And Daddy Makes Three: The Father's Impact on Mother and Young Child'. *Child Development*, 49: 466–79.

Cleary, J. and Shepperdson, B. (1979) 'Fatherhood in Fynone'. Paper presented at BSA Conference on Fatherhood. Warwick University, February.
          (1981) 'The Fynone Fathers'. Supplementary Paper No. 2, Motherhood in Swansea Project. Swansea, University College.

Clulow, C. F. (1982) *To Have and to Hold: Marriage, the First Baby and Preparing Couples for Parenthood*. Aberdeen, University Press.

Cohen, L. and Campos, J. (1974) 'Father, Mother and Stranger as Elicitors of Attachment Behaviours in Infancy'. *Developmental Psychology*, 10: 146–54.

Coley, S. B. and James, B. E. (1976) 'Delivery: A Trauma for Fathers?' *Family Coordinator*, 25 (4): 359–63.

Cowan, C. P. and Cowan, P. A. (1981) 'Couple Role Arrangements and Satisfaction during Family Formation'. Paper presented at the Society for Research into Child Development. Boston, March–April.

Cowan, C. P., Cowan, P. A., Cole, L. and Cole, J. D. (1978) 'Becoming a Family: The Impact of a First Child's Birth on the Couple's Relationship'. In W. Miller and L. Newman (eds.), *The First Child and Family Formation*. Chapel Hill, Carolina Population Centre: 296–324.

Cowley, J. C. P. and Daniels, H. A. (1981) *A Feasibility Study Concerning the Viability of Developing Parenthood/Child-Development/Family-Life Education in Schools through In-Service Education of Teachers Part 1*. Inset Section, Continuing Education. Milton Keynes, Open University.

Craven, E., Rimmer, L. and Wicks, M. (1982) *Family Issues and Public Policy*. London, Study Commision on the Family, Witley Press.

Cronenwett, L. (1982) 'Father Participation in Child Care: A Critical Review'. *Research in Nursing and Health*, 5: 63–72.

Cutter, J. E. (1916) 'Durable Monogamous Wedlock'. *American Journal of Sociology*, 22 (2): 226–57.

Daniel, W. W. (1980) *Maternity Rights: The Experience of Women*. London, Policy Studies Institute (No. 588).

Davidoff, L. (1976) 'The Rationalization of Housework'. In D. L. Barker and S. Allen (eds.) *Dependence and Exploitation in Work and Marriage*. London, Longman.

Davids, D. S. and Brannon, R. (eds.) (1976) *The Forty-Nine Percent Majority: The Male Sex Role*. Reading, Addison-Wesley.

Davis, A. (1961) Letter to the *British Medical Journal*, 1: 594–5.

De Frain, J. (1975) 'The Nature and Meaning of Parenthood'. Unpublished Ph.D. Madison, University of Wisconsin (University Microfilms no. 75–20759).

——— (1977) 'Sexism in Parenting Manuals'. *Family Coordinator*, 26 (3): 245–51.

Deutscher, M. (1970) 'First Pregnancy and Family Formation'. In D. Milman and G. Goldman (eds.), *Psychoanalytic Contributions to Community Psychology*. Springfield, Ill. C. C. Thomas.

Dickens, W. and Perlman, E. (1981) 'Friendships over the Life-Cycle'. In S. W. Duck and R. Gilmour (eds.) *Personal Relationships 2: Developing Personal Relationships*. London, Academic Press.

Dickie, J. R., Gent, E. V. Hoogerwerf, F. K., Martinez, I. and Dietermans, B. (1981) 'Mother–Father–Infant Triad: Who Affects whose Satisfaction?' Paper presented at the Society for Research in Child Development. Boston, April.

Dick-Read, G. (1934) *Childbirth without Fear*. London, Heinemann.

Dinnerstein, D. (1978) *The Rocking of the Cradle and the Ruling of the World*. London, Souvenir Press.

Dodendorf, D. M. (1978) 'A Developmental Framework for the Analysis of Expectant Fatherhood'. Unpublished Ph.D. Department of Educational Psychology and Measurements, Graduate College, University of Nebraska.

Dosanjh, J. S. (1976) 'A Comparative Study of Punjabi and English Child-Rearing Practices with Special Reference to Lower Juniors (7–9 Years). Unpublished Ph.D. University of Nottingham.

Douglas, M. (1975) *Implicit Meanings*. London, Routledge & Kegan Paul

Dyer, E. (1963) 'Parenthood as Crisis: A Re-Study'. *Marriage and Family Living*, 25: 196–201.

Ehrensaft, D. (1985) 'Dual Parenting and the Duel of Intimacy'. In G. Handel (ed.) *The Psychosocial Interior of the Human Family* (3rd edn). New York, Aldine.

Eiduson, B. T., Kornfein, M., Zimmerman, I. L. and Weisner, T. S. (1982) 'Comparative Socialization Practices in Traditional and Alternative Families'. In M. E. Lamb (ed.) *Non-Traditional Families*, Hillsdale, Erlbaum.

Einzig, J. E. (1980) 'The Child Within: A Study of Expectant Fatherhood'. Smith College *Studies in Social Work*, L, March: 117–64.

Eiskovits, R. (1983) 'Paternal Child Care as a Policy Relevant Social Phenomenon: The Questions of Values', In M. E. Lamb and A. Sagi (eds.), *Fatherhood and Family Policy*. Hillsdale, NJ, Erlbaum.

Elder, R. A (1949) 'Traditional and Developmental Characteristics of Fatherhood'. *Marriage and Family Living*, 11: 98–100, 106.

Employment Gazette (1981) 'Working Mothers and their Families'. 89 (2): 84.

English, O. S. and Foster, C. (1953) *Fathers are Parents, Too*. London, Allen & Unwin.

English Tourist Board (1979) *Forecasts of Tourism by British Residents 1985–1995*.

Entwisle, D. and Doering, S. (1981) *The First Birth: A Family Turning Point*. Baltimore, Johns Hopkins University Press.

Equal Opportunities Commission (1980) Study 230. Manchester, November: 18.
    (1982) *Parenthood in the Balance*. Manchester.

Eriksen, J. A., Yancey, W. L. and Eriksen, W. P. (1979) 'The Division of Family Roles'. *Journal of Marriage and the Family*, 41: 301–13.

Everslea, D. and Bonnerjea, L. (1982) 'Social Change and Indicators of Diversity'. In R. Rapoport, M. Fogarty and R. Rapoport (eds.), *Families in Britain*. London, Routledge & Kegan Paul.

Fagot, B. (1974) 'Sex Differences in Toddlers' Behaviour and Parental Reaction'. *Developmental Psychology*, 10: 554–8.
    (1978) 'The Influence of Sex of Child on Parental Reactions to Children'. *Child Development*, 49: 459–65.

Farrell, W. (1974) *The Liberated Man*. New York, Random House.

Fasteau, M. (1974) *The Male Machine*. New York, McGraw-Hill.

Fein, R. A. (1976) 'Men's Entrance into Parenthood'. *The Family Coordinator*, 25: 341–50.
    (1978a) 'Considerations of Men's Experiences and the Birth of a First Child'. In W. Miller and L. Newman (eds.), *The First Child and Family Formation*. Chapel Hill, Carolina Population Center.
    (1978b) 'Research on Fathering: Social Policy and an Emergent Perspective'. *Journal of Social Issues*, 34 (1): 122–35.

Feiring, C. (1976) 'The Preliminary Development of a Social Systems Model of Early Infant–Mother Attachment'. Paper presented to the Eastern Psychology Association. New York, April.

Feldman, H. (1971) 'The Effects of Children on the Family'. In A. Michel (ed.), *Family Issues of Employed Women in Europe and America*. The Netherlands, E. F. Brill.

Feldman, H. and Rogoff, M. (1968) 'Correlates of Change in Marital Satisfaction with the Birth of the First Child'. Paper to APA, San Francisco. Unpublished m.s. Ithaca, Department of Child Development and Relations, Cornell University.

Feldman, S. and Ingham, M. (1975) 'Attachment Behavior: A Validation Study in Two Age-Groups'. *Child Development*, 46: 309–30.

Fenwick, P. and Fenwick, E. (1978) *The Baby Book for Fathers: All the Expectant Father Needs to Know*. London, Angus & Robertson.

Finer, M. (1974) *Report of the Committee on One Parent Families* (Cmnd 5629). London, HMSO.

Fock, N. (1967) 'South American Birth Customs in Theory and Practice'. In C. S. Ford (ed.), *Cross-Cultural Approaches: Readings in Comparative Research*. New Haven, HRAF Press.

Frazer, J. G. (1910) *Totemism and Exogamy*. London, Macmillan.

Gardner, L. P. (1943) 'A Survey of the Attitudes and Activities of Fathers'. *Journal of Genetic Psychology*, 63: 15–53.

Gladieux, J. D. (1978) 'Pregnancy – the Transition to Parenthood: Satisfaction with the Pregnancy Experience as a Function of Sex Role Conceptions, Marital Relationship and Social Network'. In W. Miller and L. Newman (eds.), *The First Child and Family Formation*. Chapel Hill, Carolina Population Center: 275–95.

Goetsch, C. (1963) 'Fathers in the Delivery Room – Helpful and Supportive'. *Hospital Topics*, 44: 104–5.

Golden, S. G. (1975) 'Pre-School Families and Work'. Unpublished Ph.D. Ann Arbor, University of Michigan.

Goode, W. J. (1963) *World Revolution and Family Patterns*. New York, Free Press.

Grace, A. M. (1983) 'Jamaican Immigrant Child-Rearing Practices: A Study of 200 Seven-year-old Children in Relation to their Daily Lives at Home and at School', Unpublished Ph.D. University of Nottingham.

Grad, R., Bash, D., Guyer, R., Acevedo, Z., Trause, M. A. and Renkauf, D. (1981) *The Father Book: Pregnancy and Beyond*. Washington, DC, Acropolis.

Graham, H. and McKee, L. (1980) *The First Months of Motherhood*. London, Health Education Council.

Greenberg, M. and Morris, N. (1974) 'Engrossment: The Newborn's Impact upon the Father'. *American Journal of Orthopsychiatry*, 44: 520–31.

Grossman, F. K., Eichler, L. S. and Winickoff, S. A. (1980) *Pregnancy, Birth and Parenthood*. San Francisco, Jossey-Bass.

Hacker, H. M. (1957) 'The New Burdens of Masculinity'. *Marriage and Family Living*, 19 (3): 227–33.

Hanson, S. and Bozett, F. (1985) *Dimensions of Fatherhood*. Beverly Hills, Sage.

Heron, L. (1981) 'Where Have All the Fathers Gone?' *The Times Educational Supplement*, 13 March: 20–1.

Herzog, J. (1982) 'Fathers and Young Children'. Paper presented to the International Association of Child Psychology and Psychiatry. Dublin, July.

Hill, D. W. (1961) 'Fathers at Delivery'. Letter to the *British Medical Journal*, 1: 430.

Hipgrave, T. (1982) 'Lone Fatherhood: A Problematic Status'. In McKee and O'Brien (1982a).

Hobbs, D. F. (1965) 'Parenthood as Crisis: A Third Study'. *Journal of Marriage and the Family*, 27: 367–72.

(1968) 'Transition to Parenthood: A Replication and an Extension'. *Journal of Marriage and Family*, 30: 413–17.

Hobbs D. F. and Cole, S. P. (1976) 'Transition to Parenthood: A Decade Replication'. *Journal of Marriage and the Family*, 38: 723–31.

Hoffman, L. W. (1977) 'Changes in Family Roles, Socialization and Sex Differences'. *American Psychologist*, 32: 644–57.

Hoffman, L. W. and Manis, J. D. (1978) 'Influences of Children on Marital Interaction and Parental Satisfactions and Dissatisfactions'. In R. Lerner and G. Spanier (eds.), *Child Influences on Marital and Family Interaction: A Life Span Perspective*. New York, Academic Press.

Hollingworth, L. S. (1916) 'Social Devices for Impelling Women to Bear and Rear Children'. *American Journal of Sociology*, 22 (1): 19–29

Holter, H. (1972) 'Sex Roles and Social Change'. *Acta Sociologica*, 14: 2–12.

Hubert, J. (1974) 'Belief and Reality: Social Factors in Pregnancy and Childbirth'. In M. P. M. Richards (ed.), *The Integration of a Child into a Social World*. London, Cambridge University Press.

International Childbirth Education Association (1965) *Husbands in the Delivery Room*. Rochester, NY, April.

Jackson, B. (1984) *Fatherhood*. London, Allen & Unwin.

Jessner, L., Weigart, E. and Foy, J. (1970) 'The Development of Parental Attitudes during Pregnancy'. In E. J. Anthony and T. Benedeck (eds.), *Parenthood: It's Psychology and Psychopathology*. Boston, Little, Brown.

Johnson, S. (1984) *The One Minute Father*. Bromley, Colombus Books.

Josselyn, I. M. (1956) 'Cultural Forces: Motherliness and Fatherliness'. *American Journal of Orthopsychiatry*, 26: 264–71.

Kaplan, E. and Blackman, L. (1969) 'The Husbands' Role in Psychiatric Illness Associated with Child Bearing'. *Psychiatric Quarterly*, 43: 396–409.

Katz, M. M. and Konner, M. J. (1981) 'The Role of the Father: An Anthropological Perspective'. In Lamb (1981a).

Kelly, J. A. and Worrell, L. (1976) 'Parental Behaviours Related to Masculine, Feminine and Androgynous Sex-Role Orientations'. *Journal of Consulting and Clinical Psychology*, 44 (5): 843–51.

Kerr, M. and McKee, L. (1981) 'The Father's Role in Child Health Care: Is Dad an Expert Too?' *Health Visitor*, 54 (2): 47–52.

Keylor, R. (1978) 'Paternal Interaction with Two-Year-Olds'. Unpublished Ph.D. Boston University.

Klaus, M. H. and Kennell, J. H. (1976) *Maternal–Infant Bonding*. St Louis, C. V. Mosby.

Klinman, D. G. and Kohl, R. (1984) *Fatherhood U.S.A.* New York, Garland.

Knox, D. and Gilman, R. C. (1974) 'The First Year of Fatherhood'. Greenville, NC, East Carolina University. Paper presented to the National Council for Family Relations. St Louis, Missouri, October (University Microfilms No. 102 471).

Komarovsky, M. (1953) *Women in the Modern World: Their Education and their Dilemmas*. Boston, Little, Brown.

Korman, M. and Lewis, C. (in preparation) *Parents' Language to their Children in the First Three Months of Life*.

Kotelchuck, M. (1972) 'The Nature of the Child's Tie to his Father'. Unpublished Ph.D. Harvard University.

Lamb, M. E. (1975) 'Fathers: Forgotten Contributors to Child Development'. *Human Development*, 18: 245–66.

(1976) 'The Role of the Father: An Overview'. In Lamb (1981a).

(1978) 'Influence of the Child on Marital Quality and Family Interaction during the Prenatal, Perinatal and Infancy Periods'. In R. M. Lerner and D. G. Spanier (eds.), *Contributions of the Child to Marital Quality and Family Interaction through the Life Span*. New York, Academic Press.

(1981a) *The Role of the Father in Child Development* (2nd edn). New York, Wiley.

(1981b) 'Fathers and Child Development: An Integrative Overview'. In Lamb (1981a).

(in press) 'The Changing Role of Fathers'. In M. E. Lamb (ed.), *The Father's Role: Applied Perspectives*. New York, Wiley.

Lamb, M. E., Frodi, M., Hwang, C.-P., and Frodi, A. M. (1983) 'The Effects of Paternal Involvement on Infant Preferences for Mothers and Fathers'. *Child Development*, 54: 450–8.

Lamb, M. E., and Levine, J. A. (1983) 'The Swedish Parental Insurance Scheme: An Experiment in Social Engineering'. In M. E. Lamb and A. Sagi (eds.), *Fatherhood and Family Policy*. Hillsdale, NJ, Erlbaum.

Landis, J. (1950) 'Effects of First Pregnancy upon the Sexual Adjustment of 212 Couples'. *American Sociological Review*, 15: 769–78.

La Rossa, R. (1977) *Conflict and Power in Marriage: Expecting the First Child*. Beverly Hills, Sage.

La Rossa, R. and La Rossa, M. M. (1981) *Transition to Parenthood: How Infants Change Families*. Beverly Hills, Sage.

Lasch, C. (1977) *Haven in a Heartless World*. New York, Basic Books.

(1985) *The Minimal Self: Psychic Survival in Troubled Times*. London, Picador.

Lawrence, D. H. (1913) *Sons and Lovers*. London, Heinemann.

Layman, E. M. (1961) 'Discussion of the International Council of Psychologists: Symposium on Fathers' Influence in the Family'. *Merrill Palmer Quarterly*, 7: 107–11.

Lederer, W. (1982) 'Counterepilogue'. In K. Solomon and N. B. Levy (eds.), *Men in Transition: Theory and Therapy*. New York, Plenum.

Leibenberg, B. (1967/73) 'Expectant Fathers'. In Shereshefsky and Yarrow (1973).

Le Masters, E. E. (1957) 'Parenthood as Crisis'. *Marriage and Family Living*, 19, November: 352–5.

Lewis, C. (1982a) 'The Observation of Father–Infant Relationships: An "Attachment" to Outmoded Concepts?' In McKee and O'Brien (1982a).

(1982b) '"A Feeling You Can't Scratch?" The Effect of Pregnancy and Birth on Married Men'. In Beail and McGuire (1982a).

(1986) 'Early Sex Role Socialization'. In A. Colley and D. Hargreaves (eds.), *The Psychology of Sex Roles*. London, Harper & Row

Lewis, C., Newson, J. and Newson, E. (1982) 'Father Participation through Childhood and its Relation to Career Aspirations and Delinquency'. In Beail and McGuire (1982a).

Lewis, R. A. (1978) 'Emotional Intimacy among Men'. *Journal of Social Issues*, 34 (1): 108–21.

Lewis, R. A. and Salt, R. E. (1986) *Men In Families*. Beverly Hills, Sage.

Lind, J. (1974) 'Observations after Delivery of Communications between Mother–Infant–Father'. Paper presented at the International Congress of Paediatrics, Buenos Aires.

Lindeman, E. C. (1942) 'Ideals for Family Life after the War'. *Marriage and Family Living*, 4: 8–9.

Little, P. and Ralston, D. (1981) *The Baby Book for Dads*. London, New English Library.

Lomas, P. (1964) 'Childbirth Ritual'. *New Society*, 4 (118), 31 December: 13–14.
     (1978) 'An Interpretation of Modern Obstetric Practice'. In S. Kitzinger and J. A. Davis (eds.), *The Place of Birth*. Oxford, Oxford University Press.

Long, S. (1978) *Attitude of Young Working-Class Men to Children and Family Formation: A Pilot Study*. Cardiff, University College Press.

Lummis, T. (1982) 'The Historical Dimension of Fatherhood: A Case Study 1890–1914. In McKee and O'Brien (1982a).

Lundberg, F. and Farnham, M. F. (1947) *Modern Woman, the Lost Sex*. New York, Harper & Britten.

Macintyre, S. (1976) 'Who Wants Babies? The Social Construction of "Instincts"'. In D. L. Barker and S. Allen (eds.), *Sexual Divisions and Society: Problems and Change*. London, Tavistock.

Main, M. and Weston, D. (1981) 'The Quality of the Toddler's Relationship to Mother and to Father: Related to Conflict Behavior and the Readiness to Establish New Relationships'. *Child Development*, 52: 932–40.

Malinowski, B. (1927a) *Sex and Repression in Savage Society*. London, Kegan Paul, Trench, and Trubner.
     (1927b) *The Father in Primitive Psychology*. London, Kegan Paul, Trench, and Trubner.

Manion, J. (1977) 'A Study of Fathers and Infant Caretaking'. *Birth and the Family Journal*, 4: 174–8.

Marquart, R. K. (1976) 'Expectant Fathers: What Are their Needs?' *American Journal of Maternal Child Nursing*, 1 (1): 32–6.

Martin, J. (1978) *Infant Feeding 1975: Attitudes and Practice in England and Wales*. London, HMSO/OPCS.

Mason, K. O. and Bumpass, L. L. (1975) US Women's Sex-Role Ideology 1970'. *American Journal of Sociology*, 80 (5), 1212–19.

Masters, W. and Johnson, W. (1966) *Human Sexual Response*. Boston, Little, Brown.

Matthews, A. E. B. (1961) 'Behaviour Patterns in Labour: A Study of 776 Consecutive Patients'. *Journal of Obstetrics and Gynaecology of the Commonwealth*, 63: 862–4.

McCorkel, R. J. (1964) 'Husbands and Pregnancy: An Exploratory Study'. Unpublished MA. University of North Carolina. Cited in Jessner *et al.* (1970).

McDougall, W. (1908) *An Introduction to Psychology*. London, Methuen.

McGuire, J. (1982) *Gender-Specific Differences in Early Childhood: The Impact of the Father*. In Beail and McGuire (1982a)

McKee, L. (1979) 'Fathers' Participation in Infant Care'. Paper presented at the British Sociological Association Fatherhood Conference. Warwick. April.
     (1980) 'Fathers and Childbirth: Just Hold my Hand'. *Health Visitor*, 53: 368–72.
     (1982) 'Fathers' Participation in Infant Care: A Critique'. In McKee and O'Brien (1982a).

McKee, L. and O'Brien, M. (1982a) *The Father Figure*. London, Tavistock.
(1982b) 'The Father Figure: Some Current Orientations and Historical Perspectives'. In McKee and O'Brien (1982a).

Mead, M. (1950/62) *Male and Female*. Harmondsworth, Pelican.
(1954) 'Some Theoretical Considerations on the Problems of Mother–Child Separation'. *American Journal of Orthopsychiatry*, 24: 471–83.

Mehl, L. E. (1978) 'The Outcome of Delivery: Research in the United States'. In S. Kitzinger and J. A. Davis (eds.), *The Place of Birth*. Oxford, Oxford University Press.

Meyerowitz, J. H. and Feldman, H. (1966) 'Transition to Parenthood'. *Psychiatric Research Report*, 20: 78–84.

Miller, B. C. and Sollie, D. L. (1980) 'Normal Stresses during the Transition to Parenthood'. *Family Relations*, 29 (3): 459–65.

Miller, J. S. (1966) 'Return the Joy of Home Delivery with Fathers in the Delivery Room'. *Hospital Topics*, January: 105–9.

Miller, R. S. (1973) 'Pregnancy: The Social Meaning of a Physiological Event'. Unpublished Ph.D. New York University.

Moen, P. (1982) 'The Two-Provider Family: Problems and Potentials'. In M. Lamb (ed.), *Non-Traditional Families*, Hillsdale, NJ, Erlbaum.

Mogey, J. M. (1957) 'A Century of Declining Paternal Authority'. *Marriage and Family Living*, 19 (3): 234–9.

Moggach, D. (1982) 'When Did You First See your Baby?' *Sunday Times*, 27 June: 34.

Monroe, R. L. and Monroe, R. H. (1971) 'Male Pregnancy Symptoms and Cross Sex Identity in Three Societies. *Journal of Social Psychology*, 84: 11–25.

Moore, D. C. and Bridenbaugh, L. D. (1964) 'Physician, Analgesia, Regional Block and Father Participation: The Ultimate in Care of Vaginal Delivery'. *Western Journal of Surgery, Obstetrics and Gynaecology*, 72, Jan.–Feb. 37–44.

Morgan, P. (1975) *Child Care: Sense and Fable*. London, Temple Smith.

Morton, J. H. (1966) 'Fathers in the Delivery Room – an Opposition Standpoint'. *Health Topics*, 44: 103.

Moss, P. M. (1980) 'Parents at Work. In P. M. Moss and N. Fonda (eds.), *Work and the Family*. London, Temple Smith.
(1981) 'Transition to Parenthood Project–Annual Report'. Unpublished m.s. Thomas Coram Research Unit, January.

Moss, P. M. and Fonda, N. (1980) 'The Future Prospect'. In P. M. Moss and N. Fonda (eds.), *Work and the Family*. London, Temple Smith.

Mowrer, E. R. (1930) *The Family: Its Organization and Disorganization*. Chicago, University of Chicago Press.

Nash, J. (1965) 'The Father in Contemporary Culture and Current Psychological Literature'. *Child Development*, 36: 261–97.
(1976/81) 'Historical and Social Change in the Perception of the Role of the Father'. In Lamb (1981a).

New, C. and David, M. (1985) *For the Children's Sake*. Harmondsworth, Penguin.

Newson, J. and Newson, E. (1963) *Infant Care in an Urban Community*. London, Allen & Unwin.
(1968) *Four Years Old in an Urban Community*. London, Allen & Unwin.
(1976) *Seven Years Old in the Home Environment*. London, Allen & Unwin.

Oakley, A. (1972) 'Are Husbands Good Housewives?' *New Society*, 19, February: 337–40.

(1974) *The Sociology of Housework*. Oxford, Martin Robertson.

(1979) *Becoming a Mother*. Oxford: Martin Robertson.

(1980) *Women Confined*. Oxford: Martin Robertson.

O'Brien, M. (1982) 'The Working Father'. In Beail and McGuire (1982a).

O'Brien, M. and McKee, L. (1982) 'Interviewing Men: Taking Gender Seriously'. Paper presented to the British Sociological Association Annual Conference on Gender and Society. Manchester University, April.

OPCS (1979) *General Household Survey, 1977*. London: HMSO.

Owens, D. (1982) 'The Desire to Father: Reproductive Ideologies and Involuntarily Childless Men'. In McKee, and O'Brien (1982a).

Paige, K. E. and Paige, J. M. (1981) *The Politics of Reproductive Ritual*. Berkeley, University of California Press.

Paloma, M. and Garland, N. (1972) 'The Married Professional Woman: A Study in the Tolerance of Domenstication'. *Journal of Marriage and the Family*, 33: 531–9.

Parsons, B. (1975/81) *Expectant Fathers*. London, Robert Yeatman.

Parsons, T. and Bales, R. F. (1955) *Family, Socialization and Interaction Process*. New York, Free Press.

Patterson, J. H. (1961) 'Fathers at Delivery'. *British Medical Journal*, 1: 594.

Pedersen, F. A. (1980a) *The Father–Infant Relationship: Observational Studies in the Family Setting*. New York, Praeger.

(1980b) 'Overview: Answers and Formulated Questions'. In Pedersen (1980a).

Pedersen, F. and Robson, K. (1969) 'Father Participation in Infancy'. *American Journal of Orthopsychiatry*, 39: 466–72.

Phillips, C. R. and Anzalone, J. T. (1978) *Fathering: Participation in Labour and Birth*. St Louis, C. V. Mosby.

Pleck, J. H. (1977) 'The Work–Family Role System'. *Social Problems*, 24: 417–27.

(1979) 'Men's Family Work: Three Perspectives and Some New Data'. *The Family Coordinator*, 28: 481–8.

Pleck, J. H. and Brannon, R. (1978) 'Male Roles and the Male Experience: Introduction'. In J. H. Pleck and R. Brannon (eds.), *Male Roles and Male Experience*. A Special edition of the *Journal of Social Issues*, 34 (1).

Power, T. (1981) 'Sex Typing in Infancy: The Role of the Father'. *Infant Mental Health Journal*, 2:226–40.

Pressman, R. A. (1980)'Father Participation in Child Care: An Exploratory Study of Factors Associated with Father Participation in Child Care among Fathers with Working Wives and their Children'. Unpublished Ph.D. Boston University School of Education (University Microfilms No. UM 80-24146).

Rapoport, R. (1964) 'New Light on the Honeymoon'. *Human Relations*, 17: 33–56.

Rapoport, R. and Rapoport, R. N. (1971) *Dual Career Families*. Harmondsworth, Penguin.

Rapoport, R., Rapoport, R. N. and Strelitz, Z. (1977) *Fathers, Mothers and Others*. London, Routledge & Kegan Paul.

Ratner, R. S. (1980) 'The Policy and the Problem: Overview of Seven Countries'. In R. S. Ratner (ed.), *Equal Employment Policy for Women*. Philadelphia, Temple University Press.

Rebelsky, F. and Hanks, C. (1971) 'Fathers' Verbal Interaction with Infants in the First Three Months'. *Child Development*, 42: 63–8.

Rendina, I. and Dickerschied, J. (1976) 'Father Involvement with First Born Infants'. *The Family Coordinator*, 25, October: 373–7.

Rich, A. (1977) *Of Woman Born*. London, Virago.

Richards, M. P. M. (1982) 'How Should We Approach the Study of Fathers?' In McKee and O'Brien (1982a).

Richards, M., Dunn, J. and Antonis, B. (1977) 'Caretaking in the First Year of Life: The Role of Fathers and Mothers' Social Isolation'. *Child Care, Health and Development*, 3: 23–36.

Richman, J. (1982) 'Men's Experiences of Pregnancy and Childbirth'. In McKee and O'Brien (1982a).

Richman, J. and Goldthorp, W. O. (1978) 'Fatherhood: The Social Construction of Pregnancy and Birth'. In S. Kitzinger and J. Davis (eds.), *The Place of Birth*. Oxford, Oxford University Press.

Richman, J., Goldthorp, W. O. and Simmonds, C. (1975) 'Fathers in Labour'. *New Society*, 34, 16 October: 143–5.

Riley, M. (1968) *Brought to Bed*. London, Dent.

Robinson, J. P. (1977) *How Americans Use Time: A Sociological Analysis of Everyday Behavior*. New York, Praegar.

Robson, K. M. and Kumar, R. (1980) 'Delayed Onset of Maternal Affection after Childbirth'. *British Journal of Psychiatry*, 136: 347–53.

Rollins, B. C. and Galligan, R. (1978) 'The Study of Child–Family Interactions'. In R. Lerner and G. Spanier (eds.), *Child Influences on Marital and Family Interactions: A Life-Span Perspective*. New York, Academic Press.

Roopnarine, J. and Miller, B. C. (1985) 'Transitions to Fatherhood'. In S. Hanson and F. Bozett (eds.), *Dimensions of Fatherhood*. Beverly Hills, Sage.

Rose, N. (1985) *The Psychological Complex*. London, Routledge & Kegan Paul.

Rossi, A. (1968) 'Transition to Parenthood'. *Journal of Marriage and the Family*, 30: 26–39.

Rubin, Z., Hill, C. T., Peplan, L. A. and Dunkell-Schetter, C. (1980) 'Self-Disclosure in Dating Couples: Sex Roles and the Ethic of Openness'. *Journal of Marriage and the Family*, 42 (2): 305–17.

Russell, C. S. (1974) 'Transition to Parenthood: Problems and Gratifications'. *Journal of Marriage and the Family*, 36: 294–301.

Russell, G. (1978) 'The Father Role and its Relation to Masculinity, Femininity and Androgyny'. *Child Development*, 49: 1174–81.

—— (1982) 'Shared-Caregiving Families: An Australian Study'. In M. Lamb (ed.) *Non-Traditional Families*. Hillsdale, NJ, Erlbaum.

—— (1983) *The Changing Role of Fathers*. Milton Keynes, Open University Press.

Russo, N. F. (1976) 'The Motherhood Mandate'. *Journal of Social Issues*, 32 (3): 143–53.

Ryder, R. G. (1973) 'Longitudinal Data Relating Marriage Satisfaction and Having a Child'. *Journal of Marriage and the Family*, 35: 604–6.

Safilios-Rothschild, C. (1969) 'Family Sociology or Wives' Family Sociology? A Cross Cultural Examination of Decision Making'. *Journal of Marriage and the Family*, 31, May 291–301.

Sandqvist, K. (in preparation) 'Swedish Family Policy: Promoting Shared

Parenting Roles'. In C. Lewis and M. O'Brien (eds.), *Problems of Fatherhood* (working title). London, Sage.

Schaeffer, G. (1964–72) *The Expectant Father*. New York, Barnes & Noble.

Schaffer, H. R. and Emerson, P. (1964) 'The Development of Social Attachments in Infancy'. *Monographs of the Society for Research in Child Development*, 29 (3), series 94.

Schlossman, S. L. (1976) 'Before Home Start: Notes toward a History of Parent Education in America, 1897–1929'. *Harvard Educational Review*, 46: 436–67.

Schulman, N. (1975) 'Life Cycle Variations in Patterns of Close Relationships'. *Journal of Marriage and the Family*, 37 November: 813–21.

Scott, J. W. (1981) 'Scott's Primary Bonding Manoevre'. *Maternal and Child Health*, September: 380.

Seidler, V. (1985) 'Fear and Intimacy'. In A. Metcalfe and M. Humphries (eds.), *The Sexuality of Men*. London, Pluto.

Shereshefsky, P. and Yarrow, L. (1973) *Psychological Aspects of a First Pregnancy and Early Post Natal Adaptation*. New York, Raven Press.

Slater, P. E. (1961) 'Parental Role Differentiation'. *American Journal of Sociology*, 67: 296–311.

Sluckin, W., Herbert, M. and Sluckin, A. (1983) *Maternal Bonding*. Oxford, Blackwell.

Smith, L. (1985) 'The Politics of Preparation for Parenthood'. In G. Walford (ed.) *Schooling in Turmoil*. London, Croom Helm.

Solomon, K. and Levy, N. B. (1982) *Men in Transition: Theory and Therapy*. New York, Plenum.

Soule, A. B. (1974) 'The Pregnant Couple'. Paper presented to the American, Psychological Association. New Orleans, August.

Spanier, G. B., Lerner, R. M. and Aquilino, W. (1978) 'The Study of Child–Family Interactions: A Perspective for the Future'. In R. M. Lerner and G. B. Spanier (eds.), *Child Influences on Marital and Family Interaction: A Life-Span Perspective*. New York, Academic Press.

Spock, B. (1967) 'What a Father's Role Should Be'. *Redbook Magazine*, February.

Stewart, R. H. (1963) 'Natural Childbirth, Father Participation, Rooming-In or What-Have-You'. *Medical Times*, 91 (11), November.

Stoltz, L. *et al.* (1954) *Father Relations of War Born Children*. Stanford, Calif., Stanford University Press.

Switzky, L. T., Vietze, P. and Switzky, H. (1979) 'Attitudinal and Demographic Predictions of Breast-Feeding in Mothers of Six-Week-Old Infants'. *Psychological Reports*, 45: 3–14.

Tasch, R. (1952) 'The Role of the Father in the Family'. *Journal of Experimental Education*, 20: 319–61.

Thoms, H. and Karloosky, E. (1954) '2000 Deliveries under Training for Childbirth Programme'. *American Journal of Obstetrics and Gynaecology*, 68: 279–84.

Trethowan, W. H. (1972) 'The Couvade Syndrome'. In J. H. Howells (ed.), *Modern Perspectives on Psycho-Obstetrics*. Edinburgh, Oliver & Boyd.

Tylor, E. B. (1965) *Researches into the Early History of Mankind*. London, Murray.

Ukoza, A. F. (1979) 'The Myth of the Nuclear Family: Historical Background and Clinical Implications'. *American Psychologist*, 34 (11): 1095–106.

Underwood, V. V. M. (1949) 'Student Fathers with their Children'. *Marriage and Family Living*, 11: 101.

Vincent, J. (1979) 'The Fathers of Illegitimate Babies'. Paper presented at British Sociological Association Conference, Warwick University, February.

Walker, K. M. and Walker, E. M. (1928) *On Being a Father*. London, Cape.

Walker, K. and Woods, M. (1976) *Time Use: A Measure of Household Production of Family Goods and Services*. Washington, DC, American Home Economics Association.

Wandersman, L. P. (1980) 'The Adjustment of Fathers to their First Baby'. *Birth and the Family Journal*, 7: 155–62.

Weingarten, K. (1978) 'The Employment Pattern of Professional Couples and their Distribution of Involvement in the Family'. *Psychology of Women Quarterly*: 43–52. New York, Human Sciences Press.

White, D., Woollett, A. and Lyon, L. (1982) 'Fathers' Involvement with their Infants: The Relevance of Holding'. In Beail and McGuire (1982a).

Willemsen, E., Flaherty, D., Heaton, C. and Ritchey, G. (1974) 'Attachment Behaviour of One-Year-Olds as a Function of Mother versus Father, Sex of Child, Session and Toys'. *Genetic Psychology Monographs*, 90: 305–24.

Winn, W. (1979) 'Fathering and Masculinity: A Conflict in Role Expectations'. In R. F. Levant and E. T. Nickerson (eds.), *Mothering and Fathering: Dispelling Myths, Creating Alternatives*. Weston, Mass., Boston Professional International.

Winnicott, D. W. (1965) *The Family and Individual Development*. London, Tavistock.

Woollett, A., White, D. and Lyon, L. (1982) 'Studies Involving Fathers: Subject Refusal, Attrition and Sampling Bias'. *Current Psychological Reviews*, 2: 193–212.

Wyeth Laboratory Publications (undated) *It's Your Baby Too!* Taplow, Maidenhead, Berks.

Young, M. and Willmott, P. (1973) *The Symmetrical Family*. London, Routledge & Kegan Paul.

Zajicek, E. and Wolkind, S. (1978) 'Emotional Difficulties in Married Women during and after the First Pregnancy'. *British Journal of Medical Psychology*, 379–85.

Zaslow, M., Pedersen, P., Kramer, E., Suwalsky, J. and Fivel, M. (1981) 'Depressed Mood in New Fathers: Interview and Behavioural Correlates'. Paper presented to the Society for Research in Child Development. Boston, April.

Zelditch, M. (1955) 'Role Differentiation in the Nuclear Family: A Comparative Study'. In Parsons and Bales (1955).

Author Index

Subject Index

DATE DUE